HARD-BOILED CRIME FICTION

& THE DECLINE OF MORAL AUTHORITY

SUSANNA LEE

THE OHIO STATE UNIVERSITY PRESS
COLUMBUS

Library of Congress Cataloging-in-Publication Data

Names: Lee, Susanna, 1970– author.

Title: Hard-boiled crime fiction and the decline of moral authority / Susanna Lee.

Description: Columbus : The Ohio State University Press, [2016] | Includes bibliographical references and index.

Identifiers: LCCN 2016023008 | ISBN 9780814213F186 (cloth ; alk. paper) | ISBN 0814213189 (cloth ; alk. paper)

Subjects: LCSH: Detective and mystery stories, American—History and criticism. | Detective and mystery stories, French—History and criticism. | Moral conditions in literature. | Authority in literature.

Classification: LCC PS374.D4 L43 2016 | DDC 813/.087209—dc23

LC record available at https://lccn.loc.gov/2016023008

Cover design by James Baumann

Text design by Juliet Williams

Type set in Adobe Minion Pro

Cover image by Chip Simons, chip@chipsimons.com

9 8 7 6 5 4 3 2 1

FOR CHARLOTTE, RYAN, AND TOMMY

CONTENTS

ACKNOWLEDGMENTS

I AM GRATEFUL to many friends and colleagues for the support and guidance they gave me while I wrote this book. Peter Brooks, Andrea Goulet, Edward Lee, Carole Sargent, Kathryn Shevelow, Andrew Sobanet, and Susan Terrio read all or portions of the manuscript and gave invaluable advice and encouragement. Thanks also to Lindsay Martin at The Ohio State University Press. I am particularly grateful to Marianna Lee, whose ministrations helped the prose of this book immensely.

A summer grant from Georgetown University supported chapter 3. A portion of chapter 5 appeared as "Scruple and State Sovereignty: Fred Vargas's Romantic Étatisme" in *Contemporary French Civilization* 34, no. 1 (2010).

I could not have completed this book without the encouragement of my friends and family. Masha Belenky, Jeremy Billetdeaux, Erin Callahan, Susann Cokal, Laura Denardis, Mia Dentoni, Nancy Doran, Debbie Eales, Anne Fleming, Angie Graham, Cynthia Hobbs, Peter Kok, Sandra Lee, Elizabeth Letcher, Katie MacKaye, Barbara Mujica, Anne O'Neil Henry, Andrew Sobanet, Michel Steiner, Erik ten Broecke, Maya ten Broecke, Sara ten Broecke, Michele Von Stein, and Paul Young cheered on me at every turn. My gratitude also goes to the intrepid running moms of 2015: Rebecca Carr, Jen Kaplan, Maggie Prieto, Morgan Pleasant, and Tammy Lowengrub. Special appreciation goes to Christina Crean, Norah Crean, and Sean Crean. Finally, the most heartfelt thanks to my best sources of inspiration: Charlotte, Ryan, and Tommy. This book is dedicated to them.

FORTY YEARS AGO in the United States, psychologist Stanley Milgram's *Obedience to Authority* (1974) was followed by Albert Ellis's *A Guide to Rational Living* (1975). In the early 1990s, educator Jonathan Kozol's *Savage Inequalities* (1991) was joined on the bestseller list by motivational guru Anthony Robbins's *Awaken the Giant Within* (1991). In France, journalist Olivier Levard's *We All Are Robots* [*Nous sommes tous des robots*] (2014) followed psychic and spiritual adviser Serge Boutboul's *How to Unleash the Spiritual Beings That We Are* [*Comment déployer l'être spirituel que nous sommes*] (2013), and on the heels of economist Thomas Piketty's *Capital in the Twenty-First Century* [*Le capital au XXI siècle*] (2013) came therapist Sylvie Bernard-Curie's *You Have What It Takes to Succeed* [*Vous avez tout pour réussir*] (2014). These titles, broadly stated, represent polarized popular perspectives on individual conduct and consequent sense of self. One perspective starts from the premise that societal forces undercut the very idea of individual autonomy. Another concentrates instead on the high importance of individual action and decision. The first strand of analysis tends to be academic in nature, while the second is more commonly directed toward a popular audience of readers who are curious (or who the authors believe should be curious) about how to be, in that hackneyed but serviceable phrase, a better person. In other words, parallel to decades of studies questioning individual agency, not to mention moral authority, comes an equally relentless insistence that individuals must make decisions, take action, and hold their futures in hand.

It is curious that sociological and psychological studies underscoring obstacles to autonomy have run for years alongside a multitude of self-help books. Against the backdrop of such contradictory strands of thought about individual accountability, I examine a genre that puts them in direct confrontation. This genre is hard-boiled crime fiction. The cynical but kind-hearted detective is the soul of the classic hard-boiled, that chronicle of world-weary urban pessimism. Whether in Los Angeles, New York, or Paris, the hard-boiled detective is the guardian of individual moral authority and the embodiment of ideals in a corrupt environment. He also incarnates the idea that the individual can be such a guardian—can act as conservator of ideals for an entire society. All hard-boiled fiction casts its protagonists in this role, but it is in the American and French traditions that crime fiction character profiles are most congruent with paradigmatic national personalities or culture heroes. Other national crime fiction traditions have subsequently produced hard-boiled literature, but these productions have neither generated nor aligned with nationally specific heroic paradigms the way that American and French crime fiction has.[1] American and French hard-boiled traditions remain notable in their pioneering deployment of individual personalities both to stand for an entire culture and to accomplish what society as a whole cannot. Furthermore, and rather paradoxically given their characters' relative solitude, they cast the hard-boiled personality as a broadly resonant beacon of morality and accountability. American and French hard-boiled fiction, in other words, uses its characters not just to conserve cultural values in a devolving modern world but also to represent, even advertise, its individuals as instinctive conservators of culturally specific attributes and values.

---

1. Even in British detective literature, where Sherlock Holmes famously incarnated the gentleman detective and Jane Marple the proper British lady, the hard-boiled authors of the 1930s and 1940s principally generated imitations of the American character model. British authors James Hadley Chase and Peter Cheyney, popular in the French publisher Gallimard's *Série noire* for their violence-soaked crime novels, sampled American vocabulary and environments rather than creating distinctly British heroes and historical scenarios. Other such notable hard-boiled authors as Kenzo Kitakata, Arimasa Osawa, and Haruhiko Oyabu (Japan), Jakob Arjouni (Germany), Yasmini Khadra (Algeria), Ian Rankin (Scotland), Karin Fossum and Jo Nesbo (Norway), Sara Blaedel (Denmark), Arnaldur Indridason (Iceland), and Maj Sjowall, Per Wahloo, Stieg Larsson, Kjell Erikson, Camilla Läckberg, and Henning Mankell (Sweden) have created maverick individualists to critical and commercial acclaim, but none of their protagonists became cultural personae as American and French characters have. The possible exception is Stieg Larsson's Lisbeth Salander, from a well-populated tradition of Scandinavian *noir*, but even this character transcends rather than represents or defines a nationally specific heroic paradigm.

The history of American and French hard-boiled fiction follows the same road: building, demolishing, and finally reconstituting an exemplary individual. For this reason, the genre functions as a singular barometer for individual accountability in the modern age. It also demonstrates, I will argue, the enduring and reparative status of such accountability across a variety of cultural circumstances. As the hard-boiled hero goes, so goes the idea of the autonomous self in its respective cultures, and when the heroic model devolves, the very conceptual validity of individual moral authority can seem to devolve as well. In tracing the history of that model through the twentieth century and on both sides of the Atlantic, I view the idea of morality as not simply represented by a historically and culturally specific character model but generated for it and dependent upon it as well. It is because of that dependence that this book is necessarily comparative in its assessment. As the history of crime fiction demonstrates, the idea of morality comes alive through character. Historical crises of accountability and moral authority become manifest when character models go off the rails, and those character models are culturally specific. They enact crises in culturally specific ways. This specificity undergirds the relevance of hard-boiled character models to the wider culture—a relevance, again, that is intensely present in the American and French traditions. American and French protagonists share empathic awareness of others, willingness to hold themselves to account, ease with violence, and sanguine resistance to corrupt atmospheres. The American model is heavier on anti-intellectualism and declarations of personal independence, whereas the French model emphasizes historical and cultural consciousness and aesthetic discernment. These variables, these behavioral indicators, are recognizable cultural markers both of hard-boiled character and of respective paradigmatic national character profiles as well. The present book charts the evolution of the hard-boiled character, the mid-century devolution of his exemplarity, and twenty-first-century gestures to resuscitate the accountable hero. The history of hard-boiled crime fiction, I argue, tells nothing less than the story of individual autonomy and accountability in modern Western culture.

Although crime fiction showcases individual personalities with particular clarity, hard-boiled character models and their deterioration through the twentieth century are not unique to crime fiction. The tough, plainspoken American cowboy and the melancholic, poetic French aesthete are basic cultural types that pervade political discourse, moral paradigms, and popular culture in both countries. They are bedrocks of national identity, and what is more, as it happens, they are bedrocks in conversation with one another. The conversation itself is embedded in popular cultures: from the farcical

Hollywood French detective to the "Old Europe" French politician cited by former secretary of defense Donald Rumsfeld, the French character model of the contemplative but ineffectual humanist has long played the foil for the American straight shooter. So too has the American cowboy, drawing his pistol first and asking questions later (as in the 2003 French play *George W. Bush or God's Sad Cowboy* [*George W. Bush ou le triste cowboy de Dieu*]), served as counterpoint to the judicious French thinker. Furthermore, crime fiction has from the start been shaped by Franco-American dialogue, a dialogue that has made for considerable overlap between hard-boiled and *noir* as generic designations and enabled the *roman noir* to be understood as a French-American hybrid. It is in France that the American hard-boiled novel has from its inception met with consistent commercial, critical, and cinematic success. And French detective fiction fascinates American readers. From Georges Simenon to Fred Vargas, to Anglophone detective fiction set in France (Martin Walker from Britain, Cara Black from the United States, J. Robert Janes from Canada), to the French television crime serial *Spiral* (*Engrenages*) to film noir, the specter of French culture is crucial to America's own hard-boiled self-image. At the same time, French film adaptations of American crime novels have proliferated for decades. What interests me in the specificity of American and French character models and in the interaction between them is the way in which their respective devolutions chart modern crises of accountability. In both national traditions, the ostentatious detachment of cultural hard-boiled markers from actual ethical conduct, the sudden meaninglessness or outright perversion of formerly beloved behavioral indicators, are crucial to the apparent devolution of the hard-boiled protagonist. On both sides of the Atlantic, crises of individual accountability are enacted through the building, breaking down, and rebuilding of culture heroes. Hard-boiled fiction diagnoses corruption as the inevitable consequence of modern disaffection and capitalist venality, of toxic parenting and mental illness, of political disenchantment and technological alienation—in other words, all those influences that decades of sociological studies on both sides of the Atlantic have identified as real obstacles to full and independent selfhood. And yet, I contend, the hard-boiled genre presents those diagnoses as shockingly and transparently disingenuous. The twentieth and twenty-first centuries narrated in hard-boiled fiction contain numerous real obstacles to accountability. But in one historical period after another, despite one mitigating circumstance after another, hard-boiled fiction refuses to let the individual off the hook. The history of the genre suggests the end of the accountable and autonomous individual not to be a historical fact, nor even an inevitable correlate of modern analyses of subjectivity and society, but a narrative effect. It is an ostensible means to make a point about the oppressive nature of insurmountable social and psychological forces, but at the same time a way to create a despondent atmosphere for which no one can really be blamed and which no one can repair. As I will argue, the hard-boiled consistently intimates that individual abdication or suspension of accountability is deliberate and is the foundation of social disorder, not its product. The intentionality of such abdication and suspension becomes most evident in contemporary attempts to redress them, to reconstitute both autonomy and accountability. In those endeavors—and this is where the hard-boiled's sociological resonance meets shades of the self-help exhortations mentioned above—individual reclaimings of agency and accountability repudiate master narratives that equate secular modernity with social decline. Continued dialogue between these national character-driven literatures has ensured the specificity of each culture's character outline, and study of those outlines illuminates the problems of accountability that arise in the hard-boiled. It is through those character models that we can best follow crises of autonomy and accountability in literature and in cultural master narratives writ large.

I do not mean this book to be a complete history of either American or French crime fiction. It does not claim that the constitution, devolution, and restoration of moral authority form the sole undercurrent of twentieth-century crime fiction, nor does it try to give an exhaustive account of that trajectory. It does show that American and French hard-boiled crime fiction galvanizes culturally specific spiritual character models, suits those models to culturally specific twentieth-century circumstances, and then dismantles their exemplary characteristics in such a way as to compel a crucial historic reckoning with the questions of individual accountability itself. It also demonstrates that in the twenty-first century, both American and French crime fiction are profoundly concerned with the loose ends of that reckoning and stand thus in a privileged position to stimulate the restoration—or more accurately the continual reconstitution—of individual moral authority. As I trace this road, I examine those instances of the genre that are the most characteristic (more on this in a moment) and that have attained the greatest commercial and critical success. Because the corpus is vast and particularly because this study is both transhistorical and cross-cultural, inclusions of certain texts mean exclusions of others. I start with the first American and French hard-boiled novels, then move to mid-century post–hard-boiled American fiction and to the French *néo-polar*, and finally to the contemporary or "restorative" hard-boiled. The final chapter concentrates on American television rather than literature, for, I contend, it is in this widely resonant medium that contemporary interrogations of individual accountability find the strongest both popular and intellectual representation. This does not mean, of course, that twenty-first-century American authors are no longer producing hard-boiled crime fiction, or that twenty-first-century literature is second to television in richness. The years since Jim Thompson have seen Ross Macdonald's Lew Archer, Robert Parker's Spenser, Rex Stout's Nero Wolfe, Sara Paretsky's V. I. Warshawski, Sue Grafton's Kinsey Millhone, and countless others. And yet, series such as *The Wire* and *True Detective* have generated questions about responsibility and the boundaries of heroism that resonate powerfully throughout popular culture and address most directly the abdications examined in this book. In turning to television, my goal is to examine the crime fiction that, at the time of this writing, is having considerable critical and commercial success, and whose success centers on the reconstruction of individual moral authority. If we take David Simon at his word when he describes *The Wire* as a "visual novel" and consider the meta-narrative character of *True Detective,* then the inclusion of literature on the French side and television on the American will seem organic.

Although I will be pointing out the romantic foundations of crime fiction and arguing that the hard-boiled casts individual moral accountability as an alternative to narratives of modern devolution, it is crucial to underscore that hard-boiled focus on individual moral choice is neither idealistic nor prescriptive. The continual or repeated emphasis on individual accountability as I read it is neither morally reactionary nor morally utopian. Rather, the hard-boiled represents individual accountability as a continual and reparative response to a diverse series of modern cultural crises. These reparations do not amount to an erasure of history and certainly do not mean a restoration of imagined sacred frameworks. Rather, they constitute a series of endeavors, exertions even, that reinsert individual moral choice into modern master narratives. It is true that there is something atemporal (in the sense of resisting chronologies) about the hard-boiled detective, the person who sees the world as it is, who wants more, yet who is content with not having more: the hard-boiled returns to this individual again and again, but that return is not counterhistorical. In a sense, hard-boiled crime fiction does for theories of modern decline what its fictional detective does for the world in such a decline: it continually reconstitutes a traditional concept of the individual even within frames that could seem antipathetic to such concepts.

A BRIEF HISTORY OF EXEMPLARITY

Although traditional nineteenth-century "whodunit" detective fiction maintained a stable social and moral landscape, the hard-boiled as a genre tends to acknowledge its loss: the detective does not preserve morality so much as reincarnate and reconstitute it for a corrupted world. As Raymond Chandler famously wrote in his iconic definition of the hard-boiled hero: "Down these mean streets a man must go who is not himself mean, who is neither tarnished nor afraid. . . . He must be, to use a rather weathered phrase, a man of honor, by instinct, by inevitability, without thought of it, and certainly without saying it."[2] The classic hard-boiled featuring such a character flourished in the American 1920s and 1930s and in the French 1940s and 1950s, in the fiction of Carroll John Daly, Dashiell Hammett, Raymond Chandler, Léo Malet, and Jean Amila. When the first American hard-boiled protagonist boasted, "My ethics are my own," he did not seem dangerous or unethical; his "own" ethics reproduced to a striking extent the traditional and even religious principles he claimed to ignore.[3] His instinctive honor, his intuitive lack of meanness, and his exceptional nature make him an iconic Western paradox, the person who combines estrangement from established forms with a narrative and philosophical form-giving position. Those paradoxical individuals, I will argue, are the direct descendants, incarnations even, of culturally specific character models of spiritual authority—the tough, plain-speaking maverick in the United States and the contemplative poet-aesthete in France—that were outlined in early nineteenth-century romantic and religious literature. These paradoxes have a powerful resonance for popular culture, both American and French, and for individual moral authority as a conceptual phenomenon. They point to an outstanding characteristic of Western culture's most treasured modern ideals, or most precious heroic commodities: the secular individual for whom spiritual ideals come naturally, unforced, and constitute durable character attributes.

The hard-boiled model of instinctual heroism that Chandler outlined devolved and deteriorated over the twentieth century. The classic American hard-boiled morphs into the post–hard-boiled of the 1950s and 1960s, which included the entropic fictions of Mickey Spillane and subsequently Jim Thompson; the French *roman noir* turns into the *polar* and then the *néo-polar* of the 1960s and 1970s, the violence-strewn novels of Jean-Patrick Manchette, Francis Ryck, and Pierre Siniac. These last novels follow classic models in their placement of an individual subject in a polluted and crime-soaked environment. But in a resounding escalation of Chandler's *The Big Sleep,* which ended with the detective admitting, "I was part of the nastiness now," the post–hard-boiled and *néo-polar* explicitly make their principal characters— who may be detectives, policemen, politicians, bored civilians, housewives,

2. Chandler, "Simple Art of Murder," 59.
3. Daly, *Snarl of the Beast,* 1.

adolescents, or hardened criminals—crucial drivers of that ambiance.[4] The traits of the exemplary hard-boiled character twist and grow out of control: the tough American maverick becomes a dangerously resentful loose cannon and the contemplative, sardonic French intellectual an indolent pessimist. In each case, these distortions correspond to simultaneous denials of accountability, to intimations that society, family, or heredity is to blame. The result of such devolution is the loss of not only a cultural paradigm but also a hero who, through his apparently innate and instinctive embodiment of traditional virtues, once guaranteed that individual moral authority would remain a bedrock in the absence of spiritual imperatives.

The hard-boiled genre in its early twentieth-century incarnation is inextricably connected with the idea of the individual as a reliably intelligible entity. The hard-boiled character simply *is:* the outside world can act upon him, but he maintains an ontological solidity that keeps him "not mean" even when on mean streets. This solidity is supported by narrative arcs that avoid any hint of the *Bildungsroman;* there is something complete from the start about the character. In this sense, he enacts Aristotelian notions of character, which Gilbert Harman describes as "relatively long-term stable dispositions to act in distinctive ways."[5] The hard-boiled joins instinctual virtues to a nonjudgmental nature. It celebrates the fusion of what Gregory Currie names "character (a person in a story) and Character (inner source of action, related to personality and temperament)."[6] The idea of inner sources parallels Chandler's "by instinct, by inevitability" by positing an individual distinct, rounded, finished, and at the same time open to the world.[7] Harman himself has argued against the existence of character traits, and the idea of character as a coherent entity has come in for much questioning in contemporary discourse.[8] The history of hard-boiled crime fiction tells the story of that conceptual dissolution of the individual. But it also repeatedly casts that story, and the notion of the porous sociological person, as a disingenuous endeavor on the part of the subject to

---

4. Chandler, *The Big Sleep.*

5. Harman, *Explaining Value,* 166.

6. Currie, "Narrative and the Psychology of Character," 61.

7. The functions of hard-boiled character are similar to the notion of *noir* authenticity outlined in Eric Dussere's *America Is Elsewhere:* as an imagined antithesis of a corrupt or inauthentic world. Dussere frames authenticity as "an ideological attempt to imagine a negation of American consumer culture," whereas the hard-boiled casts authenticity as happening in and through the character. Like Dussere's authenticity, the hard-boiled character is a world unto itself and its "long-term stable dispositions" are "relative" and exist as an "effect." Eric Dussere, *America Is Elsewhere: The Noir Tradition in the Age of Consumer Culture* (Oxford: Oxford University Press, 2013), 4.

8. Peter Callero's *Myth of Individualism (2009),* for instance, argues persuasively for identity, thought, and emotion as sociological phenomena.

avoid responsibility. As a result, the hard-boiled in fact sustains a traditional concept of the individual, one based on "long-term stable dispositions."

SUBJECTIVE FACTS

Here, I want to return to the earlier statement that classic hard-boiled characters are secular versions of nineteenth-century character models of spiritual authority. I will argue that the hard-boiled's treatment of the individual *qua* individual plays out particular cultural anxieties about secular morality, so its synthesis of ideals and character attributes is crucial. To frame that synthesis historically and philosophically, I want to consider the classic hard-boiled's foregrounding of the individual paragon as reminiscent of Georg Lukács's account of the genesis of the novel: an account that focuses on the rise of the individual as repository of ideals. In Lukács's formulation, the epic—as distinct from and anterior to the novel—had presumed an abiding alliance of individual and world. As he notes, the epic hero is, "strictly speaking, never an individual." His description of the novel's dissolution of that alliance is germane to the hard-boiled's singular reconciliation of individualism and cultural heroism. He states:

> If the individual is unproblematic, then his aims are given to him with imme-
> diate obviousness, and the realisation of the world constructed by these
> given aims may involve hindrances and difficulties but never any serious
> threat to his interior life. Such a threat arises only when the outside world is
> no longer adapted to the individual's ideals and the ideas become subjective
> facts—*ideals*—in his soul. The positing of ideas as unrealizable and, in the
> empirical sense, as unreal, i.e. their transformation into ideals, destroys the
> immediate problem-free organic nature of the individual. Individuality then
> becomes an aim unto itself because it finds within itself everything that is
> essential to it and that makes its life autonomous—even if what it finds can
> never be a firm possession or basis of its life, but is an object of search.[9]

The hard-boiled air of "constructed nostalgia," as Dean MacCannell puts it, which can also be read as an equally constructed mood of loss, makes the hard-boiled hero a durable conservator of ideals "without thought of it." In the early hard-boiled, "ideas as subjective facts" are lived by the character as "aims given with immediate obviousness," with the certitude, if not the vocab-

---

9. Lukács, *Theory of the Novel,* 66, 78.

ulary, of epic forms.[10] An "aim given" implies a larger aim-giving framework, but when an autonomous individual takes over the conservation and animation of ideals "by instinct, by inevitability, without thought of it and certainly without saying it," their "obviousness" becomes limited to him—their solidity as given aims becomes subjective. And yet, their obviousness to the individual character—their sturdiness as subjective facts—gives the narrative impression, because the character is the protagonist and often narrator, of being shared and valued by the world of the novel. This narrative valorization of the hero's inclinations, this impression of sharing created by his centrality, is not at all the same as the total and totalizing "immediate obviousness" that for Lukács was characteristic of the epic world. Rather than operating from the outside in, meaning that the individual is valuable because of what he embodies, it operates primarily from the inside out. In other words, the embodied characteristics seem valuable because they are borne by the individual *qua* individual, and because they are borne entirely without the supporting foundation of transcendent meaning.

For Lukács, the transition from the epic to the novelistic world was intertwined with the transition from a religious to a secular or modern world. He describes his vision of this transition as "essentially determined by Hegel, e.g. the historico-philosophical view of what the epic and the novel have in common and what differentiates them." The diachronism of the epic-novel distinction resonates throughout *The Theory of the Novel*—one need look no further than the statement that "once this unity disintegrated, there could be no more spontaneous totality of being"—and in some sense echoes the mood of loss that reverberates through the hard-boiled. The "giver" of aims in the epic world was (past tense) the "roundness of the value system which determines the epic cosmos." The hard-boiled character is (present tense) much more likely to declare the absence of moral ideals than their presence. At the same time, I contend, even when it represents absence, the hard-boiled unites Lukács's diachronic account of transition with a consistently vital subjectivity through that transition—a subjectivity that counteracts the sense of loss. Lukács further states that "the present in *The Theory of the Novel* is not defined in Hegelian terms but rather by Fichte's formulation, as 'the age of absolute sinfulness.'"[11] As Axel Honneth writes of Fichte's formulation, "What is methodologically significant about this kind of philosophy of history is that it seems to allow one to make a negative judgment on the present without basing it explicitly on a value judgment."[12] This postulation of value-free judg-

---

10. MacCannell, "Democracy's Turn," 280, quoted in Dussere, 10.
11. Lukács, *Theory of the Novel,* 18.
12. Honneth, *Pathologies of Reason,* 97.

ment, I would propose, is crucial to the hard-boiled; indeed, it is the ground from which hard-boiled subjectivity and ethics are drawn.

Judith Butler describes the Hegelian subject—one without a persisting identity that endures through various phases—as "not a self-identical subject who travels smugly from one ontological place to another; it is its travels, and is every place in which it finds itself."[13] I read in the hard-boiled a subject conscious of his own actions, and whose consistent presence rests on that consciousness throughout his travels. He resides in the negativity of the outside world as in a permanent home, even as he counteracts that negativity through his own conscience. Chandler's "Simple Art of Murder" puts forth a historical and comparative account of detective fictions but represents the "mean streets" as a given: those mean streets surround the subject rather than negating him. As Lukács writes, "Art always says, 'And yet!' to life."[14] The hard-boiled as I read it in this book says "And yet!" to theories of secular modernity as decline and to the determinism of cultural circumstances, as well as to the utopian dream of warmer historical periods. Dean Moyar, noting in *Hegel's Conscience* that "the distinctive mark of conscience is that it is reasoning from *the first person perspective,*" writes, "In understanding modernity and the nature of ethical content within modern societies, we inevitably aim to give an account of the true nature of practical reasoning, but that should not blind us to the fact that conscience in all its forms is a fragile achievement."[15] In its resistance to narratives of decline and in its instinctive insistence on accountability and ethics, the hard-boiled foregrounds conscience, that "fragile achievement," as a continual regenerator of autonomous subjectivity. In so doing—and here again are shades or tones of the self-help books cited earlier—it insists on the abiding importance of individual moral choice across historical periods and circumstances.

In one sense, the hard-boiled character is an existential hero who does not know or care that he is one. Chandler's description implies an involuntary and indeed automatic heroism—an exemption from atmospheric contamination but also an exemption from any subjection to or even consciousness of morality or ethics as concepts. At the same time, the concept of moral choice is as crucial as it is paradoxical. The hero's "honor without thought of it" cannot mean goodness without exertion. On the contrary, I contend, it means more precisely "exertion without thought of it." The most persuasive critical treatments of hard-boiled subjectivity have argued for the detective's individualism being a critical response to the possible dangers of political collectivity

---

13. Butler, *Subjects of Desire*, 8.
14. Lukács, *Theory of the Novel*, 72.
15. Moyar, *Hegel's Conscience*, 14.

(McCann), to a corporate capitalism that alienated even as it enclosed the individual (Breu), to the diminishing of sentimental affiliations and group traditions (Cassuto), to modernity's critical stance (Rolls), and to crises of postwar nation-building (Gorrara). In such treatments, the detective's character emerges both as psychologically determined and as culturally or environmentally driven. He exists within and in response to his circumstances, which are almost invariably dispiriting. The character must engage with the desolation of the outside landscape, the hopelessness of institutions, and the indifference of the general public. What is more, the meanness of the mean streets necessarily affects the character, so that the envisioning of aims and the embodiment of ideals is not automatic. If conscience is a "fragile achievement," it is also a conscious and continually repeated one; this necessary repetition and the intention implied in "achievement" preclude moral utopianism. Autonomy and accountability are at a premium because these are as hard-won as they are necessary.

THE DANGER OF SUBJECTIVE FACTS

Putting aside the rather dispiriting notion of a shared culture for which one person or even group of people is responsible, the principal problem of the hard-boiled may be that the primacy of the individual imbues him with considerable power and thus, by extension, with menace. If honor becomes a matter of instinct, if it is a character attribute or what Currie names "an inner source of action" within the hard-boiled hero, what happens when the individual turns bad, as he ultimately does in the course of the twentieth-century hard-boiled? And what happens when theories of character as a concept, as a series of "relatively long-term stable dispositions" come apart, as they ultimately start to along the same timeline? It is when the soul, that ideal repository, becomes itself a source of contamination, that a *noir* grimness settles not only on modern crime fiction but also on its cultural master narratives.

In examining American and French crime fiction alike, my focus is on the culturally specific resonances of early nineteenth-century spiritual paragons and on their dissolution. In considering the French *néo-polar* and the American post–hard-boiled, their purposeful renunciations of individual accountability, and their casting of complex (and accountability-undermining) models of subjectivity as the inevitable correlates of modern existence, I focus nonetheless on what remains of a traditional concept of the individual. This is intentional, and indeed represents the central argument of this book, because even without recourse to a sacred frame, the long history of the hard-boiled nonetheless encourages a reading of individual moral choice as durable and vital. The complex ideological models of the political *néo-polar* and of Jim Thompson's postmodern psychopaths may seem difficult to reconcile with a traditional concept of the individual (and of society as a grouping of individuals), but this incompatibility is precisely my point. Those traditional concepts continue to intrude, to assert themselves, and even as the *néo-polar* and the mid-century American post–hard-boiled deconstruct the traditional subject they continue, in their exchange with nineteenth-century models, to resurrect it. The surprising result of such resurrections is that poststructuralist theories of subjectivity appear as so many disingenuous distractions. When individual conduct and the conceptual sturdiness of character devolve in concert, the result is a spectacular threat to the idea of accountability.

Because it focuses on character and on questions of accountability, this book privileges certain ancestries of the hard-boiled over others. In the French domain, I concentrate more on the romantic antecedents of hard-boiled character than on the urban chronicles of Balzac and Hugo that laid the ground for crime fiction's settings and social formations. Alistair Rolls notes, "Crime fiction is a genre (if indeed it can properly be called a genre) that was born in the modern city, and indeed in Paris in particular," and underscores the detective "as a trope, alongside the *flâneur,* of mid- to late-nineteenth-century Parisian modernity."[16] Thus the urban foundation of crime fiction runs alongside a strongly retrospective romanticism at the level of character. Indeed, insofar as nineteenth-century Paris is a site of inchoate modernity, crime fiction's evocation of romantic roots and its insistence on respecting their outlines speak to a charged ambivalence about that modernity. It also informs an abiding and sometimes nostalgic authority the genre accords to individual personality. Outside the scope of the present study are the numerous film adaptations of hard-boiled novels and the evolution of the female hard-boiled hero.[17]

---

16. Rolls, *Paris and the Fetish*, 29.

17. John Irwin, Stephen Faison, Gene Phillips, Paula Rabinowitz, Alastair Phillips, and Alistair Rolls and Deborah Walker, among others, have given film noir rich consideration. And while choosing to limit the discussion to masculine hard-boiled subjectivity, I nonetheless address the question of the hard-boiled character's romantic and sexual relationships and his treatment of women, reading in these expressions or dilutions of empathy, honesty, and consciousness of others.

OVERVIEW

The first chapter examines nineteenth-century American and French sermons, romantic literature, and traditional nineteenth-century works of crime fiction. It outlines the respective character portraits of each culture's ideal spiritual authority and follows the transformation of spiritual authorities into romantic heroic exemplars. Just as American romantic literature turns into innate American character traits such elements of preaching as unpretentiousness, plainspokenness, and an instinctive sense of right, so French romantic literature turned into sentimental attributes the sensitivity and poeticism of the preacher's message. These characteristics born in romantic and religious literature were the fruits of historical specificity, but they have nonetheless turned into durable character models. It has been a long time since an American frontiersman crashed through the forest or a Frenchman wandered mountain paths, and yet these are canonical models, points of reference, culture heroes, and modern foundations for each nation's vision of character and of spiritual authority. That lineage is shared by both countries, fused on the French side with Balzac and Hugo and in the process establishing the heroes of France's urban streets. That coincidence of secular psychology and spiritual authority, that rendition of virtue as personality and of personality as virtue, anticipates the hard-boiled accidental paragon, the man of honor "without thought of it." This chapter also locates in early nineteenth-century texts the seeds of crime fiction's eventual twentieth-century contamination of this ideal model. French religious writings warn against amoral aestheticism and nihilistic lassitude. In the American model, on the other hand, a greater source of concern was the perversion of the spiritual message by a theatrical narcissism.

The second chapter focuses on the first hard-boiled crime fiction novels in the United States and France, concentrating on the principal detective. In *The Snarl of the Beast* (1927) by Carroll John Daly, the narrator, Race Williams, is at once the lone pioneer and the garrulous revival preacher, announcing on the first page: "Right and wrong are not written on the statutes for me, nor do I find my code of morals in the essays of long-winded professors. My ethics are my own. I'm not saying they're good and I'm not admitting they're bad, and what's more I'm not interested in the opinions of others on that subject."[18] Though Race Williams makes no claim for the universal value or prominence of his "ethics," the very use of the word indicates at least a nodding familiarity with systems, schools of thought, and the idea of an absolute. Displaying

---

18. Daly, *Snarl of the Beast*, 1.

restraint, psychic fortitude, anti-intellectualism, empathic capacity, and intuitive morality, he functions as an ideal respondent to a fragmented and alienating New York as well as to a postwar America. In Léo Malet's *120, rue de la Gare* (1943), Nestor Burma reanimates the nineteenth-century postrevolutionary poet for contemporary wartime. Through a nuanced sense of the aesthetic and its ethical limitations, through an understatement of his own problems and an empathic response to those of others, and through reliance on literary, cultural, and architectural history to solve a murder, Burma uses his status as outsider private detective to advocate for an entire culture under attack. The German occupation engenders an ethical stance that at the same time conserves French cultural hegemony. Although the idea of the exemplary outsider has always resonated more problematically in a European context than in an American, the occupation allowed the outsider to become an exemplary cultural insider. At the same time, Burma's fusion of aesthetic sensibility, empathic capacity, narrative mastery, and heroic exemplarity, so resonant for occupied France, powerfully underscores the importance of individual heroic models to the conservation of a culture under assault.

Chapter 3 examines the deterioration of the American character model in *The Killer Inside Me* (1952), the best known of Jim Thompson's post–hard-boiled novels. Jim Thompson's drifters, con artists, alcoholics, and psychopathic small-town sheriffs have been read as "only the most extreme examples of a whole world gone wrong" and "wriggling past private madness, or American rot, to universal horror."[19] And yet, what renders Thompson's name synonymous with a hard-boiled turn toward hopelessness is his simultaneous insistence on and evacuation of individual responsibility: a constant alternation between the Race Williams model of determined centrality and grand gestures of nihilistic powerlessness. Lou Ford, the Texas sheriff who narrates *The Killer Inside Me,* refers to the "sickness" that he calls dementia praecox (schizophrenia) and which drives him to murder. Numerous intertextual parallels between Lou Ford's narrative and Daniel Paul Schreber's 1903 *Memoirs of My Nervous Illness*—written by an actual dementia praecox patient— cast him as overdetermined by an accountability-erasing diagnosis and by the traumatic memory of a Foucauldian panopticon-like childhood. These parallels conjure two major threats to individualism and even to the idea of character. One is psychic trauma—an experience that resists and derails narrativization and results in a splintered self—and the other an overwhelming and ongoing social control. "Universal horror" comes from narrative manipulation of these specters: from the disillusion that arises when Ford's insistence

19. McCauley, *Jim Thompson,* 242; Polito, *Savage Art,* 456.

on narrative control clashes with his calculated surrenders to traumatic memories and mad impulses, and with his enthusiastic imitations of a dumbed-down American lexicon. Similar strategies to both master one's narrative and undercut accountability emerge in Jim Thompson's *Pop. 1280,* in the novels of Horace McCoy and Patricia Highsmith, and in American political actors of the last fifty years. As Stephen King writes in his foreword to Thompson's novel, "Looking back at the record, one would have to say that [the description of Ford] . . . also describes a generation of politicians: Joe McCarthy, Richard Nixon, Oliver North, Alexander Haig, and a slew of others. In Lou Ford, Jim Thompson drew for the first time a picture of the Great American Sociopath."[20]

The fourth chapter considers the French *néo-polar,* the violent and politically jaundiced descendant of the *roman noir,* focusing on its principal author and theorist, Jean-Patrick Manchette. The *néo-polar* launches the same double-pronged assault on the classic hard-boiled French character model as did the American. First, it practices a point-by-point undoing of French heroic characteristics, namely, an ethical sense of the aesthetic and its limits, a respect for French cultural and literary history, and an empathic and readerly interest in other people. At the same time, it blames that undoing on social, political, or philosophical forces, casting what Dominique Manotti calls "existential disenchantment" as an inevitable accompaniment to political disillusion.[21] And just as Thompson's characters turn the direct, plain-speaking individualist into an unhinged hayseed, so Manchette's characters turn the melancholic aesthete into a bored, destructive, self-absorbed nihilist. In *L'affaire N'Gustro,* Manchette's first sole-authored novel, sometime narrator Henri Butron echoes the disgruntled protagonists of Roger Nimier and Albert Camus but in so doing distorts the nineteenth-century romantic model by beating up strangers, embracing reactionary politics, and urinating on historic Parisian monuments. All the while he contemplates, or pretends to contemplate, his own character, value, and existence. These contemplations build up character as such—the "fictional character" that Robbe-Grillet outlined in his writings on the *nouveau roman*—as an absent narrative center.[22] Dismantling or deconstructing the subject is in fact the subject's most important and most intentionally dispiriting accomplishment. Similar distortions emerge in the principal character of *Morgue pleine* and *Que d'os!,* Manchette's most traditional private detective novels. The very characteristics that make detective Eugène Tarpon so subdued a specimen—disenchantment, lassi-

---

20. Thompson, *Killer Inside Me* (1989), n. pag.
21. Frommer and Oberti, "Dominique Manotti," 46.
22. Robbe-Grillet, *Pour un nouveau roman,* 26.

tude, confusion—are precisely those of the early nineteenth-century romantic heroes, in hyperbolic form.

The last chapter considers contemporary efforts on both sides of the Atlantic to redress the collaborative problems of exaggerated autonomy and hamstrung accountability. It focuses on Fred Vargas's novels, particularly *Seeking Whom He May Devour* [*L'homme à l'envers*], in which Commissioner Adamsberg is described as having "many scruples, but few principles." In keeping with Jacqueline Hodgson's descriptions of the French republican tradition as one in which "the sovereignty of the people becomes the sovereignty of the state," Adamsberg valorizes and incarnates a symbiotic republican ideal of the state as representative of the people.[23] The privileging of scruple over principle demonstrates that individual interiority can become— both reflect and morph into—the character of the state. It brings crime fiction back to the Chandler model of "honor without thought of it" and to a rendition of principles as instinctual traits, reinserting the early nineteenth-century romantic model in the midst of contemporary judicial operations. In the United States, where the hard-boiled mantle has increasingly been taken up on television as well as in novels, crime dramas similarly reconcile reclamation of individual responsibility with the myriad psychic, institutional, and discursive challenges to that reclamation. Almost without exception, crime television grapples with tensions between individual accountability and the leaden weight of judicial and procedural norms. HBO's *The Wire* (2002–2008) and *True Detective* (2014) showcase the endeavor to make autonomy matter and to arrive at an enlivening rather than destructively entropic result. *True Detective* acknowledges and even underscores that hard-boiled moments of empathic, philosophical cool are indeed ideals rather than sustained modes. *The Wire* reproduces the pervasive hopelessness of the *néo-polar* but nonetheless sustains the accountable subject, insisting on self-examination as an unavoidable element of the living mind.

THE CHALLENGE OF HARD-BOILED CRITICISM

Before moving to a discussion of early nineteenth-century heroic models, I want to put in a few words about attempts to analyze the hard-boiled genre, which has known an enduring popularity and been the subject of much recent academic analysis. Urban-centered and touched with nihilism and violence, it lends itself to political and historical analyses of modern capitalist

---

23. Hodgson, *French Criminal Justice*, 16.

alienation. Featuring an independent detective and abandoning the murder-investigation-resolution structure of the armchair detective novel, it dovetails with critiques of institutional processes and of cultural understandings of the law as well as with investigations of narrative structure. Character-driven and focused on the individual, it opens itself to studies of the intersection of the sociological and the psychological and to analyses of cultural mythology. And since hard-boiled fiction belongs, for the above reasons as well as for its association with film noir, to a marginally literary "shadow" category, it has inspired examination of the very nature of the canon and the tension between marginal and universal in the cultural imagination. Criticism of this particular genre is always somewhat circular in nature. On the one hand it examines and situates individual novels within the hard-boiled corpus and at the same time resituates that corpus within literature and culture, taking into account the particular novel at hand. All such criticism has to negotiate with the fact that the genre is an apparent whole made of disparate parts as well as to acknowledge the genre's marginal nature—all of which makes its place in the world of literature and literary studies a necessarily vexed one.

At times, for instance, criticism of crime fiction has argued that a particular novel or author had transcended the pulp marginality of the genre and should be counted as "literature." Raymond Chandler and Dashiell Hammett have come in for much commentary of this sort. And yet, as Uri Eisenzweig contends in *Le récit impossible,* claiming that crime fiction has always occupied a critical and conceptual place between "bad literature" and "paraliterature," the appeal of crime fiction lies in its resistance to such elevations. He writes, "It was particularly in the 1890s, when the detective novel exploded onto the literary scene, that its negative characterization correlated unambiguously to its new perception as a generic unit" [C'est surtout au cours des années 1890, alors que le roman policier surgit massivement sur la scène littéraire, que s'affirme sans ambiguïté la corrélation entre sa caractérisation négative et la perception nouvelle de son unité générique].[24]

What Eisenzweig describes as the "negative characterization" associated with the genre goes a long way toward explaining the unavoidably ambivalent as well as Sisyphean nature of endeavors to elevate it. Arguments for the literary and cultural importance of a literature whose very importance resides in its refusal to embrace traditional concepts of "importance" are doomed to a certain amount of self-contradiction. The genre's marginal and at times anti-intellectual nature is absorbed into, becomes in the end the foundation of, its place within the world of literature. Indeed, in part as a result of critical attention, its readiness to trawl the bottom of the canon becomes crucial

---

24. Eisenzweig, *Le récit impossible,* 32.

to its place in it. Its deliberate urban marginalism, combined with repeated critical introductions into the realm of literature, amount to a sort of edgy advertisement for the genre. The place of the hard-boiled, one foot in the world of literature and the other in paraliterature, is especially relevant to the present study because that place is characteristic of its protagonist as well. It is a critical commonplace that the toughness and moral ambiguity of its characters represent an authorial indictment of social corruption—in other words, the character is responding to a dangerous, disordered, or demoralizing cultural habitat. Raymond Chandler's famous "mean streets" statement presented the tension between overweening meanness and individual moral solidity as the foundation of the hard-boiled. So it is too, I would contend, with the individual hard-boiled novel within the hard-boiled canon.

Because of its storied place in the margins of literature, as well as in the margins of law, culture, family, and psychology, criticism stops short of fully integrating the hard-boiled into the world of literature. Although directing literary criticism to a genre that wholeheartedly sidesteps the literary may not qualify as a literary critical endeavor, what makes the hard-boiled a compelling focus of academic study is precisely its almost coincidental, surprising, or precarious literary nature. It is even an accidental literature, much as its character is an accidental hero. Its precarious capacity to transcend the genre and join the mainstream ranks of literature becomes the foundation of its academic (because anti-academic) appeal.

THE TOO-FAMILIAR HARD-BOILED OUTLINE

The occasionally antiliterary and anti-intellectual hue of the hard-boiled, combined with its sheer numbers, has created peculiar problems in the analysis of individual novels and characters, as well as a curious circularity in discussions of the genre. One such problem, which arises indirectly from the very number of novels, is that not every novel that conforms to generic definitions of the hard-boiled is either good or interesting enough to be woven into the practice of literary criticism and welcomed into the club of literary elevation. At the same time, because it is a genre, and because it is read and sought and celebrated as such, the practice of exclusion tends to threaten the integrity of the totality more so than in other forms less about outline and ambiance. John Milton, in his 1963 study of the western novel, had written of the cowboy:

> This was the golden era of the cowboy, a short and frantic era which ended abruptly in the severe winters of 1886–87 and the accompanying drought,

but which left behind a myth, or at least an image of the cowboy-hero, riding the range in loneliness and courage. The image has been built upon general impressions and somewhat isolated facts, because no one cowboy lives on in legend or fact to take his place beside the notable hunters and scouts such as Carson, Boone, Glass, and Buffalo Bill. What remains in literature (as it also remains in the movies and in television) is simply the "typical" cowboy, the stereotype which has ridden his faithful horse at a gallop through a large number of bad novels and a very few good ones.[25]

Even aside from its dependence on sometimes mediocre foundations, the predominance of "type" has its problematic implications. With crime fiction in general, and with the hard-boiled in particular, the "image" seems greater than and in some sense independent of the sum of its component parts. Characters are specific, their particular actions and words distinct, but "the hard-boiled character" is an outline, within an atmosphere, within a mood. The phenomenon of a type that supersedes individual examples, the dominance of the "typical" that John Milton describes in his study of the cowboy, is as characteristic of the hard-boiled as it was of the cowboy western. And it is characteristic for some of the same reasons: the connection of the hard-boiled genre to film noir (analogous to the cowboy novel's connection to western movies) underscored the interchangeability of faces, not to mention insinuated the hero literally as a silhouette, a trench-coated form in the evening. One could know the hard-boiled hero by his cigarette, his inscrutable glance, and the shadows and rain that surrounded him. This familiarity has proved profitable for the hard-boiled's place in popular culture and by extension in academic studies, since it accords the form a strong cultural currency that interacts well with its high-low literary nature, yet at the same time defends itself from critical examinations. From a twenty-first-century perspective, it is almost impossible to unknow what has become such a familiar cultural image that, no matter how schematic, has virtually become visual and conceptual shorthand for the urban underworld. Or perhaps it is more correct to say that it is difficult to see how much the familiarity of the outline precludes knowing what resides within—much as Shklovsky meant when he wrote, "We apprehend objects only as shapes with imprecise extensions; we do not see them in their entirety but rather recognize them by their main characteristics. We see the object as though it were enveloped in a sack."[26] In the case of the hard-boiled character, that sack takes the form of clichés ("a man of honor," "mean

---

25. Milton, "Western Novel," 80–81.
26. Lemon and Reis, *Russian Formalist Criticism*, 11.

streets," "urban wasteland") that abound both in the literature and in criticism of it. The problem with an excessive familiarity with the hard-boiled outline is that discussion of its component parts—that is, examination of the protagonist's character, thoughts, words, ideas—often veers into reification of that general and rather schematic personality outline. Because of the large number of hard-boiled novels and characters, because of the many variations on the theme, because of the sometimes clichéd nature of the theme itself, such criticism often turns into a repeated list of characteristics, of plot and character outlines. Criticism that situates an individual novel or character within the hard-boiled canon and then re-delineates that canon based on the reading of that individual novel or novels—which most criticism does to some extent, including this present endeavor—must be aware of its tendency to move in a circle, thus to both pursue and create a moving target.

EVOLUTION OF FORM AND CHARACTER

Because so many early authors of the hard-boiled have vanished into the historical ether, and because the genre has gained what Milton called a "recognizable pattern," the historiography of the hard-boiled often reads the genre as "evolving." As Robert Skinner writes, "The writers who shaped the hard-boiled hero in the early years were a diverse group whose writing was rough and volatile, like raw petroleum, but which, over time, was refined and filtered into a smooth, high-grade product."[27] We can recall John Milton's description of the "cowboy" as a "stereotype which has ridden his faithful horse at a gallop through a large number of bad novels and a very few good ones." That characterization demonstrates the dependence of proliferation and mediocrity—the way in which abundant production, and a consequent profusion of mediocre examples, dull or blur the substance of the hard-boiled "type" even as it solidifies its outlines. What is more, in the realm of the hard-boiled, some of the early writers who are best at creating an "outline"—contributing to the firm contours of the hard-boiled character as a type, or to what Lee Horsley called "the most characteristic narratives"[28]—are at the same time not terribly good at creating either a multifaceted individual character or a fictional world. I will be making an argument for the unsung psychological complexity of the much-maligned Carroll John Daly, the first hard-boiled author. Critics have declared, and not without some justification, that Daly was "a dreadful

---

27. Skinner, *New Hard-Boiled Dicks,* 10.
28. Horsley, *Noir Thriller,* 16.

writer" and "impossibly crude."[29] Daly, it would seem, was entirely aware of writing a "first" and establishing which would be its "most characteristic narratives." And numerous authors followed close on his heels, authors who were not "firsts" but who wrote with similar crudeness—a crudeness that, paradoxically enough, contributed to the fixed canonical contours of hard-boiled mood and vocabulary. Subsequent critical treatments of Hammett and Chandler acknowledged their debt to Daly. In some readings, Hammett and Daly are presented as equally primitive, with Chandler contributing more stylistic sophistication.[30] According to these evolutionary scenarios, a schematic or poorly written character and novel could nonetheless gain value through its subsequent resonances in other novels, echoes in now-canonical authors, and thus an eventual contribution to the groundwork of the hard-boiled "type." Hammett's improvements on Daly are instances of such contribution, as are Chandler's on Hammett. Because the hard-boiled outline has become both more familiar and more abstract, and because its tributaries have multiplied, assessments of the hard-boiled sometimes point, as Skinner's does, to a process of evolution and refinement. It is important, however, to note that the "smooth, high-grade product" to which Skinner refers is hard-boiled *writing*—writing that was "rough and volatile" in the first decade of the genre, when paper (a product in its own right) was inexpensive and the disposable weekly magazine the most popular publication forum. The hard-boiled character as modern individualist embodiment of morals and ethics, on the other hand, follows a very different sort of arc, one that is quite the opposite of refinement and can more properly be called "devolution"—the rotting of the object within its familiarizing sack. For all the alternation and ultimate fusion between the marginal and the literary, the main event of the hard-boiled as I read it is not the refinement of a form but rather the weakening both of the idea of individual embodiment and of shared ideals as conserved or conservable by individuals, and at the same time a blueprint for reinstatement of that embodiment. Contemporary crime fiction endeavors to reanimate individual autonomy, to correct for the excesses that made that autonomy dangerous, and to restore the notion of responsibility for the common good. In other

---

29. William Nolan writes of Daly, "The writing was impossibly crude, the plotting labored and ridiculous, and Race Williams emerged as a swaggering illiterate with the emotional instability of a gun-crazed vigilante." Nolan, *Black Mask Boys*, 35.

30. According to Sigelman and Jacoby, "the low-brow character of the readership imposed on hard-boiled writers the imperative of simplicity—the need to use simple words joined in simple sentences strung together in simple chronological order. The pioneering hard-boiled mysteries of Carroll John Daly and Dashiell Hammett did precisely that, and little more. Chandler's achievement was to graft stylistic complexity and sophistication onto the rudimentary hard-boiled format." Sigelman and Jacoby, "Not-So-Simple Art of Imitation," 15–16.

words, it underscores the importance of reviving the concept of "honor" that in fiction stands "without thought of it." When narrative insistence on individual agency is inseparable from the presence of shared moral responsibilities, that alliance allays certain hopeless tendencies not just in crime novels but more broadly and importantly in modern cultural and political master narratives.

FROM VIRTUE TO HONOR

A Nineteenth-Century Paradigm Shift

CONSTRUCTING A CULTURE HERO

I wrote earlier that one of Western culture's most treasured modern ideals is the secular individual for whom spiritual ideals come naturally, unforced, and constitute durable character attributes. I read such embodiment of ideals and possession of personality attributes as simultaneous functions of novelistic character rather than as distinct historical roles. And yet the early nineteenth century was witness to a moment in literary history that expressly blended those perspectives on character, actively situated exemplarity within psychology, and, not coincidentally, gave rise to crime fiction as a genre. Both France and America saw a decline in religious enthusiasm in the immediate aftermath of their respective late eighteenth-century revolutions.[1] Both countries saw endeavors to reanimate that enthusiasm on a national-cultural scale during the early nineteenth century. And in the literature of both, that reanimation singled out a principal character that retained its appeal as a cultural type long after the religious framework had faded. Although the transition from a religious to a secular society was an actual and well-documented lived sociohistorical phenomenon, literary romanticism retained a nostalgic remi-

---

1. Finke and Stark write, "The characterization of the religious situation in the immediate aftermath of the American Revolution as the 'lowest ebb-tide' in our history was used nearly word for word by all the leading authors from Robert Baird in 1844 to Sydney Ahlstrom in 1972." Finke and Stark, *Churching of America*, 2.

niscence that portrayed transition as redolent of loss and defeat. This portrayal aligned with the inclination of contemporaneous sermons and religious writings to describe secularism as decline. It also aligned with the advent of social and political changes (industrialism, capitalism, urbanization) that did in fact give rise to as much lament as optimism. The transition to a secular society thus became not just a historical phenomenon but also a story, replete with melancholic reminiscence, dramatic warning, and—importantly for the present study—strong individual characters who could mediate that social evolution.

Whereas American religious revival went the way of evangelicalism, revival meetings, and a devaluing of clerical gentility, France saw the return of Old Regime ecclesiastics and an aesthetic-poetic argument for religion. The French emphasis on lyrical grace was in contrast to an American preference for religious dynamism, with the artist and the evangelist serving as respective cultural models of spiritual standing and strength. These models amounted to character portraits of each country's ideal believer, or ideal moral leader—models that emerged solidified through nineteenth-century sermons in both countries. At the same time they are precisely the respective heroic models that populated both nineteenth-century romantic literature in the two countries and crime fiction, especially the hard-boiled.

American and French hard-boiled protagonists are direct descendants of nineteenth-century models of spiritual authority who emerged from the sermons and religious writings of the first quarter of the nineteenth century, as well as of the romantic heroes who carried those same characteristics. In this chapter I describe how nineteenth-century models of spiritual authority morphed into particular cultural heroic models—the frontier individualist in America and the contemplative poet-aesthete in France—and how those foundational heroes in turn became cornerstones of the hard-boiled. In examining the hard-boiled character as a descendant of the spiritual-romantic hero, I focus on the sort of persona and individual qualities that each nation associated with spiritual connection, in order to demonstrate to what extent these were codified by the time of their rendition in crime fiction.

This is not to suggest that romantic and religious writing were the sole precursors to crime fiction. Nor does it mean that hard-boiled fiction reminisces about anterior historical frames or turns around to recuperate abandoned religiosities. It means instead that hard-boiled exemplarity and early nineteenth-century spiritual exemplarity function in analogous ways: by combining the embodiment of virtue with the possession of individual characteristics and by casting those characteristics as antithetical to narratives of modern degeneration. It is true that in romantic literature, that antithesis can resonate as recuperative and thus both historical and counterhistorical in nature. But the innate characteristics themselves, which in the hard-boiled emerge connected to the notion of ideal embodiment, function in that genre as emblems of individual capacity for moral choice and action across a variety of historical circumstances.

In the early nineteenth century, cultural models of right and power were drawn with surprising clarity as character portraits—as actors in a historiographical narrative. It is worth a moment to trace the evolution of these portraits, these paragons able to temper the winds of historical transformation simply by being who they are, since their enactment of "honor without thought of it" constitutes, somewhat paradoxically, the dominant thought of the hard-boiled and the aim to which it would reach. Lukács wrote that "if the individual is unproblematic, then his aims are given to him with immediate obviousness." The hard-boiled detective is not an unproblematic individual, but the early nineteenth century hands him the aim of individual conscience, that "fragile achievement" that has continued for centuries to remain an aim in and of itself. Indeed, by the time they appear in the hard-boiled, the attributes outlined in this chapter function as markers of an abiding subjectivity. The pertinent personae set the stage for respective cultural incarnations of Raymond Chandler's "honor without thought of it" as well as for the stakes of individual choice and for reparative hard-boiled returns to accountability.

FRENCH RELIGIOUS WRITING

Broadly stated, French emphasis on introspection contrasted with American preference for religious dynamism. The contrast between the contemplative poet and the vigorous revival preacher pervades religious and romantic portraits as well as crime fiction in America and France. The seventeenth century had been known as the "time of the beautiful sermons" [temps des beaux sermons], but the postrevolutionary period brought renewed attention to the voices and personae of religious authority.[2] French nineteenth-century religious writings interweave spiritual connection with sensitivity, artistic sensibility, and intellectual finesse. That affiliation remains whether the preacher is Catholic or Protestant, the tone of the sermon wistful or vigorous. For priest and philosopher Félicité de Lamennais, for instance, the element of sentiment and especially of sadness was paramount: "Man's life on earth is full of

---

2. Landry, *Le temps des beaux sermons.*

pain, misery, and suffering . . . In that state, human wisdom has a choice to make: harden oneself against nature and deny the torment, or seek distraction in the pleasure of it" [La vie de l'homme sur la terre est pleine de douleurs, de misères, de souffrances . . . Or, en cet état, la sagesse humaine n'a vu que le choix entre deux partis: ou de se raider contre la nature et de nier le supplice, ou d'y chercher une distraction dans la volupté].[3] He echoed many of his Catholic contemporaries in his 1817 *Essay on Indifference in Matters of Religion* [*Essai sur l'indifférence en matière de religion*], declaring the feeling of divine love more important than the act of penitence. Henri Lacordaire, an admirer of Lamennais and another precursor of modern Catholicism, counseled as well the importance of love and affirmed the value of verbal eloquence as both product of and incitement to passion.[4] Just as spiritual connection is said to evoke love and sensitivity, the converse is also true. According to Athanase Coquerel, Protestant theologian and pastor, "a moral, intellectual, perceptive, religious being cannot be happy unless he sees a path of knowledge, holiness, and love rising continually before him. To give him less, to offer him other riches, would be to wrench him from his very nature: created for light, he would be forced to seek his happiness in the dark" [un être moral, intellectuel, sensible, religieux, ne peut être heureux sans qu'il soit tracé devant lui une ligne sans cesse ascendante de science, de sainteté, d'amour. Lui donner moins, l'enrichir autrement, ce serait le jeter avec violence hors de sa nature; créé pour la lumière, ce serait l'envoyer chercher sa félicité dans la nuit].[5] The interconnection between moral, intellectual, perceptive, and religious sets forth a character model for the ideal believer in nineteenth-century France.

The above-cited priests are either proponents of liberal Catholicism (Lamennais and Lacordaire) or of liberal Protestantism (Coquerel). Sentimental theology coexisted with the dire and menacing remonstrations of more conservative preachers. Alexandre Soulier, for instance, a Protestant predicator from Andouze, adopted the voice of God to proclaim the discourse of hellfire: "Go on, false disciples, go accursed into that eternal flame that awaits the devil and his angels" [Allez donc, méchans serviteurs, allez donc, disciples prétendus, allez maudits, au feu éternel, préparé au diable et à ses anges!].[6] There was menace to be found in Catholic writings, too, through less

---

3. Lamennais, *L'imitation de Jésus-Christ,* 197. Translations are mine unless otherwise noted.

4. Lacordaire, *Conférences du révérend père Lacordaire,* 4:149, and *Conférences du révérend père Lacordaire,* 4:149, 64.

5. Coquerel, *Sermons,* 1:543.

6. Soulier, *Les jugements de Dieu,* 103.

apocalyptic vocabulary, however.[7] Love and lyricism correlated with a liberal side of theology, whereas dire menace, with its proliferation of capital letters and italics, remained the property of the conservative wing. One of the earliest and most powerful lines in that battle of style was drawn by François-René de Chateaubriand, who not only celebrated the association of lyricism with religion but also aligned both with the heroic character portraits of French romanticism.

CHATEAUBRIAND AND FRENCH ROMANTICISM

One of the best-known instruments of French nineteenth-century religious revival, Chateaubriand's *Génie du christianisme*, underscores the interconnections among beauty, musical rhetoric, romanticism, and mystical intensity. *Génie*, which Napoleon would call the "work that had done the most harm to his power" [l'ouvrage qui avait le plus nui à son pouvoir], also definitively blends spiritual and romantic literature and identifies lyricism as its instrument of conversion. Intended as a gentler alternative to heavy-handed doctrinal admonition, *Génie* declared in its preface: "We had to prove . . . that of all the religions that had ever existed, Christianity is the most poetic, the most human, and the most propitious to liberty, to art, and to literature" [On devait chercher à prouver . . . que de toutes les religions qui ont jamais existé, la religion chrétienne est la plus poétique, la plus humaine, la plus favorable à la liberté, aux arts et aux lettres].[8] The very titles of its chapters reinforce the reliance of spiritual connection on the interdependence of the "moral, intellectual, perceptive, and religious": "Song of Birds," "The Poetic of Christianity Is Divided into Three Branches: Poetry, the Fine Arts, and Literature" [Que la poétique du christianisme se divise en trois branches; poésie, beaux arts, littérature], "Of Some French and Foreign Poems," "Music," "Sculpture," and "Architecture."[9] The words "beauty," "tenderness," "sweetness," "song," "music," and "poetry" appear again and again in *Génie*, as they do in sermons of the period. Chateaubriand sold his readers on the lyrical value of the scriptures, and his defense of the use of Latin in the Church is as much aesthetic as historical. Chateaubriand was of course not

---

7. Cf. Freppel, *Cours d'éloquence.*
8. Chateaubriand, *Génie du christianisme*, 1:12.
9. The emphasis on lyricism responded expressly to Hughes Old's description of the last days of French classical preaching: "The forms themselves were worn and tired. Even worse, the homiletical forms were compromised by their association with absolutism." Old, *Reading and Preaching of the Scriptures*, 6:16.

the first French author to wed religious feeling with poetry.[10] He continues Fénelon's tradition in declaring that a precondition of belief—or a precondition of openness to his argument for belief—is an appreciation of poetry and art.

The gentle and lyrical arguments presented in *Génie* amounted to a sort of modern liberal evangelical methodology. "God does not forbid us to tread the flowered paths, if they serve to bring us back to Him" [Dieu ne défend pas les routes fleuries quand elles servent à revenir à lui], wrote Chateaubriand, creating both a sermon and a metasermon.[11] Importantly, *Génie* also served to create an emotional character portrait of the author's ideal Christian, defining the sort of personality or character that would respond to his arguments. First, he paints people as fond of mysterious phenomena. "Considering man's natural attraction to the mysterious, it is hardly surprising that the religions of all nations have had their impenetrable secrets" [Il n'est point étonnant, d'après le penchant de l'homme aux mystères, que les religions de tous les peuples aient eu leurs secrets impénétrables]. Once he has declared that people are constituted to embrace Christianity, he outlines the "perfect harmony of feeling and thought, of imagination and understanding" [parfait accord du sentiment et de la pensée, de l'imagination et de l'entendement] that makes them so. He then zeroes in on the precise characteristics, inclinations, and dispositions that form the groundwork for the romantic heroic model. These include a taste for the bucolic, for "the voice of the zephyr or the storm, of the eagle or the dove, that called man to the temple of the God of nature" [la voix du zéphyr ou de la tempête, de l'aigle ou de la colombe, qui appelait l'homme au temple du Dieu de la nature]. He also declares that "there is in man an instinctive melancholy, which puts him in harmony with scenes of nature. Who has not spent hours on end seated on the bank of a river, watching its passing waves?" [Il y a dans l'homme un instinct qui le met en rapport avec les scènes de la nature. Eh! Qui n'a passé des heures assis sur le rivage d'un

---

10. In his 1713 *Treatise on the Existence of God* [*Traité de l'existence de Dieu*], Fénelon had famously argued for the existence of God by comparing the world to an epic poem: "Let one reason as subtly as he wants; no man in his right mind will be persuaded that the *Iliad* had no other author than accident. Cicero said as much of the *Annales* of Ennius, and he added that chance would never write a single verse, much less an entire poem. Why then should this reasonable man believe of the entire universe, which is doubtless much more marvelous than the *Iliad*, what his good sense would not let him believe of this poem?" [Qu'on raisonne et qu'on subtilise tant qu'on voudra, jamais on ne persuadera à un homme sensé, que *l'Iliade* n'ait point autre auteur que le hasard. Cicéron en disoit autant des *Annales* d'Ennius; et il ajoutait que le hasard ne feroit jamais un seul vers, bien loin de faire tout un poème. Pourquoi donc cet homme sensé croiroit-il de l'univers, sans doute encore plus merveilleux que *l'Iliade*, ce que son bon sens ne lui permettra jamais de croire de ce poème?]. Fénelon, *Œuvres complètes*, 10.

11. Chateaubriand, *Génie du christianisme*, 1:13.

fleuve, à voir s'écouler les ondes?]¹² I have quoted these declarations about human nature at some length because what sermons had set forth as spiritual counsel and method, these phrases describe as inborn human inclinations. In using the vocabulary of instinct, imagination, and understanding (*entendement*), Chateaubriand creates a character who is, to borrow Chandler's phrase, religious "without thought of it," someone to whom the aim of "harmony with nature" is both obvious and immediate. At the same time, crucially, that innateness or "immediate obviousness" accompanies an existential isolation. The experiences described are solitary. In other words, this is not an epic hero at one with vast spiritual expanses, whose "lesser strength is guided to victory by the highest power in the world,"¹³ but rather someone existing well outside the realm of sacred frames. The sensitive and melancholic young man who finds beauty in nature and classical music and loves literature and melodious sounds emerges as a collage of innate attributes and tastes. Combining spiritual virtues with instinctive character traits, he also becomes an enduring cultural type.

Within *Génie*, of course, Chateaubriand declares that the principal interest of sensitivity and artistic tastes is their connection to God and religion. Yet the sensitive, sentimental, and poetic aspects of his ideal reader/believer are precisely those of his secular romantic heroes as well. One of Chateaubriand's most important legacies is precisely that subtle move in focus from the spiritual to the sentimental. Rather than being in touch with God—or perhaps as the most remarkable and celebrated manifestation of being thus in touch—the romantic hero is in touch with his emotions. This shift in focus has been variously interpreted. Alain and Arlette Michel write of Chateaubriand, "His work is among those that have contributed most to passing the Christian tradition on to romanticism. The author does this not with the dilettantism of the aesthete or the dreamer, but with the sharp lucidity of an intelligence conscious of all its movements, an intelligence often visionary" [Son œuvre est l'une de celles qui concourent le plus largement à transmettre la tradition chrétienne au romantisme. Il ne le fait point avec le dilettantisme de l'esthète ou du rêveur mais avec la lucidité aiguë d'une intelligence consciente de tous ses mouvements, intelligence souvent visionnaire qui s'exerce].¹⁴ Other critics of romanticism deny this view of the spiritual within the sentimental, proposing instead that the very blending of sentimental and spiritual leads to a repudiation of the divine.¹⁵ The change in emphasis from the religious to

---

12. Ibid., 1:16, 86, 135, 298.
13. Lukács, *Theory of the Novel*, 98.
14. Michel and Michel, *La littérature française*, 23.
15. Cf. Lacoste, "Un substitut théologique," 224.

the romantic and from matters of virtue to matters of temperament took the form of a growing focus on the heart and mind. *Génie* casts spiritual connection as supremely desirable, but its author nonetheless contributed (whether intentionally or not) to the romantic displacement of religious discourse into the domain of the literary and also, importantly, of virtue into the domain of individual character attributes.[16]

There is perhaps no better example of this displacement than Chateaubriand's own *René*, a romantic novella embedded within *Génie du christianisme*. Placing this sentimental book within *Génie* amounts to inserting the sentimental into the religious—an insertion that gradually leads the reader from spiritual ideals to the portrait of an individual personality. As *René* opens, it is clear that the principal interest of the story lies in the movements of the psyche. "[The elders of the tribe] were all only the more ardent in exhorting him to open his heart to them. They showed so much discretion, tenderness, and authority that he was obliged in the end to satisfy them. He therefore spent time with them, not in recounting the adventures of his life, since he had had none, but the secret feelings of his soul" [Ils n'en furent que plus ardents à le presser de leur ouvrir son cœur; ils y mirent tant de discrétion, de douceur et d'autorité, qu'il fut enfin obligé de les satisfaire. Il prit donc jour avec eux, pour leur raconter, non les aventures de sa vie, puisqu'il n'en avait point éprouvé, mais les sentiments secrets de son âme]. The emotions and sensations are valuable in and of themselves rather than as conduits to spirituality. Religion functions in the service of melancholic nostalgia rather than the other way around. René's fleeting attraction to the monastic life bears out this orientation: "My heart moved by these pious conversations, I wandered often toward a monastery, close to my new abode; for a moment I was even tempted to hide my life away there" [le cœur ému par ces conversations pieuses, je portais souvent mes pas vers un monastère, voisin de mon nouveau séjour; un moment même j'eus la tentation d'y cacher ma vie]. Despite this temptation, however, René decides to pursue solitude in other ways. "Either by an inconstant nature or a prejudice against the monastic life, I changed my intentions; I resolved to travel" [soit inconstance naturelle,

---

16. As Guilhem Labouret notes of the mid-nineteenth century, "An outdated form, sermons no longer move crowds. Lacordaire had no successor at Notre-Dame. And yet, religious discourse continues to echo in different forms, from Claudel to Maritain. In other words, if religious discourse was powerful in the nineteenth century, it had doubtless left sermon and homily behind" [Forme passée de mode, le sermon ne touche plus les foules: Lacordaire n'a pas trouvé son successeur à Notre-Dame. Pourtant, le discours religieux conserve un large écho, mais à travers des formes différentes, de Claudel à Maritain . . . Autrement dit, si le discours religieux fut puissant au XIXe siècle, sans doute est-il sorti des sphères du sermon et de l'homélie]. Labouret, "Les mutations du discours religieux," 39.

soit préjugé contre la vie monastique, je changeai mes desseins; je me réso-
lus à voyager].[17] This rejection of monasticism engenders both his voyage to
America and the present narrative. Indeed, there are numerous instances in
René where religious meditation is subsumed to a melancholic contemplation
that becomes the nucleus of the narrative.

The early nineteenth-century turn from religious writing to romantic literature combines spiritual virtues with secular character attributes. By the
time these attributes surface in the twentieth-century hard-boiled, they are
no longer taken to signify "goodness" per se but rather to characterize the
protagonist's way of being—the steadiness of character that marks his ongoing and active subjectivity. To contemplate, walk along a river, lean against a
tree, peruse a volume of poetry—these actions become markers of his ability
to observe an insufficient material world and yet still flourish within it. Open
and evolving, he nonetheless carries into the twentieth century a dependable
regenerative force of conscience and the courage to maintain his subjectivity
"without thought of it."

ROMANTICISM AND THE SECULAR CHARACTER MODEL

Chateaubriand is not the only author whose romantic personages distill spiritual virtue into individual characteristics and mood. The writings of Lamartine, Hugo, Vigny, and other nineteenth-century romantics imbue their
characters with sadness, solitude, contemplation, love, and remorse, echoing the models outlined in sermons and in Chateaubriand's *Génie.* Alphonse
de Lamartine, in "Cours familier de littérature: un entretien par mois," narrates his encounter with a young poet whom he describes thus: "The young
Provençal was at ease in his talents as he was in his clothes; nothing bothered him, because he sought neither to inflate himself nor to rise above his
natural position. Perfect propriety, that instinct for precision that gives both
shepherds and kings a dignity and grace in speech and posture, governed
his entire person. He had that seemliness that truth confers; he was pleas-
ing, interesting, moving" [Le jeune provençal était à l'aise dans son talent
comme dans ses habits; rien ne le gênait, parce qu'il ne cherchait ni à s'en-
fler, ni à s'élever plus haut que nature. La parfaite convenance, cet instinct
de justesse dans toutes les conditions, qui donne aux bergers, comme aux
rois, la même dignité et la même grâce d'attitude ou d'accent, gouvernait
toute sa personne. Il avait la bienséance de la vérité; il plaisait, il intéressait,

17. Chateaubriand, *Œuvres,* 1:65, 68, 69.

il émouvait].[18] Although this description of Provençal poet Frédéric Mistral reveals a secular profile, it is strikingly similar to Rousseau's description of Jesus, reproduced and paraphrased in countless sermons throughout the nineteenth century: "What elevation in his maxims! What profound wisdom in his speeches! What presence of mind, what delicacy, and what precision in his responses! What mastery over the passions! Where is the man, where is the sage, who could thus act, suffer, and die without weakness or ostentation?" [Quelle élévation dans ses maximes! quelle profonde sagesse dans ses discours! quelle présence d'esprit, quelle finesse et quelle justesse dans ses réponses! quel empire sur ses passions! Où est l'homme, où est le sage qui sait agir, souffrir et mourir sans faiblesse et sans ostentation?].[19] What mattered in Lamartine's formulation (and also in Rousseau's, for that matter, but not for the priests who cited him) was the disposition of the poet, his mood, his comportment. Virtue as such distills into temperament, and the story of the individual psyche as such begins to dominate the story as an end in and of itself. Attributes like the "seemliness that truth confers" are within his personality rather than in the outside realm of rules or first principles; they are organic elements of his character. Because these attributes are combined with virtues and appear in romantic literature during a transition to secularism, they appear imbued with a spiritually representative function. But they are nonetheless his own reliable features and as such are not representative of anything outside or anterior to him. They are elements of his personality and form the foundation of his subjectivity.

AMERICAN RELIGIOUS WRITINGS

Just as French romantic literature turned the conduct and personae outlined in religious writings into romantic personality portraits, so too did American romantic literature distill the counsel of American sermons. There was no American literary equivalent of *Génie du christianisme*, a seminal text that introduced a literary genre even as it expressly promoted religion and presented a romantic author even as it offered a guiding voice of spiritual authority. Indeed, the absence of an American literary equivalent is a testament to the relatively antiliterary nature of American religious revival compared with the intensely literary nature of its French counterpart.[20] The American

---

18. Lamartine, *Cours familier de littérature*, 238.
19. Rousseau, *Œuvres mêlées*, 3:72.
20. The Bible is of course the notable exception to this rule. An American minister writes of a visit to Paris in 1803, the year that *Génie* was published: "In Paris, it required a search

contemporary and equivalent of *Génie*—equivalent in the sense that it too instructed vast audiences of believers on how to find God and act in relation to God, and also instructed other clerics how best to spread the word of God—is the Second Great Awakening series of revival meetings, which embodied a singularly American model of spiritual exemplarity. This revival movement, theatrical in nature, generated a strong connection between personality and spiritual authority—a connection that on the French side was nourished primarily through literature.

The Second Great Awakening (1790–1840s) was promoted mainly through camp meetings. As historian John Finger recounts, during the camp meetings, "people would gather from miles around to spend anywhere from a night to a week or so listening to hell-fire and damnation sermons and joyfully experiencing the presence of God. . . . Peter Cartwright, a famous preacher, noted with satisfaction that he had seen more than five hundred people at a time convulsing in ecstasy."[21] The revival meetings offered spiritual exercises designed to encourage conversion as well as vigorous and theatrical preaching. Thomas Abernethy writes, "It was not theological abstractions, nor yet the simple gospel of love with which the itinerant Samsons slew their tens of thousands. It was with the fires of hell, and the vengeance of God that they accomplished it. . . . Thundered at with all the stentorian verbosity of the primitive evangelist . . . they [attendees at the meeting] listened in awed stupefaction until their nerves failed."[22] Where French sermons deployed the discourse of truth, beauty, sensitivity, and love, the American counterpart both encouraged and performed unpretentiousness, plainspokenness, and an appreciation of fear. The theatrical nature of preaching was, it should be noted, particular to revival meetings; outside that arena, the vocabulary of fire and brimstone was delivered with relative calm.

Because the camp meetings constituted such a public and theatrical venue, message and persona overlapped considerably. Even sermons that were not performed before the masses accentuated the importance of personality and insisted on powerful, plain-speaking simplicity. Jonathan Pomeroy, in his 1800 metasermon "On the Folly of Denying a God," insisted not only that sermons should inspire fear but also that threats of suffering be earthly and immediate rather than vaguely celestial: "A prospect of immediate suffering, deters more from outward acts of sin, than any thing which can be threatened, as coming

---

among the booksellers of four days, to find a single Bible. We fear this is also the awful situation of the greater part of France, and other countries formerly connected with the see of Rome." New York Missionary Society, *Interesting Account*, 4.

   21. Finger, *Tennessee Frontiers*, 174.

   22. Abernethy, *Frontier to Plantation*, 218.

after death."[23] Warren Fay, a pastor in Massachusetts, similarly insisted that preachers convey force: "Can [ministers] rouse the conscience and affect the heart, unless their discourses glow with warmth, strike with force, seize and melt the affections, and estamp the seal of divine truth?"[24] American sermons like these were often metadiscourses about spiritual modeling; that is, they instructed listeners how to act as spiritual authorities. But sermons intended for audiences of believers, rather than for audiences of other Second Great Awakening preachers, also drove home the elements of menace and fear with such titles as "The Guilt and Danger of Unbelief," "Guilt of those who strengthen the Wicked," "Destruction of those who despise the Gospel," and others similar in tone.[25]

God in American sermons was a more menacing prospect than in France's liberal Catholicism. And connection with that God aimed at individual salvation rather than nuanced emotional connection. It could be argued that the American emphasis on individual exhortation had to do with the distinctions between Protestantism and Catholicism. Such nineteenth-century evangelicals as Charles Finney, Lyman Beecher, and Francis Asbury focused on sin as a choice and on the notion that humans had the power to turn away from sin and embrace moral action. This message shifted away from a Calvinist theology based on predestination and toward a belief that people were responsible for their own destiny.[26] But comparison of French to American preachers, Catholics, and Protestants reveals contrasts along national rather than religious lines. What most distinguishes the discourse of American sermons and public revivals is its righteousness, its use of fear as an instrument of persuasion, and, in the realm of persona, its emphasis on both charisma and unpretentiousness. Indeed, to praise an American orator for plainspokenness was to contrast American practicality with European intellectualism, or American frankness with European lyrical ornamentation. This preference for simplicity was largely political in nature, since the refusal to embellish separates the preacher from the upper class and thus by extension from English authority. For this reason, and because of contemporaneous American frontier literature that also foregrounded individual choice and audacious action, spiritual exemplarity was united with such

23. Pomeroy, *Folly of Denying a God*, 15.

24. Fay, *A Sermon*, 10.

25. See Lathrop, *Sermons on Various Subjects*.

26. Cf. Lyman Beecher's writings on Unitarianism, including his citation of articles stating that "men are free agents, in the possession of such faculties, and placed in such circumstances, as to render if practicable for them to do whatever God requires. . . . Such ability is here intended as lays a perfect foundation for government by law, and for rewards and punishments according to deeds." Beecher, *Sermons Delivered on Various Occasions*, 312.

choice and action—a union that predicts the combination of right and violence featured in the hard-boiled. But what I want most to underscore in the citation of American sermons is precisely the conflation of the sermonizing voice with the force of individual subjectivity. The declaration of right expresses individual conscience in much the same way as the French romantic heroes, as voices and persona existing in various cultural circumstances. The nationally resonant American character model thus connected, as it did on the French side, to the fact of being as an individual and subjective act— even when that being seemed volatile or susceptible to adverse forces. Once again, this connection is not intended to indicate that the American character model is "really" religious in nature or that ideals embodied must stand within a sacred frame. Rather, I am arguing that the historical phenomenon of religious revival, aligning with romantic literature to create canonical cultural voices, contributed materially to the enduring valorization of individual subjectivity, particularly in times of historical transition. The result was a cultural personality outline that functioned as an indicator of existential sturdiness.[27]

AMERICAN ROMANTICISM

Just as French romantic literature turned the love, sensitivity, and lyricism of the preachers' counsel into natural attributes, so American romantic literature casts unpretentiousness, plainspokenness, practicality, and an instinctive sense of right as innate American character traits.[28] James Fenimore Cooper's Leatherstocking (1823–1841) and John Kennedy's Horse-shoe Robinson (1835) are two examples. The description of Hawkeye in *The Last of the Mohicans* (1826) codifies woodsy simplicity: "The frame of the white man, judging by such parts as were not concealed by his clothes, was like that of one who had known hardships and exertion from his earliest youth. His person, though muscular, was attenuated rather than full; but every nerve and muscle appeared strung and indurated by unremitted exposure and toil." And yet, for all this duress, he is open and straightforward: "The eye of the hunter, or scout, or whichever he might be, was small, quick, keen, and restless, roving while he spoke, on every side of him, as if in quest of game, or distrusting the sudden approach of some lurking enemy. Notwithstanding these symptoms of habitual suspicion, his countenance was not only without guile, but

---

27. See Cotkin's *Existential America*, particularly chapter 2.

28. See Jason Shaffer's discussion of the Western romantic hero as a descendant of the Revolutionary-era comic character in *Performing Patriotism*, 9.

at the moment at which he is introduced, it was charged with an expression of sturdy honesty."[29] With a "keen," "guileless," and "honest" countenance, Hawkeye possesses at once acute sensitivity to his surroundings and a solid character within them. Perception of the outside world accompanies steadfast existence in its midst, which allows the subject to evolve without the "smugness" that Butler had cited. Kennedy's Horse-shoe in turn is "as brave a man as you ever fell in with," and the narrator notes that "the men have great dependence on what he says."[30] Like Cooper's Leatherstocking, Horse-shoe is simple and courageous:

> The habits of the experienced soldier were curiously illustrated in the thoughtful and sober foresight with which Robinson adapted his plans to the exigencies of his condition, and then in the imperturbable light-heartedness with which, after his measures of safety were taken, he waited the progress of events. His watchfulness seemed to be an instinct, engendered by a familiarity with danger, whilst the steady and mirthful tone of his mind was an attribute that never gave way to the inroads of care. He was the same composed and self-possessed being in a besieged garrison, in the moment of a threatened escalade, as amongst his cronies by a winter fire-side.[31]

"Instinct," "attribute," and "composed" indicate a subject who comes on the scene fully assembled and complete. "Foresight" and "watchfulness," similar to Hawkeye's "keen" and "roving" eye, indicate at once both sensitivity to and openness to one's surroundings, which echoes a subjectivity elastic but secure. It also echoes Chateaubriand's formulation of an "instinct" that admits openness to nature, as well as Lamartine's description of Mistral as having "that seemliness that truth confers." These literary formulations address the relationship of subjectivity to constitution, and in turn to endurance within adverse circumstances both individual and historical. As in the French example, character attributes can appear imbued with a spiritually representative function: Horse-shoe's influence over others resembles that of the preacher, but his character traits are nonetheless his own natural possessions and as such retain a strong cultural significance. Whereas the French romantic hero carried tomes of poetry and rested dreaming against a tree, the frontier hero—the American romantic—carried a gun, strode through the forest, and remained sparing with his words. And these personae, fruits of cultural and historical specificity, have produced durable character models

---

29. Cooper, *Leatherstocking Tales*, 1:501.
30. Kennedy, *Horse-Shoe Robinson*, 112, 273.
31. Ibid., 127.

and indeed "culture heroes." It has been a long time since an American frontiersman crashed through the woods or a Frenchman wandered forest paths,
yet these are canonical models, points of reference, modern foundations for
each nation's vision not just of spiritual authority but of conscience "without
thought of it." The reason for that durability, it seems, is precisely the coincidence between spiritual authority and individual character—a coincidence
borne of the congruence of romanticism and religious writings and of the
attendant elevated value of individual subjectivity.

As in the French example, the coincidence between character attributes
and spiritual virtues emerges through the common vocabulary that American romantic literature shares with American sermons. Cooper, for instance,
described an army "saved from annihilation by the coolness and spirit of
a Virginian boy [George Washington], whose riper fame has since diffused
itself, with the steady influence of moral truth, to the uttermost confines of
Christendom." The boy's "spirit" and "moral truth" contrast with the menace
of his enemies, as the passage continues: "A wide frontier had been laid naked
by this unexpected disaster, and more substantial evils were preceded by a
thousand fanciful and imaginary dangers. The alarmed colonists believed that
the yells of the savages mingled with every fitful gust of wind that issued from
the interminable forests of the west."[32] The stormy vocabulary of this battle is
strikingly reminiscent of numerous sermons against the "lurking enemies" of
sin. For instance, as Lyman Beecher famously intoned against intemperance
in the same year as Cooper's novel: "It is here, then, beside this commenc-
ing vortex, that I would take my stand, to warn off the heedless navigator
from destruction. . . . Loud thunders should utter their voices—and lurid fires
should blaze."[33] Eli Meeker also compares sin to a dangerous spark of fire: "In
a moment, massy walls of wood and stone, the pride of war, and the labour
of years, yield to the dreadful explosion, and scattered in ten thousand fragments, spread terror and destruction around."[34] In romantic literature, the
spiritual adversary gives way to the human one, but the dominant character
elements of vehemence and temper, cornerstones of American Western and
frontier literature as of the hard-boiled, remain in place. The frontier hero
can be read as what Alexander Saxton calls a "natural Jacksonian," or "a vernacular character of lower-class status to whom is attributed class consciousness in the form of egalitarian values."[35] But he is at the same time, in style
and temperament, a counterpart of Pomeroy's direct, declarative preaching.

---

32. Cooper, *Leatherstocking Tales*, 1:481–82.
33. Beecher, *Six Sermons*, 29.
34. Meeker, *Sermons*, 77.
35. Saxton, *Rise and Fall of the White Republic*, 186.

On the American as on the French side, the intersections of religious writings with romantic literature turn spiritual virtues into secular character attributes. As in Cooper's earlier-cited description of George Washington, for instance, the phenomenon of "spirit" functions in American romantic and religious writings much as "sensitivity" does in the French. Lyman Beecher declaims: "The Spirit of God revives the tender feelings of childhood and brings into the fold his wandering lambs."[36] This phrase situates "spirit" as God-given and thus external to the human subject. On the romantic side, American literature of the early to mid-nineteenth century subordinates the element of the divine to natural courage. Cooper's above-cited "coolness and spirit of a Virginian boy," referring to George Washington's role in salvaging the "unexpected disaster" of a French and Indian victory, is one such instance.[37] Bird's *Nick of the Woods* has one man deride another's hesitancy: "The man has some spirit now and then; but whar's [*sic*] the use of it, while he's nothing but a no-fight quaker?"[38] Washington Irving, Nathaniel Hawthorne, and John Kennedy (author of *Horse-Shoe Robinson*) also use the word extensively to denote both divine energy and force of character, even bellicosity. Rather than being the force of righteousness, "spirit" in these instances can mean vigorous independence or a simple desire to fight; and it is these qualities just as much as an explicit God-consciousness that have come to identify the American culture hero. Recall that for the French, in a similar turn, Coquerel wrote that a being "created for light" "cannot be happy unless he sees a path of knowledge, holiness, and love continually rising before him." But secular romantic characters, who are the early nineteenth century's more enduring personae, cast the search for knowledge and love as innate impulses and narrative themes.

FROM SERMONS TO ROMANTICISM TO THE HARD-BOILED CHARACTER MODEL

What romantic literature transmitted was not a teleological blueprint for spiritual salvation or even connection but rather the contours of human experience, the outlines and adventures of a personality. Romantic characters do

---

36. Beecher, *Sermons Delivered on Various Occasions*, 136.
37. Cooper, *Leatherstocking Tales*, 1:481. The emphasis on toil emerges also as a metaphoric thread in American sermons: "The apostle Paul was a bold, intrepid, and zealous preacher of the gospel. How extensive are the blessed effects of his unwearied labours." Meeker, *Sermons*, 67.
38. Bird, *Nick of the Woods*, 52.

not themselves have an ideological or religious agenda. Their authors may have such an agenda, or their narrators may, but representation is not the character's own intention. Indeed, the absence of such intention, whether from nonchalance, nihilism, self-absorption, or (mainly in the case of American fiction) the pressing demands of survival, is often a crucial aspect of his character. And yet, when these accidental heroes emerge in their twentieth-century hard-boiled incarnations, their function as characters is precisely to represent ideals that have gone missing—*because* they have gone missing— from society and its institutions. Once again, this representation is neither idealist nor utopian in nature. It is the return of instinctual conscience rather than idealism that enables the hard-boiled to counter historical master narratives of modernity in decline.

In most traditional crime fiction, returning to moral and legal order is the point of the plot. Although the novel in general, as Peter Brooks has remarked, presented a narrative order that replaced the absent master plot, crime fiction rendered its absence as an atmospheric and judicial starting point.[39] It is therefore not surprising that the crime fiction genre was born at a time of political change and religious uncertainty on both continents. Certainly, there were other circumstances that drove the development of crime fiction. Roger Caillois, for instance, noting the importance of urban development to the genre, observed the echoes of Cooper's *Leatherstocking Tales* in crime fiction's representations of the city. Describing the "transformation of the adventure novel into the detective novel," he writes, "it is a fact that the City's metamorphosis stemmed from the transposition of the savannahs and forests of Fenimore Cooper into the urban setting. In his novels, every broken branch signifies a particular anxiety or hope, and every tree trunk conceals an enemy's rifle or the bow of an unseen, silent avenger" [Il faut tenir pour acquis que cette métamorphose de la Cité tient à la transposition dans son décor de la savane et de la forêt de Fenimore Cooper, où toute branche cassée signifie une inquiétude ou un espoir, où tout tronc dissimule le fusil d'un ennemi ou l'arc d'un invisible et silencieux vengeur].[40] The character traits that are our focus gained value within that anxious atmosphere, and it is not surprising that the appearance of the detective in literature coincided with that of the romantic individual as spiritual authority and individual. The hard-

---

39. Brooks, *Reading for the Plot*, 6.

40. Caillois, *Edge of Surrealism*, 178; *Le mythe et l'homme*, 157. Eugène Sue, author of *Les mystères de Paris* (1842), declared his intention to "mettre sous les yeux du lecteur quelques épisodes de la vie d'autres barbares aussi en dehors de la civilisation que les sauvages peuplades si bien peintes par Cooper" (1). Sue's *Mystères* inspired Léo Malet's *Les nouveaux mystères de Paris*. See also Stierle and Starobinsky, *La capitale des signes*.

boiled conflation of psychology and embodiment is rooted in the two roles, the simultaneous frameworks for reading individual character in the early nineteenth century. The rest of this book examines the return of the character models through the twentieth- and twenty-first-century hard-boiled; to start, here are a few examples of their incarnations.

Cynthia Hamilton has noted that the Western genre and the American hard-boiled share an emphasis on individualism, though she points out that where the Western "pays homage to the need for progress," the hard-boiled "man of conscience" lives in essential isolation.[41] Some of the most fundamentally canonical American characteristics are unpretentiousness, bravery, and an instinctive and anti-intellectual certitude. *The Last of the Mohicans's* Hawkeye announced, "I am no scholar and I care not who knows it."[42] The preface to the first edition of *Nick of the Woods* states: "It is not to be denied that men of education and refinement were to be found among the earlier settlers of Kentucky; but the most prominent and distinguished founders, the commanders of the Stations, the leaders of the military forces,—those who are, and must continue to be, recollected as the true fathers of the State, were such persons as we have described, ignorant but ardent, unpolished and unpretending, yet brave, sagacious, and energetic,—the very men, in fact, for the time and the occasion."[43] The first American hard-boiled hero, Race Williams, echoed this sentiment when he proclaimed: "Right and wrong are not written on the statutes for me, nor do I find my code of morals in the essays of long-winded professors. My ethics are my own."[44] Exemplary character is connected in American religious and romantic writings as well as in the hard-boiled to anti-intellectualism; the most valuable truth is the truth one *knows* rather than the truth that must be learned.

Modesty also emerges as an ideal American characteristic that passes from sermons to romanticism to crime fiction. Cooper's Hawkeye declared, "I am not a prejudiced man, nor one who vaunts himself on his natural privileges," as though in anticipation of Chandler's "honor without thought of it, and certainly without saying it."[45] Horse-shoe Robinson shares this humility: "He was a man of truth—every expression of his face showed it. He was modest besides, and attached no value to his exploits."[46] Hard-boiled detectives evince this same unassuming manner. Sam Spade in *The Maltese Falcon*

41. Hamilton, *Detective Fiction in America*, 16, 29.

42. Cooper, *Leatherstocking Tales*, 1:502.

43. Bird, *Nick of the Woods*, 28. Owen Wister's Virginian also announced, "I have got no education and must write humble against my birth." Wister, *The Virginian*, 371.

44. Daly, *Snarl of the Beast*, 1.

45. Cooper, *Leatherstocking Tales*, 1:502; Chandler, "Simple Art of Murder," 59.

46. Kennedy, *Horse-Shoe Robinson*, 297.

declares to Cairo, "You're not hiring me to do any murders or burglaries for you, but simply to get [the falcon] back if possible in an honest and lawful way."[47] Philip Marlowe announces to General Sternwood, "I'd like to offer you your money back. It may mean nothing to you. It might mean something to me. . . . It means I have refused payment for an unsatisfactory job."[48] Both these statements echo the sense of the detective as moral commodity and as participant in a redemptive economy. In *Farewell, My Lovely*, Marlowe notes, "I'm getting a hundred dollars for doing nothing. If anybody gets conked, it ought to be me." Positive action becomes more crucial than good intention, and to "be" is to be of service to others. In addition to a modest vision of one's worth, clarity and plainspokenness are also at a premium. When in *Farewell, My Lovely*, Mrs. Grayle tells Marlowe that "there's such a thing as being just a little too frank," he responds, "Not in my business."[49] In *The Maltese Falcon*, Gutman admires Spade, noting: "It never occurred to me that you'd hit on such a simple and direct way of getting at the truth."[50] In word and in the act of detection, the main character functions as an instrument and example of intuitive understanding.

In French crime fiction, by contrast, even maverick detectives tend to come—as romantic heroes do—from a humanist tradition of philosophical contemplation and aesthetic consciousness. This is even the case for Eugène Vidocq, the criminal turned first chief of police, then founder of the first detective agency, then inspiration for Balzac's Vautrin (among other characters), and author (albeit via a ghostwriter) of the *Mémoires*. The editor of the 1869 edition of the *Mémoires* casts them as a realistic alternative to "sentimental mush"—which they are—but the book nonetheless puts forth the recognizable outlines of romantic character.[51] The narrator compares himself to the biblical Prodigal Son,[52] and his description of Christiern, a fellow prisoner, is a virtual echo of the romantics earlier cited: "His intelligence seemed to divine our very thoughts: he was sad, thoughtful, and kind; in his features there was a mixture of nobility, candor, and melancholy that was at once seductive and moving. . . . Although a smile was often on his lips, Christiern appeared beset by the deepest sorrow; but he kept his chagrin to himself, and no one even knew why he was in prison" [Son intelligence semblait deviner

47. Hammett, *Maltese Falcon*, 53.
48. Chandler, *Big Sleep et al.*, 180.
49. Ibid., 245, 306.
50. Hammett, *Maltese Falcon*, 204.
51. His 1869 editor describes the *Mémoires* as containing "un réalisme palpitant qui s'offrait tout à coup à une société blasées sur les mièvreries sentimentales." Vidocq, *Mémoires*, 6.
52. "L'aumônier . . . me cita la parabole de l'enfant prodigue: c'était à peu près mon histoire." Ibid., 13.

la pensée; il était triste, méditatif, bienveillant; dans ses traits, il y avait un mélange de noblesse, de candeur et de mélancolie, qui séduisait et touchait en même temps. . . . Quoique le sourire fût souvent sur ses lèvres, Christiern paraissait en proie à un profond chagrin, mais il le renfermait en lui, et personne ne savait même pour quelle cause il était détenu].[53]

When Émile Gaboriau (who himself was inspired by Vidocq in creating Lecoq, as was Maurice Leblanc in creating Arsène Lupin) introduced the troubled, ambivalent *juge d'instruction* in *L'affaire Lerouge,* he focused similarly on the character's melancholic nature: "Kind despite his coldness; his countenance sweet and a little sad. This sadness had remained with him since his grave illness two years before, which had nearly been the end of him" [Sympathique malgré sa froideur, d'une physionomie douce et un peu triste. Cette tristesse lui était restée d'une grande maladie qui deux ans auparavant avait failli l'emporter].[54] *Douceur* and *tristesse* are reminiscent of Chateaubriand's René, while mention of the "grave illness" recalls Chateaubriand's account in *Mémoires d'outre-tombe* of the malady born of a "disordered life."[55] Come the twentieth century, Georges Simenon's iconic Maigret is himself given to meditation and nocturnal ramblings: "He walked along the embankment, stopping from time to time. He looked at the sea, at the multicolored silhouettes that abounded in the waves on the bank" [Il marchait le long du remblai, en s'arrêtant de temps en temps. Il regardait la mer, les silhouettes multicolores qui devenaient de plus en plus nombreuses dans les vagues du bord].[56] Fred Vargas's *commissaire* Jean-Baptiste Adamsberg embodies the solitary and contemplative wanderer: "Adamsberg turned off the road to get to the narrow path that had a crop of sprouting maize on one side, and on the other flax. . . . He stopped walking and sat for a long while with his back propped against a tree trunk as he sounded out his thoughts" [Il quitta la route et rejoignit le chemin étroit qui passait entre un champ de jeunes maïs et un champ de lin. . . . Il s'arrêta, s'assit un long moment contre un arbre, explorant la solidité de ses pensées].[57] In this description, rumination on the criminal investigation is not unlike Chateaubriand's contemplation of the church bells in his town: "On Sundays and holidays I often heard, through the trees in the great woods, the sound of distant bells calling men in the fields to prayer. Leaning against the trunk of an elm, I listened in silence to the pious murmuring" [Les dimanches et les jours de fête, j'ai

---

53. Ibid., 130.
54. Gaboriau, *L'affaire Lerouge,* 10.
55. Chateaubriand, *Mémoires d'outre-tombe,* 257.
56. Simenon, *Œuvres romanesques,* 3:14.
57. Vargas, *Seeking Whom He May Devour,* 269–70, and *L'homme à l'envers,* 298.

souvent entendu, dans le grand bois, à travers les arbres, les sons de la clo-
che lointaine qui appelait au temple l'homme des champs. Appuyé contre
le tronc d'un ormeau, j'écoutais en silence le pieux murmure].[58] The image
of a man leaning against a tree and gazing into the distance as if listening
to a "pious murmuring" became the iconic illustration of Chateaubriand by
Anne-Louis Girodet de Roussy-Trioson—an image not of a spiritual icon but
of romantic melancholy. Vargas's Adamsberg offers a virtual *tableau vivant* of
that painting, though again the detective's intention is neither to pose nor to
represent. Rather, his instinctive contemplation, like Marlowe's modesty, is in
the service of understanding. Similarly, in *Sous les vents de Neptune,* the *commissaire* is described as "walking away slowly, a thin, dark, stooping figure,
steering a slightly irregular course through the night" [s'éloigner d'un pas
lent, mince silhouette noire et courbée, tanguant légèrement dans la nuit],[59]
an image that recalls Alfred de Vigny's association of the night with a sub-
lime and divine solitude.[60] These characteristic actions and positions taken,
marking exemplarity in their respective national traditions, return throughout the history of the hard-boiled.

THE FRAGILITY OF CONSCIENCE

I said earlier that the concept of moral choice necessarily contains an element
of conscious effort, and that what Chandler calls "honor without thought of
it" constitutes more precisely an acceptance of that sustained effort. In the
nineteenth century, religious writing takes a romantic turn and develops a
personality figure as the embodiment of internal spiritual (or even doctrinal) virtues. But as the century progresses, the assumed spiritual/doctrinal
context fades, leaving the persona standing largely on its own, attractive or
compelling in and for itself. As the twentieth century begins, this persona is
taken up by writers who claim no religious or doctrinal foundation but find
instead a natural paradigm for stories about individuals confronting the mean
streets. That natural paradigm becomes valuable not because it promises to
restore anachronistic sacred frames but because it constitutes the capacity of
individual conscience and subjectivity to create an alternative narrative. How-

---

58. Chateaubriand, *Œuvres,* 1:67.

59. Vargas, *Wash This Blood Clean from My Hand,* 20, and *Sous les vents de Neptune,* 29.

60. "The sentiment of solitude, of silence, of a waking dream in the night is poetry itself
for me, and the revelation of man's angelic future existence" [Le sentiment de la solitude, du
silence, du rêve éveillé dans la nuit est la poésie même pour moi et la révélation de l'existence
angélique future de l'homme]. Vigny, *Les destinées,* 190.

ever, precisely because the hard-boiled embodies and perpetuates the idea of instinctual exemplarity, it risks the possibility of that instinct faltering. As an evolving genre, the hard-boiled places the individual in a position of narrative, moral, and judicial authority and then, over the course of the twentieth century, proceeds to threaten the notion of the individual *qua* individual as an incarnation of anything, any institution or abstraction, any sense of truth and right. The unraveling of the force of individual conscience proves much more demoralizing than the now-familiar notion of lost sacred frames. Curiously enough, nineteenth-century religious and romantic writings themselves predict the vulnerability of conscience as well as the necessity—and possibility—of its continual reconstitution.

French and American nineteenth-century writings insinuate eventual faults in the very character models they put forth, suggesting that surmounting such faults will demand "thought of it" on the part of the character. These potential faults are as culturally specific as the character models themselves. From the standpoint of the nineteenth century, they are associated with the faltering of virtue, but in the hard-boiled, they mark the faltering of conscience—a conscience that the principal character, like the hard-boiled genre itself, then moves to reassert. According to French religious writings, the potential underside of artistic contemplation and sensitivity is an amoral aestheticism, an excessive reclusiveness. Chateaubriand specifically decried the person who wanted to write a beautiful work of literature without regard to God, pointing to "that moral tint without which nothing is perfect" [cette teinte morale sans laquelle rien n'est parfait] and thus warning against the peril of a pretty but empty envelope. As I noted earlier, he also insisted that "God does not forbid us to tread the flowered paths, if they serve to bring us back to Him," subtly warning that the aesthetic pleasures of "flowered paths" can lead one astray. Indeed, the question of aesthetics detached from religion or morality permeated the nineteenth and twentieth centuries. It permeates the hard-boiled in the late twentieth century, when—as the chapter on Jean-Patrick Manchette will demonstrate—we meet fiction describing violence as spectacle, using the aesthetic as either coy excuse or ironic instrument of perversity. Another troubling seed in the French romantic model, one that comes into full bloom in the late hard-boiled, is the dangerously alienated nature of the solitary young man. This nature is rooted in the romantic model, and although it can indicate an admirable restraint and contemplativeness, it can also become a dangerous twentieth-century *néo-polar* outsider. Examples of such a morphosis are Manchette and his disgruntled anticapitalists, Michel Steiner and his self-absorbed psychoanalyst, Daniel Pennac and his sadistic Monoprix clerks.

American writings, on the other hand, find risk not in overvaluation of the aesthetic but in perversion of the spiritual message via messianic egos. One Baptist leader in 1802, concerned that attendees at the revival meetings could fall victim to demagogic manipulators of popular opinion, writes: "A number of hot-headed young men, intoxicated with the prevailing element of excitement, and feeling confident of their own powers and call to the work— though entirely destitute of any suitable education—assumed the office of public exhorters and instructors. When once this door was opened it was found difficult to close it."[61]

Another potential American pitfall is overvaluing anti-intellectualism and instinctive certitude. The same is true in the grandiosity of the individual—that is, the interest of the individual in himself as a character in the drama of conversion and spiritual awakening. A letter from one Second Great Awakening convert to the preacher who converted him, cited in McClymond's *Embodying the Spirit,* reads: "I fear they [revivals] are fast becoming with you a sort of trade, to be worked at so many hours every day and then laid aside. Dear brother do you not find yourself running into formality, a round of formality in the management of revivals?"[62] McClymond goes on to cite Jimmy Swaggart's offer of a free satellite dish to any church that would broadcast him instead of listening to a live local preacher. The contradiction of the egomaniac claiming exemplary humility (or the self-aggrandizing person claiming to "embody the spirit") has become a commercial (and religious) commonplace, but it is a contradiction nonetheless and one that—as the chapter on Jim Thompson will illustrate—the American hard-boiled develops to theatrical and catastrophic effect. In American crime fiction, it is not the blithe aesthete, the cold intellectual, or the philosophical recluse who poses a threat, but rather the egocentric power driver, the hot-headed actor and orator in whom natural vigor transforms into a volatile and perilous blast of emotion.

In the aforementioned instances, nineteenth-century writings warn against precisely those personality failings and excesses that would come to fruition in the late hard-boiled. In the nineteenth century, such excesses are cast as threats to virtue, whereas in the hard-boiled they are the lurking enemies of conscience. Indeed, at times they pose as evidence that conscience is an unsustainable anachronism. The abandonment or demolition of accountability is crucial to the bleak atmosphere of the late twentieth-century hard-boiled. And yet, crucially, abandonment of accountability is as much a

---

61. Murray, *Revival and Revivalism,* 177.
62. McClymond, *Embodying the Spirit,* 17.

deliberate narrative choice as is its maintenance, and the hard-boiled novel makes that choice on every page.

DALY AND MALET

The history of the hard-boiled is that of the assertion of individual moral agency as well as of the vulnerability of that agency—a balancing act between the "fragile achievement" of conscience and obstacles to it. Although those obstacles are in the air from the start, the hard-boiled in both the United States and France starts out by celebrating individual moral choice as remarkably reliable and instinctual. In the very first hard-boiled novels from those two countries, the nineteenth-century coincidence of romantic character and spiritual exemplarity, as well as the nineteenth-century background of cultural upheaval, are transposed into and suited for the twentieth century. In American literature, the postwar 1920s are characterized by the emblem of the returning soldier, the specter of shell shock, and the rise of free-market capitalism. These factors place a premium on psychic fortitude, self-reliance, physical courage, and instinctual morality. In France, the first hard-boiled was published during the Nazi occupation, and the salient attributes of the principal character were sensitivity to French literary and cultural history and an empathic response to suffering. Also fundamental was a clear sense of the ethical limitations of hard-boiled nonchalance and aesthetic distraction. In each case, the canonical character traits rooted in a nineteenth-century atmosphere of postrevolutionary nation-building arise in periods of similar crises of national identity. The first hard-boiled novels demand much in the way of empathy, fairness, historical sensibility, and self-awareness from their subject. And in each case, that subject delivers those character attributes and exemplifies the reliability of individual morality.

CHAPTER 2

CARROLL JOHN DALY AND LÉO MALET

The First Hard-Boiled Heroes

THE FIRST AMERICAN hard-boiled novel was Carroll John Daly's *The Snarl of the Beast* (1927), the first French hard-boiled Léo Malet's *120, rue de la Gare* (1943). In each of these works the principal characters reincarnate the heroic characteristics of their early nineteenth-century romantic predecessors, and they do so in response to the particular modern needs and circumstances of their culture. Crises of national and cultural self-definition in a burgeoning capitalist postwar period (United States) and in a period of wartime occupation (France) enable or invite the reemergence of the nineteenth-century model of exemplary character. Carroll John Daly's Race Williams reembodies the characteristics of self-reliance, plainspokenness, anti-intellectualism, and an instinctive sense of right. Léo Malet's Nestor Burma represents a literary sensibility, an aesthetic discernment, and an epigrammatic nonchalance. In each case the familiar qualities at hand, markers of an active conscience, are tailored to the era of publication. The American 1920s saw the return of the soldier and the phenomenon of shell shock, as well as a laissez-faire economy and the rise of organized crime. France in 1943 was under Nazi occupation, which raised the stakes of national identity, cultural patrimony, and ethical sensitivity. Just as the hard-boiled detective rushes in to do what he can against the crime at hand, doing society's dirty work and sometimes being sullied in the process, so the hard-boiled as a genre acts as mediator and protector from present cultural circumstances.

In each case, the principal character represents a model of moral individualism, claiming accountability for his actions and remaining conscious of himself as an autonomous actor and narrator. This consciousness may seem to contradict Chandler's idea of honor "without of thought of it." Even the most modest of honorable characters inevitably thought about the rightness of their actions. And if they were narrators they almost inevitably said it or hinted at it; "The Simple Art of Murder" is an essay, not a work of fiction. But by the time the individuals Chandler described came to the page in the 1920s, it was entirely common for characters to be conscious of their impact, of their properties and parameters as characters. That consciousness is innate; detached from the nineteenth-century discourse of religion and virtue, it takes the form of an automatic impulse to *be* a subject, to act autonomously, and what is more to recognize others as subjects as well. In the case of Race Williams, he is responsible for standing apart from corrupting currents, whether these are social, such as the venality of capitalism and crime, or personal, such as anger and pessimism. In the case of Nestor Burma, his responsibility is to stand apart from ongoing assaults on French soil and French culture and to carry France's humanist heritage aloft through them. In both these protagonists, that awareness of accountability, sometimes thought and said as such and sometimes not, blends with nineteenth-century character outlines to constitute a model of secular moral authority. This chapter examines that combination, reading each of these characters as a model for the character-based nature of modern morality. It locates in these respective "first" novels a startlingly clear blueprint for conscious subjectivity as a vital response to modern cultural crises.

THE SNARL OF THE BEAST

In the traditional nineteenth-century detective story à la Sherlock Holmes or Gaboriau, an individual commits a crime, upsetting the moral and judicial order of a normally intact world. That upset also carried a spiritual resonance: Jeffrey Mahan writes that "the classical detective story reflects a disruption of God's orderly creation."[1] When the police or an associate then apprehends the criminal, order is restored and the problematic individual removed. In the hard-boiled, on the other hand, rather than an ordered world and a disordered individual, we see the opposite: a disordered, corrupt world and an ordered (narrative-driving, narrative-structuring, principle-maintaining)

---

1. Mahan, "Hard-Boiled Detective," 90.

individual. This is the case in both the American and French hard-boiled, though what passed for order and disorder varied between the two. Social distortion that in the traditional detective story was embodied in and eliminated with the criminal is now projected and represented outward, and it is the detective who remains ordered, intact, and articulate.

By the time *The Snarl of the Beast* was published as a novel in 1927, Carroll John Daly had already written stories for *Black Mask,* many featuring detective Race Williams.[2] As early as 1923, Daly's editor had embraced the idea of Race Williams as a serial character and as a model for other writers. In 1927 the serial *Snarl of the Beast* was published as a novel. Daly has been criticized for the crudeness of his writing; as William Nolan remarks, "Daly produced what may be termed 'instant clichés,'" and indeed *The Snarl of the Beast* is as much a hard-boiled statement of intent as it is a hard-boiled story in itself.[3] This very crudeness, however, coming in the form of declarations to the reader, lends a directness and transparency to his philosophy. It also furnishes a model for the hard-boiled combination of conscious accountability and maverick nonchalance and allows the reader to measure his words against his actions. Although "my ethics are my own" is in some sense a blustering throwaway line, it nonetheless marks a clear turn away from rules and first principles. As such, it raises questions about the intersection of accountability and autonomy and about the possible moral authority of one who admits no authorities. The phrase proposes an individualist dismissal of norms, and yet to speak of ethics, associated as the word is with morality and right and wrong, implies an appeal to or at least a nodding familiarity with the transcendent. Every definition of the word *ethics* includes some component of morality, principle, and governance. Even the most individualistic sense of ethics includes an element of guidance, a subdivision of the individual into governor and governed, id and superego. Race Williams does not say, "I do what I want" or even "I do what I think is right" but rather uses a term evocative of those very ancient Greek philosophers and long-winded professors whose writings he dismisses. His claim to ethics is neither parodic nor perverse—Williams is erratic and bombastic but does nothing to demonstrate

---

2. Daly's short-story "Three Gun Terry," published in 1923, introduced the first hard-boiled detective, Terry Mack, who beat Race Williams to the pages of *Black Mask* by two weeks. As William Nolan remarks, "Terry Mack is the prototype for ten thousand private eyes who have gunned, slugged, and wisecracked their way through ten thousand magazines, books, films, and TV episodes. . . . The pioneer private-eye tale is remarkable in that almost every cliché that was to plague the genre from the 1920s into the 1980s is evident in 'Three Gun Terry.'" Nolan, *Black Mask Boys,* 43.

3. Nolan, *Black Mask Boys,* 43.

that he is unethical—but it does introduce an uneasy fusion of the autonomous and the absolute, of moral values and natural character attributes.

Stephen Faison notes, "The private detective is not ethical to the extent
that ethics are defined as a set of established rules and standards of conduct. . . . The detective obeys his own personal code." But as Race Williams's
conduct bears out, there is little practical difference between ethics as "a set
of established rules and standards of conduct" and ethics as one's "own personal code." Although one definition situates the source of the imperative
outside the individual, in the abstract or in the firmament, and another situates that source within the individual, yet both share an absoluteness of decision. The latter may be less grandiose than the former, less couched in the
vocabulary of transcendence, but the subsequent actions and their consequences may not be different at all. Still, it is almost impossible to talk about
the hard-boiled without reproducing this same collapsing distinction, the
same sense that ideas transposed into subjective facts gain in grandeur. Faison continues, "The hard-boiled detective believes in justice and fairness but
not as abstract concepts. He practices these virtues in particular situations
with specific individuals who demonstrate that they deserve these consider-
ations. In a world in which ethics are impossible, self-determined personal
integrity is all that remains."[4] "Self-determined" implies containment within
the individual, but to "believe in" implies an external existence, and what are
"these virtues," or indeed any virtues, if not "abstract concepts"? And yet to
talk about the hard-boiled, and indeed to talk about individual morality at
all, is inevitably to bump up against these contradictions. What makes the
character intelligible and vital is a consistency of conduct—an instinctive
awareness of and responsibility for treating others well.

THE HOMAIS PROBLEM

To return to Chandler's "honor without thought of it," even if the "it" in
question is not called honor per se, it nonetheless signifies some standard
of decision. But to examine more closely the potential contradictions in
Race Williams's statement and furthermore the potential collapses of meaning therein, I want to turn to a rather unlikely rhetorical counterpart to this
hard-boiled detective. There is a moment in Flaubert's 1857 *Madame Bovary*
when the Yonville innkeeper Madame Lefrançois admonishes the pharmacist
Homais: "You are an infidel! You have no religion" [Vous êtes un impie! vous

---

4. Faison, *Existentialism*, 88, 89.

n'avez pas de religion]. To this, Homais protests: "I have a religion, my religion, and I even have more than any of them, with their mummeries and their juggling!" [J'ai une religion, ma religion, et même j'en ai plus qu'eux tous, avec leurs mômeries et leurs jongleries!][5] Whereas Race Williams's ethics are his own, Homais's religion is his own. And just as Race Williams's statement lines up with the moral disillusionment of his time, so the pharmacist's claim lines up with the religious transition in progress in 1857, namely, the disconnection of religion-as-social-institution from religion-as-personal-experience. From Madame Lefrançois's accusation to Homais's response, however, the meaning of religion undergoes a subtle but problematic change. For the innkeeper, to "have religion" means to be a good Catholic and to respect the institution of religion with its social rules and norms. On the other hand, to "have a religion, my religion" means to have one's own doctrine and one's own sense of spirituality. Again, this is not a particularly scandalous idea, for it represents the sort of personal theism that many theologians had already deemed crucial to the maintenance of faith in the midst of secularization. But when Homais says, "I even have more than any of them," the meaning of his "religion" starts to waver, for to have "more than any of them" implies once again a public and socially recognized commodity. If what Homais has "more of" is his own doctrine or code, it makes sense that he would have "more" of it than anyone else. But in that case, the fact that he even makes the claim becomes questionable, for it goes without saying that he would have "more" than others of something that is by definition his alone. On the other hand, if what he has "more of" is a faith that others would share or recognize, then his individualistic brandishing of "my religion" loses meaning, and the sincerity and personal value of that religion decline.[6]

Race Williams's declaration about ethics combines the personal and the universal in a manner similar to Homais's. But rather than ending up with a parodic and meaningless middle ground, as Homais does, Williams—and here we see *The Snarl of the Beast* as a hard-boiled statement of intent conscious of autonomy and accountability for action—manages both. On the one hand, this is because Race Williams is the novel's sole voice of judicial, moral, philosophical, and narrative authority, and thus the insouciant autonomy of the individualist necessarily claims a more universal moral value. Furthermore, the hero who rejects intellectual arguments and eschews "long-winded" humanism to find his own ethical path is a classic American type. In the context of historic dismissals of scholarship as articulated by preachers,

---

5. Flaubert, *Madame Bovary,* 116.
6. Lee, *A World Abandoned By God,* 70–72.

romantics, and vernacular writers, "my ethics are my own" is more promising than dangerous. But this historical background and Race Williams's narrative dominance alone would not suffice to hold his statement above water: what matters is that his "own" ethics bear a surprising resemblance to establishmentarian ethics and thus set up a comforting vision of individualism. Much as nineteenth-century romantic sentimentality echoed the spiritual exemplarity outlined in religious writings, so Race Williams's echo of received definitions of ethics prepares the reader of the hard-boiled to trust this notion of an ethics "of my own."

The principal factor that prevents Race Williams from becoming a sort of Homais with a handgun is not the theoretical or historical foundation of his claim, or even its appurtenance to American character traditions, but simply his conduct. He treats other people well and thinks about the effect of his actions on others. Although Race claims no interest in other people's notions of morality, and he systematically detaches the word "ethics" from all the ideas and markers commonly associated with it, he nonetheless acts in a way that corresponds to received definitions of the word. The coincidence of word, action, and consequence—the fact that the violent, relentlessly autonomous, statute-ignoring maverick reaches the same desirable crime-solving result and manages the same empathy as teams of policemen and principled armchair detectives did in the nineteenth century—makes the hard-boiled detective a viable and desirable embodiment of otherwise lifeless ideals.

TRAUMATIC MEMORY, OR THE ENEMY FROM THE PAST

It is a sign of the times as well as of American individualism that the idea of ethics originating with "someone else" is so disagreeable to Williams. To write one's own script and make one's own rules is a conscious response to the corruption of the 1920s. At the same time, Williams's embodiment of early nineteenth-century American personality characteristics combined with his ethical conduct constitute him as a cultural type, even commodity, much needed in modern America: the subject conscious of his own accountability. Throughout the novel, we see references to the historical and cultural value of Williams's conscience.

William's trustworthiness as character and as ethicist results in part from the traditional dominance of the American anti-intellectual maverick, but it also comes from the personal background and cultural resonances of his self-control. On the cultural front, Race Williams's particular brand of fortitude and reliability corresponds to the figure of the soldier or, more precisely, the former soldier. The novel encourages that association, according considerable importance at once to empathy and psychic resilience in the face of danger and violence. Uri Eisenzweig has described detective fiction as being connected to a crisis of realism, as the dramatic enactment of the very difficulty of narrating. "In any case, the idea of a genre whose entire thematic raison d'être centers on the impossibility of telling the truth corresponds historically to growing frustrations within Western accounts of the real" [En tout état de cause, c'est incontestablement au moment des difficultés grandissantes de la narration occidentale du réel qu'émerge et se constitue, historiquement, l'idée d'un genre dont toute la raison d'être thématique tourne précisément autour de l'impossibilité de raconter la vérité].[7] The historic circumstances surrounding the hard-boiled connect this comment, this impossibility of telling the truth, to the phenomenon of post–World War I crises of narration, and more precisely to the difficulty of narrating violence. Race Williams's principal stock-in-trade is how easily he encounters, assimilates, and narrates violence. Indeed, it is perhaps for this reason that Joseph Shaw, veteran of World War I and editor of *Black Mask* from 1926 to 1936, was so fond of the Race Williams character and encouraged the production of more Race Williams stories as well as the publication of this novel. Williams's particular brand of fortitude is perfect for a postwar audience conscious of the psychic perils of war as well as of the outlines of modern psychological discourse. This is not to say that the readers of *Black Mask* were simultaneously reading the works of Freud, but rather to suggest that some awareness of war's psychic aftermath, as well as of the phenomenon of the unconscious, was part of the cultural imaginary in the mid-1920s. Different historical periods valued different precise manifestations of individual conscience. Early nineteenth-century writings featured honesty and spirit on the frontier, while the early twentieth century, having formed an idea of the intact psyche, valued the conscious subject who would not come undone in the face of violence. The core notion of a subject who exerts himself to ethical action and whose "fragile achievement" improves the lives of others, however, has not changed.

On the personal front, Race Williams recounts a grim childhood, one that underscores the absence of any ethical foundation as such. Toward the end of the novel, when Milly—a friend of Williams's client—kisses Race Williams in gratitude, he writes, "Was it the warm kiss of a woman who loves, or the cold kiss of a woman who plays? Neither—more like the soft lips of a young child—memory must serve me there—for such a feeling knocks off the years and brings a picture of dirty, unkempt children—a hard, cruel face—and the

---

7. Eisenszweig, *Le récit impossible*, 29.

bleak walls of the orphanage where I learned to coldly calculate the frailties of man."[8] This childhood experience, mentioned in passing, solidifies the impression of Race Williams's unforced character attributes. My contention is that he can be read as courageous and heroic because of his capacity to transcend experiences that were known at the time of the novel's writing to produce either shell shock (encounters with violence) or persistent fear (a loveless childhood). One salient characteristic of such experiences, which today are called traumatic, is their ahistoricity, their ability to transcend or compress time, reaching across time into the present and even into the future, across generations.[9] Psychiatrists and psychoanalysts have noted that trauma does not (at the instant of its occurrence) enter the conscious or unconscious mind in the same way as other experiences do. Cathy Caruth connects this resistance to the Freudian phenomenon of "Nachtraeglichkeit," or belatedness: "Traumatic experience suggests a certain paradox: that the most direct seeing of a violent event may occur as an absolute inability to know it; that immediacy, paradoxically, may take the form of belatedness."[10] Experience that was not assimilated and incorporated may end up resisting historicization, thus bleeding into the present.

To a surprising extent, *The Snarl of the Beast* articulates Williams's experience in the terms of contemporary understanding of trauma and of 1920s accounts of war-related neurosis. These representations raise problems of accountability that Race Williams addresses head-on, with a directness that makes him a model of conscience for the posttraumatic era. Hard-boiled toughness has become a well-worn cliché, as has the idea of the hard-boiled character as morally ambiguous or autonomous. What is significant about *The Snarl of the Beast,* particularly in its role as "first hard-boiled novel," is that it represents such toughness as coterminous with a successful assimilation of loss and violence. Such assimilation then becomes the foundational condition for autonomy and its exemplarity—not just because toughness is an enviable characteristic but also because obstacles to it are at the forefront both of the novel and of contemporary discourse.

---

8. Daly, *Snarl of the Beast,* 156. Subsequent references to this work will be given parenthetically in the text.

9. Laub and Auerhahn. "Forms of Traumatic Memory."

10. Caruth, *Unclaimed Experience.* Laplanche et al. define this belatedness: "The subject revises past events at a later date, and that revision invests them not only with a new meaning but also with psychical effectiveness. . . . It is not lived experience in general that undergoes a deferred revision but, specifically, whatever it has been impossible in the first instance to incorporate fully into a meaningful context. The traumatic event is the epitome of such unassimilated experience." Laplanche, Pontalis, and Nicholson-Smith, *Language of Psychoanalysis,* 111–12.

What *The Snarl of the Beast* represents as psychic intactness is a twentieth-century, Freudian-era version of nineteenth-century American frontier courage. As John Kennedy had said of Horse-shoe Robinson, "His watchfulness seemed to be an instinct, engendered by a familiarity with danger, whilst the steady and mirthful tone of his mind was an attribute that never gave way to the inroads of care. He was the same composed and self-possessed being in a besieged garrison, in the moment of a threatened escalade, as amongst his cronies by a winter fire-side."[11] And as Mabel announces to Pathfinder, "Your truth, honour, simplicity, justice, and courage are scarcely equaled by any on earth."[12] In Daly's twentieth century, the courageous person who can stand up to "a threatened escalade" (or what Caillois called "an unseen, silent avenger") is the one who embodies mental strength in the service of national protection and in smaller-scale kindnesses to others. *The Snarl of the Beast* opens: "It's the point of view in life that counts. For an ordinary man to get a bullet through his hat as he walked home at night would be something to talk about for years. Now, with me; just the price of a new hat—nothing more. . . . My position is not exactly a healthy one. The police don't like me. The crooks don't like me. I'm just a halfway house between the law and crime; sort of working both ends against the middle" (1). In this formulation, the first image we encounter, the bullet in the hat, is remarkable for not being remarkable—the event that will *not* dominate this narrative. What separates this narrator from the "ordinary man" becomes his neutral and nonchalant vision of a traumatic event, his ability to transcend or detach himself from it. The entire first chase scene can be read as a dramatic enactment of that detachment. In that scene Race Williams is pursued by the Beast, the novel's snarling and literally inarticulate predator. Besides the symbolic fact of sneaking up from behind, the Beast explicitly represents a disturbing past, for he is the abusive stepfather of Williams's client Daniel Davidson; as such, he constitutes the past and present threat to both client and detective, and the impetus for the case. As Davidson describes him to Williams, "The man that [my mother] left my father for was little short of a beast. He dominated her life and mine" (29). And further on: "A beast who beat me as a child until I lay a helpless heap upon the floor. I see him yet—his flaming eyes, great hairy hands" (31). Daniel Davidson, who lacks the narrator's capacity to surmount past incidents and in a sense incarnates compromised subjectivity, is immersed in the memory of the man: "I see him now—Raphael Dezzeia—my stepfather—the snarling lips—the great teeth—those hands—those hands . . ." (31). Race Williams

---

11. Kennedy, *Horse-Shoe Robinson,* 52.
12. Cooper, *Leatherstocking Tales,* 2:279.

himself describes the Beast in similar terms, as a "reeking mass of rottenness. No way to describe it" (6). And yet, Williams is not undone by this sighting as his client is. Several pages later, the Beast has murdered a policeman and menaced Williams; Williams has escaped and goes on to meet his client: "When a thing is done it's done. So I dismissed the incident from my mind" (16). He later explains his rapid detachment from the haunting vision of the Beast with the statement, "He wasn't related to me, you see, and I had little to fear" (32).

One of the real advantages of Daly's "crude writing" is the heavy-handed obviousness of his allegories and symbols, and the "Beast" comes to represent a persistent childhood fear in which Davidson is ensnared but from which Williams is free. Thus it becomes important to learn that Race Williams once had as much to fear as Davidson—that the detective's own childhood unfolded within "the bleak walls of the orphanage where I learned to coldly calculate the frailties of man." Williams does not mention this background until much later in the novel, nor does he dwell on it, but it underscores the organic and automatic nature of Williams's fortitude.

The sense of being able to escape a problematic past is also aligned with the use of narrative time in Daly's novel. *Snarl*, which starts in the present tense for its action and its philosophizing, moves suddenly to the past tense as Williams gains the upper hand over the Beast: "I don't have to turn to know that my shadow has quickened his pace and now takes two steps to my one; fast, short strides of a heavy body that swings from side to side. Things were getting interesting. I slipped off my thick gloves and wound my fingers about the heavy forty-four in my coat pocket" (3). This shift to the past tense is almost imperceptible, but it is placed so as to remove the narrator from danger both physical and mental. Not only has Williams survived long enough to make it beyond the past tense, he has gained a mental remove: a distance that allows both synthetic distancing ("things") and intellectual observation ("were getting interesting"). This remove contrasts furthermore with the distress of his client Daniel Davidson, the terrified drug addict whose dominant punctuation is the dash and whose submersion in fear makes him barely able to finish a sentence. He starts accounts in the past tense and finishes them in the present, demonstrating the ahistorical persistence of his recollections. Lewis Moore calls the Beast "a possible allusion to the orangutan in Poe's 'Murders,'"[13] and indeed his "snarl" underscores the primal and preverbal nature of the threat he poses. As the Beast represents the menacing past— gunshots and a traumatic childhood contained in one monstrous presence—

---

13. Moore, *Cracking the Hard-Boiled Detective*, 9.

the narrator's escape from him and his movement to the past tense represent a post-posttraumatic moment, a literal and symbolic creation of liberating historical distance. Furthermore, of course, the actual action that Williams narrates is that of pulling out the gun. As Sean McCann notes, for Daly, "gunfire and rhetorical power are virtually identical forces,"[14] and in this scene, the one allows deployment of the other. Victory over the Beast is explicitly framed both as a victory of mental fortitude over an amorphous adversary from the past and as a victory of present consciousness over the transhistorical reach of violence.

SHELL SHOCK

The intimation that detachment from a traumatic childhood is a condition for hard-boiled toughness is initially surprising in this "crudely written" novel, though it lines up with psychoanalytic discourse published at the time. But on a more national-cultural scale, the insistence on transcending the past resonates with the postwar nature of the hard-boiled. As Lee Horsley describes:

> The noir thriller began to develop as a popular form in the aftermath of one devastating war and came to maturity in the two decades that terminate in a second world war. In its most characteristic narratives, some traumatic event irretrievably alters the conditions of life and creates for its characters an absolute experiential divide between their dependence on stable, predictable patterns and the recognition that life is, in truth, morally chaotic, subject to randomness and total dislocation.[15]

Race Williams the character is neither a soldier nor a former soldier, unlike Dashiell Hammett's Nick Charles and Charles Todd's Rutledge, who both fought in World War I, and Mickey Spillane's Mike Hammer, who would come to the page after the end of World War II.[16] Still, the hard-boiled does tend to cast the contemporary urban scene as a sort of battlefield and to use a military vocabulary. *The Snarl of the Beast* uses this lexicon, as do the novels of Hammett and particularly Chandler. But what interests me here is the

---

14. McCann, *Gumshoe America*, 58.

15. Lee Horsley, http://www.crimeculture.com/Contents/Hard-Boiled.html (accessed February 17, 2016).

16. The phenomenon also appears in British crime fiction. Charles Rzepka describes Dorothy Sayer's Lord Peter Wimsey as a "shell shocked" veteran officer "feeling guilty for having sent so many of the men enlisted under him to their deaths during the war." Rzepka, *Detective Fiction*, 164.

way in which Williams remains empathic and stable in the midst of violence as well as the ways in which surmounting violence functions in the public service.

As Jon Adams describes in *Male Armor,* "War provides a pivotal arena for actualizing masculinity." He labels "soldierly masculinity" the particular brand of traditional male function associated with heroism—courage, suppressed emotion, strength, and clearheaded decisiveness. Men who exhibit these behaviors are soldier-heroes."[17] The First World War wedded "soldierly" to "courage" with renewed force, but for the first time the "suppressed emotion" had a sense of emotional peril not previously present in public discourse. By the end of World War I, the American army had had to face more than eighty thousand cases of shell shock. The phenomenon of shell shock was examined in 1915 by the British psychiatrist Charles Myers, who had initially described it not as a psychological but rather sensory disorder resulting from exploding shells. At the same time, he wrote, "The close relation of these cases to those of 'hysteria' seems fairly certain."[18] *Snarl's* description of Daniel Davidson, his drug addiction (he is described in the novel as a "snowbird"), and his jumpiness are almost verbatim repetitions of what medical literature of the postwar period had to say about traumatic neuroses: "I got a look at his face. White, drawn, sunken cheeks, colorless lips—and far distant, somber, searching, roving eyes. . . . Haunted eyes followed me. . . . But our snowbird was talking; gulping it, coughing it and squeaking it out" (26). As J. Rogues de Fursac wrote in 1918, shell shock was marked by "panting, irregular and shallow breathing; stammering, scanning, or explosive speech" and "motor reactions [that] are slow, uncertain, feeble."[19] Davidson shows these same symptoms: "His breath came in uncertain gasps" (24); "uncertain feet—feet that stumbled" (45); "his feeble step and his jerking body told their story" (45). Davidson's symptoms are attributed to the "ravages of dope," but they become most obvious when he describes his stepfather: "I see him now—Raphael Dezzeia—my stepfather. . . . He clung suddenly to me like a frightened child, but his bony fingers still pointed and his weird, wild, searching eyes glared past me at the door" (31). So it was with de Fursac's patient: "A shot fired in the distance, the sight of an airplane, a simple conversation about the war, suffice to let loose manifestations of anxiety. Thus another patient of mine, upon hearing several cannon shots, though fired at a great distance, was seized with such trembling that he had to be put to bed."[20]

17. Adams, *Male Armor,* 9.
18. Myers, "A Contribution to the Study of Shell Shock," 320.
19. De Fursac, "Traumatic and Emotional Psychoses," 37, 34.
20. Ibid., 37.

Myers describes a patient "still very jumpy and alarmed, even at the sound of a footstep," citing the "recurrence of such terror that a special nurse was considered necessary that night."[21] Race Williams, on the other hand, unruffled by the threat from his past, "had tramped through the woods like a regiment of soldiers—cavalry, more like. I guess I made nearly as much noise as an army bringing up the heavy artillery" (207).

At the time of the hard-boiled genesis, war neurosis, which would later come to be called battle fatigue and then posttraumatic stress disorder,[22] was initially associated with "generally excessively emotional" subjects.[23] Race Williams seems to subscribe to this idea (echoed in Myers's comparison of shell shock to hysteria), describing Davidson's trembling as antithetical to masculinity: "There's only one cure and that's manhood; a will power which is so seldom built into the racked brain of the weakling who becomes a sleigh rider" (42). The experience of shell shock was either seen with suspicion—thought to be a sort of malingering—or associated with a weak emotional constitution. As Anthony Babington writes, "It had once been believed that shell shock patients could be divided into two classes: firstly, those who had a pre-existing form of mental deficiency, and secondly, those who were exhibiting a type of hysterical manifestation."[24] At the same time, numerous scholars and doctors argued that the nature and duration of modern war posed more challenges than had earlier wars. William Hocking argued in 1918 that "the strains of war on nerve and courage are not less but more severe than in previous wars. . . . The prevalence of shell shock means not that human quality has declined, but that it can deliberately expose itself to more inhuman and longer suffering than men have ever before in large numbers been called on to endure."[25] In recent decades, the soldier model and the fact of military experience become closely intertwined—in public and psychiatric discourse—with the threat of posttraumatic stress. As Cathy Caruth noted in her seminal study of trauma and narrative, "The experience of the soldier faced with sudden and massive death around him, for example, who suffers this sight in a numbed state, only to relive it later on in repeated nightmares, is a central and recurring image of trauma in our century."[26]

---

21. Myers, "Contributions to the Study of Shell Shock," 608.

22. Not all combat sequelae are PTSD.

23. De Fursac, "Traumatic and Emotional Psychoses," 30.

24. Babington, *Shell Shock*, 70.

25. Hocking, *Morale and Its Enemies*, 7. Babington also notes that "it was a rarity for soldiers in past generations to suffer from the types of war neuroses which might be classified today as 'battle fatigue' or 'battle exhaustion,' owing to the much shorter duration of the encounters between opposing armies." Babington, *Shell Shock*, 10.

26. Caruth, *Unclaimed Experience*, 11. But even in the 1920s, public consciousness of shell

THE ENEMY TO THE REAR

To return to Williams's position in the first action scene, between the Beast and his decoy: this position, facing one enemy while turning one's back on another, further connects Race Williams to the soldier who stands between the battlefield and the civilian world. As James Daughton describes it, a sense of being menaced from all sides, of being unsupported at home and in the command center, was often characteristic of the soldier's sense while at war: "The ineptitude of military officials and the callous indifference of the civilian population drove soldiers to imagine 'an enemy to the rear.'"[27] The impression of adversaries to the front and indifference to the rear represent the soldier's vulnerable and indeterminate place between home and war. This impression also describes the shell shocked soldier in the aftermath of war, between an inescapable past and a worrisome future: it is not a coincidence that the Beast, Raphael Dezzeia, with his un-American name, represents a foreign menace as well as a traumatic memory. At the time of *Snarl*'s publication, the specter of the war continued to loom both psychologically and financially. In his State of the Union address in 1926, Calvin Coolidge remarked that in the midst of a flourishing economy, "The one weak place in the whole line is our still stupendous war debt. In any modern campaign the dollars are the shock troops. With a depleted treasury in the rear, no army can maintain itself in the field. A country loaded with debt is a country devoid of the first line of defense. Economy is the handmaid of preparedness."[28] In this formulation, war debt becomes itself an "enemy to the rear." Furthermore, his Italian-sounding name and the association of the Beast with criminal "gangs" associate him with organized crime. In 1926 Al Capone and his associates killed the prosecutor who was pursuing him for the 1924 murder of another gangster. The Beast becomes a menacing floating signifier, his snarl the myriad intrusions upon the American national psyche, law, and economy. Yet Race Williams, standing between a cold orphanage and a threatening urban landscape, is remarkably at ease with enemies to the front and rear. His position between decoy and beast in his first street scene corresponds to his own self-proclaimed position "working both ends against the middle." And rather

---

shock increased over the decade. According to Eric Dean, "In the United States, the number of veterans receiving hospital care for neuropsychiatric disorders stood at 7,499 in 1921 and increased over the subsequent ten years to 11,342 in 1931. . . . In 1944, almost half of the 67,000 beds in VA hospitals were occupied by the psychoneurotics of World War I." Dean, *Shook Over Hell,* 39.

27. Daughton, "Sketches of the *Poilu's* World," 61.

28. Calvin Coolidge, "State of the Union," December 7, 1926. In Kalb, *State of the Union,* 158.

than sensing abandonment by social structures, he finds a welcome independence: his physical and economic self-reliance make him a microcosm of instinctive preparedness on a personal and a national level. While Race announces on the first page that his position is "not exactly a healthy one," he nonetheless seems much healthier (and in the end, more alive) than most of those around him. Daniel Davidson has died of a heart attack and the Beast has been killed.

THE EMPATHIC OUTSIDER

The idea of trauma as an experience that resists conscious incorporation into an individual's personal narrative is an extreme psychological phenomenon, but even when he does not experience shell shock, the soldier is situated outside society even as he is emblematic of it. Studies of the psychology of the soldier published during and just after World War I underscore this separation. As William Hocking writes, "The mind of the soldier is marked off from the mind of the same man in civil life. Soldiering is a life having its own special strains, and its own standards. . . . The army is a world of peculiar structure: the conditions of success and the meaning of success are not the same as elsewhere; consequently it is not always the same men who come to the top."[29] Studies of the military discuss this separateness extensively.[30] And yet, of course, although it is understood that war has its own rules and laws, the soldier is also expected to incarnate and defend the national principles that make civilian existence possible.[31] The hardboiled reincorporates or reintegrates that paradoxical position, as it takes battlefield effectiveness and improvisation and transplants them—has them thrive within and become beneficial to—a civilian landscape. The soldier's strength, formed in the midst of a quintessentially patriotic but at the same time often almost incomprehensible experience, connects national virtues with outsider status—with a sense of independence or alienation from the social mainstream. This independence-as-national-paradigm corresponds both to the model of soldierly masculinity and to the hard-boiled character. Hard-boiled subjectivity is thus linked, paradoxically enough, with a class of national protectors.

29. Hocking, *Morale and Its Enemies*, 97.
30. See Samuel Huntington, *The Soldier and the State*; Keegan, *History of Warfare*; Weber and Eliasson, *Handbook of Military Administration*.
31. See Weber and Eliasson, *Handbook of Military Administration*; Snyder, *Citizen-Soldiers*.

Race Williams, surmounting enemies from front and rear, moving beyond an orphan's upbringing and surviving the onslaughts of snarling pan-European monsters, embodies classic American notions of masculine courage, at the same time joining outsider status to posttraumatic mental fortitude. As such, he situates "soldierly masculinity" in the modern era and in a civilian environment, which makes him not just a successful soldier on urban streets but, more crucially, a successful *former* soldier and thus a proven one: a person who can survive the onslaught of violence and maintain control of the narrative. To be sanguine and matter-of-fact in the face of violence is of course both a classic American masculine trait and also a soldierly characteristic. Various scholars have located this quality in the hard-boiled hero as well as in the American Western. John Cawelti writes, "This narrative pattern—a protagonist placed in a situation where some form of violence or criminality becomes a moral necessity—is one of the basic archetypes of American literature."[32] But ease in violence and the successful assimilation of a traumatic past are not enough to make a character the trusted conservator of ideals as "subjective facts." *The Snarl of the Beast* showcases with equal insistence the importance of ongoing empathy and accountability.

In time of war, the enemy is the adversarial nation. But in its aftermath, the internalization of traumatic experience becomes in turn another enemy, one that perpetuates the first. Race Williams, as he repeats ad infinitum, is in his element in violence, yet he demonstrates a discerning use of force, drawing the line between people who are part of the criminal world and people who are not. Such discernment is fundamental because it establishes a sense of awareness, of conscious responsibility for his actions and their consequences. "That the end justifies the means was made for me all right—but no end would justify the taking of an innocent life" (136). Toward the end of the novel, he repeats that he shoots "to protect my life or the life of another. But I don't go out to kill" (151). When a "derelict of the night"—actually the Beast's decoy—approaches him to ask for money, "The temptation to lift my gun and smack him one was strong but I didn't. It wasn't a big heart or a sensitive conscience that made me hesitate. Just common sense and the hope of a long life" (3). Here again, an evocation of the future ("hope of a long life") and of a capacity for reason ("just common sense") contrasts with the traumatic sense of being stuck in the past, dominated by volatile emotion. When he then goes to meet with Davidson, he is kind to him and understands his demons. "I'm not one for sympathy, but I stretched out a hand and tight-

---

32. Cawelti, "Myths of Violence," 529.

ened it on his wrist. . . . This thing was real enough to him" (29). Later, he contemplates Davidson as a therapist might: "Danny might have been lying, but unconsciously. He believed every word he told me" (62). Williams values authentic expressions of feeling: "Here was real emotion" (35); "there was sincerity in them all right" (38).

In a historical era that saw the recognition of shell shock as a medical phenomenon and the rise of psychoanalysis as a discipline this narrator who could claim instinctual fortitude and maintain kindness to others makes of himself an ideal American hero.[33] The capacity for empathy keeps him from being "hardened," from being desensitized or indifferent to violence. Davidson embodies an almost parodic rendition of posttraumatic defenselessness, whereas Williams incarnates strong emotional constitution. Since the discourse around shell shock initially described it as a problem for the weak rather than as a broad situational hazard, Williams's coping mechanisms read as natural and unforced—a strength "built in," as he puts it. This instinctive empathy recalls the combination of virtue and character attributes that nineteenth-century writings had established. Virtue as such is absent from the present calculation, but it is important to note that nothing is lost through this absence. A strong empathic presence is necessary to constitute this novel's exemplary protagonist, but it is also sufficient.

The empathic presence and emotional generosity that he shows is also shared by Milly, the "girl of the night" who works hard to rescue Davidson. Milly also seems touched by something similar to shell shock as Williams describes her "uncertain, animal doubt and watchfulness of danger" (36). But she concentrates on supporting Daniel "as one who is used to meet with and tackle the abuses of life—but nothing haunted in her eyes" (35). When Daniel dies, Milly receives his inheritance and sails for Europe. Race Williams contemplates joining her, both of them compensated by the narrative for their kindness and courage (49). Indeed, insofar as Race Williams's treatment of Milly is emblematic of the hard-boiled treatment of women, this novel set a standard that began almost immediately to decline. He distrusts Milly initially, but his kindness to her (as well as to the woman who breaks into his home) shows a basic inclination to give others the benefit of the doubt. Lewis Moore cites Williams's "chivalric relationship to women" and notes that few hard-boiled writers "have the Victorian image of women that Race Williams demonstrates in *The Snarl of the Beast*."[34] He alternates between crusty and

---

33. Freud's *Beyond the Pleasure Principle* (1920), *The Ego and the Id* (1923), and *Inhibitions, Symptoms and Anxiety* (1926).

34. Moore, *Cracking the Hard-Boiled Detective*, 81.

sentimental in his musings on women, but he does them no harm and denies them no dignity or autonomy.

The nineteenth-century outsider was an example to others not because he had eluded the shroud of violence and uncertainty that covered the present day, but because he had not eluded it; he had simply learned, or grasped through instinct and a tough constitution, how to exist within it. So it is with Williams and his inauspicious childhood, his solitary position on the mean streets of New York. As Butler puts it, "he is his travels," which means that he lives and functions fully within the historical present rather than as an anachronistic ideal. In the case of the hard-boiled character, competence in contemporary culture demanded acceptance of that culture, whatever its form. The combination of a troubled past and an emotionally intact present became a heroic paradigm in the post–World War I period, which coupled national intactness and national identity with the successful assimilation of violence and traumatic experience.

If I have talked at some length about the circumstances of Race Williams's strengths, and about the background of shell shock as a neuropsychiatric phenomenon, it is because the solidity of the character *as* character is also at a premium. The concept of "war neurosis" associates soldierly masculinity with the risk of pathology, thus introducing dubious undercurrents into the courageous persona of the soldier. It sows a seed of doubt and dissolution that will germinate in the post–hard-boiled and ultimately threaten to subvert both accountability and character as such. Gregory Currie talks in terms of "character (a person in a story) and Character (inner source of action, related to personality and temperament)."[35] The hard-boiled character opens and closes the novel with a certain stasis—indeed, "hard-boiled" implies a character capable of sustained exertions of conscience. What Gilbert Harman describes as "relatively long-term stable dispositions to act in distinctive ways"[36] remains intact, at the level of the individual protagonist and at the metalevel of the hard-boiled character as phenomenon. Hard-boiled character, in other words, is disposed over the long term to admit the outside world without disintegrating in response to it. Williams narrates that stability as if it were a matter of innate ease, but his constant talking underscores the element of conscious effort.

---

35. Currie, "Narrative and the Psychology of Character," 60.
36. Harman, *Explaining Value*, 166.

WHAT COULD GO WRONG?

The Snarl of the Beast is not the best written of the American hard-boiled novels, nor is it now the best known. Yet during the 1920s and 1930s, every hard-boiled writer built upon or cribbed from the Race Williams model, and Daly is the undisputed originator of the hard-boiled character. In this first instance of the hard-boiled novel, the nineteenth-century frontier maverick becomes a modern urban soldier able to assimilate a miserable background and stop past perils from spoiling the present. Charles Rzepka, among others, points out the self-reliance implicit in the hard-boiled character:

> Despite America's postwar economic gains, new insecurities were undermining public confidence in the promise of the American Dream. Writers for pulp magazines like *Black Mask* responded by portraying an America in which no one could be trusted, least of all wealthy society types. . . . Lacking the respect for "tradition" and "history" that helped motivate his Golden Age English counterpart to defend an idealized prewar way of life, the American tough-guy detective knew he could count on only one thing: himself.[37]

The Snarl of the Beast's representations of escape from traumatic history underscore the notion that the detective who counts on "himself" has gained a victory. He remains ostentatiously dismissive of tradition, education ("longwinded professors," "I'm not quoting from books"), and authority ("empty as a congressman's head," "I always like to play the game outside the law"), but he nonetheless generates ethical and empathic decisions through his individualism. Sean McCann's *Gumshoe America* attributes that victorious individualism to an anticollectivist mentality. Outlining the linkage between the hard-boiled genre and the decline of New Deal liberalism, he ventures that Race Williams's individualism does not just coincide with national intactness but actually works crucially in its service, in a manner consistent with contemporary political ideas:

> For the politically unsubtle Daly, labor unions and liberal politicians assume the same status as the Klan. Each represents a corrupt form of political solidarity. Each aspires to a spurious *national* status. . . . Thus, while Race Williams's refusal to be a joiner undermined the Klan's vision of native community, the potential endpoint of such a commitment was a radical skepti-

---

37. Rzepka, *Detective Fiction*, 186.

cism about all forms of social organization—one that would invalidate not just Klannish fantasies of community, but every idea of civic obligation or human solidarity.[38]

As McCann further notes, when political communities were the problem, the individual who eschewed communities was the solution. The idea that any community could become problematic gives political resonance to the common observation that the dominant quality of the hard-boiled "world," with its institutions and its people, is one of contamination and corruption: the sort of corruption, that is, to which only the unaffiliated individual could be an antidote.

Without contesting McCann's astute political reading of hard-boiled responses to corruption, I would underscore as well the enormous responsibility that the unaffiliated individual now carries. As a genre the hard-boiled puts great emphasis on the extent of corruption and particularly on the critical vocabulary of contamination and loss. *Snarl* contributes to this wide attribution, describing "gun fights [as] a nightly affair in most any section of the city, and the killing of a policeman no longer a national event" (18) and New York buildings "whose only claim to distinction was the glories of the past" (105). Because that sense of a desolation at once spiritual, medical, and environmental is so pervasive and now iconic, the dominant hard-boiled problem, at first glance, would seem to be not whether or not individualism and individual incarnation of "subjective facts" are well advised but whether individualism is even possible. It is because of this contamination—be it political, as in McCann's reading, or psychological—that the exceptionalism of the individual resonates as a triumph over such an environment. Subsequent hard-boiled novels encourage this sense of struggle against contamination. ("Anybody that brings any ethics to Poisonville is going to get them all rusty," states Hammett's Continental Op in *Red Harvest*. "I was part of the nastiness now," concedes Chandler's Marlowe at the end of *The Big Sleep*.[39]) The problem that Race Williams actually sets up, however, is not just contamination from the outside in. Rather, it is the complications of grounding "ethics"—and eventually law—in an individual in the first place.

When Race Williams says, "My ethics are my own," he sets himself up as spokesperson and bodyguard—for the novel has no other—not just of social principles and national ideals (as in the cowboy model, for instance), not just of sentimental connection and historical consciousness, as Leonard Cassuto

---

38. McCann, *Gumshoe America*, 62.
39. Hammett, *Red Harvest*, 549. Chandler, *The Big Sleep*, 197.

describes, but of ideas and principles themselves—of their very meaning and content. This appropriation, of principles in general and of ethics in particular, will become a major hard-boiled selling point. No one else in Daly's novel mentions ethics at all, so the narrator's appropriation has a conservationist function. At the same time, "my ethics are my own" points to an immediate and fundamental problem with the maverick nature of the hard-boiled detective and with a "nonconformist authority" in general, namely, that these constitute a contradiction in terms. In Williams's early declaration, the dismissal of "statutes" and "essays of long-winded professors" amounts to a distancing of "my ethics" from legal and philosophical frameworks, respectively. And the reluctance to qualify those ethics as "good" or "bad" seems indeed to eschew any moral system of evaluation, including but not limited to the theological. The Homais problem, in other words, always looms. In distancing himself from philosophical, legal, social, and moral contexts, Race Williams makes principles coterminous with "subjective facts." This coincidence functions well when the subject is willing and able to perform such embodiment. In this section, I have been examining Williams as both untraumatized soldier and conservator of ethics to demonstrate that the hard-boiled reconstitutes the nineteenth-century culture hero and establishes an individualistic American response to disorder. At the same time, the "emotional psychoses" Davidson introduces continue to threaten. The fears and suspicions evoked when shell shock was first diagnosed—fears of incurability, suspicions of malingering, equation of symptoms with excessive emotionalism—rise again in the post–hard-boiled novel. The various specters of posttraumatic distress that *Snarl* enumerates, the "bleak walls of the orphanage," the ravages of drug addiction, the encroaching criminal atmosphere, the menacing and inarticulate "Beast" signifying menace within and without: these all emerge in the post–hard-boiled novel of the mid-twentieth century to threaten the psychic intactness of the character as such. As the century progresses, in other words, the self as such becomes unreliable, as character and accountability deteriorate from within and the subject begins to doubt whether he actually is one.

120, RUE DE LA GARE

In this section I will focus on *120, rue de la Gare,* the first Nestor Burma novel by former surrealist poet Léo Malet. Widely considered the first French hard-boiled novel, *120* combines the often antiheroic pessimism of mid-century *noir* fiction with the certitude and exemplarity of the American hard-boiled. The French *roman noir* is a cultural hybrid, and its French lineage runs from the *Memoirs* of Vidocq through the urban forests of Balzac, Hugo, and Sue, then to the roaring Parisian streets of Baudelaire. Michelle Emanuel observes that Malet "writes of Paris with a surrealist eye and a popular sensibility."[40] Alistair Rolls and Deborah Walker note that Malet's "texts bear many traces of [Baudelaire's] prose poems, which will pave the way for the more fully fetishistic *Weltanschauung* of 1945," and echoes of surrealist referents arise in the course of *120*.[41] Malet's novel does for France much of what the first American hard-boiled did for America. That is, it reconstitutes the nineteenth-century culture hero for the needs of the twentieth century and brings the model of spiritual authority and romantic heroism into the modern era. *120, rue de la Gare* was published in 1943 during the occupation. Nestor Burma, the novel's hero, heads the detective agency, Fiat Lux, whose operations have been suspended by the Second World War. Burma is as verbose as Race Williams and as conscious of himself as a character. Perpetually ready for a close-up, he announces: "Suddenly, I was no longer the POW . . . but Nestor Burma, the one and only, the director of the Fiat Lux agency, Dynamite Burma" [Subitement, je ne fus plus le *Kriegsgefangen* . . . mais Nestor Burma, le vrai, le directeur de l'Agence Fiat Lux, Dynamite Burma].[42] Breaking into a moment of English to posture for his readers: "What do you want? I'm Burma, the man who can knock a mystery out flat" [Que voulez-vous? Je suis Burma, l'homme qui a mis le mystère knock-out] (89).[43] Anne Mullen and Emer O'Beirne note that the French antihero is more often a criminal or a policeman than a private detective and that Nestor Burma is the exception to this rule. Like Race Williams, he is a thorn in the side of criminals and police alike, and at ease in violence.[44]

Whereas Race Williams's claims to a nationally resonant ethical intactness are an anti-intellectual manner and a soldierly resistance to violence, Nestor Burma's are a contemplative aestheticism, sardonic understatement, and a quintessentially French *esprit*. The timing of publication, moreover, allows Burma to function as a mainstream culture hero at a time when cultural frameworks are being dramatically shut down. These circumstances are

---

40. Emanuel, *From Surrealism to Less-Exquisite Cadavers*, 28.

41. Rolls and Walker, *French and American Noir*, 23. Malet is not the only detective novelist to dovetail with surrealism; Robin Walz notes that "*Fantômas* was surreal before the letter, and surrealists later recognized the 'Lord of Terror' as their confrère." Walz, *Pulp Surrealism*, 45.

42. Malet, *120, rue de la Gare*, 20. Subsequent references to this work will be given parenthetically.

43. The movie version of *120, rue de la Gare* (1946) is more cartoonish in its representation of Burma's posturing: the character karate-chops his own valet and flexes his muscles for the camera. At the end of the film, he and his secretary Hélène, united in romance, face the camera and recite the movie's title.

44. Mullen and O'Beirne, *Crime Scenes*, 233.

crucial to Burma's role, to the "first-ness" of this novel, and to the cultural resonance of Burma's heroism. At the same time, the occupation demands a certain ethical tact. The American hard-boiled detective had declared ethical independence after a war, and what is more, after a war that had never threatened American soil. Nestor Burma, on the other hand, conducts his investigation during an occupation that assailed French culture as such—literature, music, theater—as well as the amorphous leisure that had made aesthetic sensibility and romantic heroism possible. To "watch the passing waves" in the midst of the occupation would be an act of poetic resistance, but it could also, depending on what is happening around, be egregiously tone-deaf. Part of Nestor Burma's responsibility, then, is to navigate the ethical parameters of the aesthetic even as he embodies the sensibilities so closely associated with the French heroic model.

THE INDEPENDENT ETHICIST

In American crime fiction, moral codes and decisions come from the individual less as they derive from historical precedent or even rumination than from an intrinsic or instinctive sense of right. In French crime fiction, by contrast, even maverick detectives tended to come from a humanist tradition of philosophical contemplation and awareness. Nestor Burma never states that his ethics are his own. And yet, he reaps the autonomy of such a claim precisely because of the occupation, which has weakened sociocultural frames, forcing ethics into the hands of the individual. As David Platten writes of the occupation-era *roman noir*, "In *L'Étranger* et *L'Être et le néant*, both published in 1943, Camus and Sartre wrote of the absurdity and loneliness of the human condition, of the inescapable burden of choice, and the impossibility of freedom beyond that individual choice. During the Occupation these were not abstract ideas, but realities rapping at the front door with such sustained regularity that a whole generation was left traumatised for years afterwards."[45] In this formulation the existence of ideals as "subjective facts"—or the postulation of virtues as personality features—gives way to a debilitating isolation. And yet, as Platten notices, the characters in *120, rue de la Gare* are far from debilitated:

> *120, rue de la Gare*, which introduces to the world of crime fiction the character of Nestor Burma, could have been written at any time in the last sixty

---

45. Platten, *Pleasures of Crime*, 79.

years. It does refer to features of occupied life, such as "Ersatz" goods and the difficulties in acquiring the "interzone" passes. . . . However, it is strikingly devoid of any political or social comment. And although commentators have identified *120, rue de la Gare* as the first properly French *roman noir*, generically, in tone and narrative design it harks back to the "innocent" age of the classic whodunit.[46]

Malet's novel does indeed "hark back" in this manner, but I would argue that its apparently retrograde innocence is not about the social forms or master narratives of the nineteenth century, but rather about the resilient individual able to live and even thrive within "the burden of choice." The hard-boiled subject that "is its travels" has moved into an era that casts such resilience as countercultural. The principal draw of the hard-boiled is its promise to deliver the solace of commitment to civil society and the functioning order of a rationalized world without the deadening effects that were often associated with each. Another draw is its postulation of a subject that experiences the burden of choice as livable rather than traumatic. This is the precise sort of fantastic scenario that Chandler provided when he described a man who is not mean going down mean streets, for he portrays that aloneness in one's decency as a tolerable condition rather than—as Platten rightly finds in Sartre and Camus—a draining and impossible one. Honneth's account of making a "negative judgment on the present without basing it explicitly on a value judgment"[47] can also be understood to describe that tolerance. Burma thus crucially combines component parts of existential aloneness and unstinting solidity, a point of balance in which a critical perspective on the whole of society does not turn into hopeless resignation, as it tended to for other *noir* authors such as Albert Simonin and August de Breton. These latter were in a sense the more seminal French *noir* authors, their respective *Touchez pas au grisbi* and *Du rififi chez les hommes* catapulting the *Série noire* to greater popularity.[48] And Rolls points out that Malet himself, in *Nestor Burma contre C.Q.F.D,* provides a "distinctly prose-poetic non-resolution" that he contrasts with the "synthetic resolution" of *120, rue de la Gare.*[49] But *120* nonetheless earns its place as first hard-boiled because it reconstitutes the conscious subject for the twentieth century.

46. Ibid., 80.

47. Honneth, *Pathologies of Reason,* 97.

48. Philips, *Rififi,* 19.

49. Rolls, *Paris and the Fetish,* 146. See also Laurent Bourdelas, who notes that "the Occupation is the literary equivalent of the fog that lends atmosphere to Anglo-Saxon detective novels" [l'Occupation est l'équivalent littéraire du brouillard qui donne leur atmosphere aux romans policiers anglo-saxons]. Bourdelas, *Le Paris de Nestor Burma,* 9.

The French hard-boiled creates a powerful union of communitarian connections, individual conscience, and national security. Claire Gorrara writes
that *120, rue de la Gare* "eschews a directly political history of the Occupation" but notes that insofar as it reveals "a social fantastic which subverts the
rational and political order of the Occupation," it can be read "as a deeply
politicized text about the state of occupied France."[50] For the purposes of
this discussion, Platten's statement that *120* could have been written any
time in the last sixty years in fact raises the value of Burma's primitive and
unstated wholeness. Assaults on the fullness of the individual's subjectivity,
constraints placed on his originality or authenticity, do not occur within the
hard-boiled world. The grievous vacuum that abandons the individual to the
"burden of choice" is the hard-boiled's vital precondition, but the detective
is born to thrive within it. Existential concerns for the individual's fullness
of being or for the dreaded abyss of a meaningless world either never come
up or have been resolved already. The external circumstances—wartime on
the French side, urban peril on the American—that force and underscore
individual responsibility for the ethical also ensure that the ethical remain
individual, instinctive, bound not to theories of subjectivity but to the mere
fact of daily living.

A CULTURAL OUTSIDER, AND A CULTURE OUTSIDE

The idea of the exemplary maverick has long been canonically and tradition-
ally American, so Race Williams was at least partly type rather than paradox. For Burma, on the other hand, the paradoxical combination of maverick
and classically French becomes possible precisely because of the occupation.
In this particular historical moment, when an entire culture comes under
assault, the wartime outsider is at the same time a French insider. He is a
conservator of culture. As Claire Gorrara writes, "In *120, rue de la Gare*, the
Occupation emerges as a period of dislocation when the everyday is radically
altered by the eruption of an alien order." Earlier, she had noted, "Censorship
. . . was more than the control of mere information; it represented a sustained
attack on French culture as the repository of values and ideals that could bol-
ster national confidence during the 'années noires' as the war years came to
be known."[51] In the political and ideological sense, the conditions of the occupation allowed the irreverent outsider—a canonically American hard-boiled

---

50. Gorrara, *Roman Noir,* 28.
51. Ibid., 25, 22.

notion—to take the form of a Frenchman standing up for French culture on French soil.[52] What is more, he does this in a particularly French way: contemplating nature, solving the murder through literary clues, and taking care not to wander into amoral aestheticism.

THE PASTORAL MUSE

Nestor Burma shares Race Williams's familiarity with violence and danger. Like Williams, he is able to transcend fear and elude self-pity. And like Williams, he uses these capacities to become, or rather be, an ethical individual. But rather than declaring outright that a bullet in the hat is nothing to talk about, Burma uses sarcastic epigrams and derisive references to bourgeois comforts. When asked why so talented a detective as he had not escaped from the POW camp, "I responded that I hadn't taken a vacation in quite some time, so prison was its substitute" [Je répondis que je n'avais pas bénéficié de vacances depuis longtemps et que, pour moi, cette captivité en tenait lieu] (15). When his partner and close friend Bob Colomer does not recognize him: "You don't know your friends any more? Burma . . . Nestor Burma . . . just back from a country holiday" [Tu ne remets plus les copains? Burma . . . Nestor Burma . . . qui revient de villégiature] (24). And then, recounting that moment of misrecognition to another person: "It took him a minute to recognize me. I must have gained weight" [Il a mis un sacré moment à me reconnaître. J'ai dû grossir] (28). These understatements and dismissals, rooted in Burma's experience as prisoner of war, have the same toughening function as Williams's blithe discounting of the bullet through the hat. That turning of pain into witticism constitutes the French version of the psychic toughness that characterized the American hard-boiled. Comic pretense at aesthetic consciousness ("I must have gained weight") and aristocratic contentment ("back from a country holiday") mock the detached contemplativeness of the romantic hero, but they serve a particularly twentieth-century psychic function. Burma, by his own admission, is the man "who can knock [any] mystery out flat!" Turning imprisonment into a quip is Burma's contribution to what Gorrara called

---

52. In a sense, the entire French hard-boiled genre constitutes such a homegrown outsider. As Michelle Emanuel describes in her study of Léo Malet, fellow writer Louis Chevance encouraged the author to write a detective novel for the Minuit collection, citing the new market for crime fiction "made in France." Emanuel, *From Surrealism to Less-Exquisite Cadavers*, 23. In a commerical sense, then, the occupation's prohibition on books from outside France created the original market conditions for French "outsiders" to flourish within France.

the "social fantastic which subverts the rational and political order of the Occupation." Since actually knocking out the intruding enemy (the occupier) was not possible (in practice or even on the page, for reasons of censorship), as knocking out the Beast was in *Snarl,* the best way to surmount the wartime experience was to turn it into the subject of an epigram. The ability to mock or understate marked a victory of intellectual creativity, which in turn marked a psychological and cultural triumph.

The idea of the individual or instinctive moral compass is fundamental to the hard-boiled. Because Burma is represented at the mercy of an occupying army, he becomes ethical by opposition to them—ethical by virtue of surviving imprisonment by the unethical. This survival allows the individual to carry his culture aloft through circumstances that suppressed the cultural as such. Burma's use of understatement in particular equates the ethical status of the prisoner of war and the ethical status of the person who can diminish his own misfortune but not that of others, and so gives to the occupied Frenchman a moral finesse. A detached or sardonic perspective that would be obscene coming from a perpetrator, or unfeeling coming from a witness, can read as a defense mechanism—and thus answer to a different ethical standard—coming from a prisoner. Crucially, Burma trains the lens of understatement on his own experience rather than on someone else's, which lends an ethical legitimacy to his mockeries.

Burma's ironic mentions of vacations and weight gain introduce the ethically problematic parameters of the aesthetic. Indeed, a crucial element of Burma's response to violence and privation, and one that can be coded as particularly French, is his aesthetic emphasis on the visual and the sensorial. The question of the ethical parameters of such concentration permeates discussions of the ethical and the aesthetic from Kant to Hegel, from Adorno to Foucault. Burma as occupation-era character and as hard-boiled innovator seems conscious of the tension between ethics and sensual pleasure. Walking that line gives him a philosophical credibility akin to Chandler's "honor without thought of it," one that we could call "a [Foucauldian] beautiful life without thought of it." Burma's aesthetic perspectives on violence and pain have an intuitive ethical sense, but they also intimate what can go wrong, and what in the *néo-polar* will go wrong, with the aesthetic perspective.

120, rue de la Gare contains various moments where the décor of wartime morphs into pastoral landscape descriptions—a combination that recalls the romantic pastoral and raises, in a seemingly intentionally provocative gesture, the ethical tension that surrounds art in wartime. Whereas Race Williams declares that a bullet in the hat is nothing to write home about, Nestor Burma ruminates on the shape of that bullet. Early in the novel, Burma articulates a pastoral appreciation for the scenery of the POW camp: "I went out to stretch my legs. . . . It was July. The weather was balmy. A warm sun caressed the barren landscape. A gentle breeze blew from the south. A sentry walked back and forth on the watchtower. The barrel of his gun shone in the sun. After a moment, I went back to my table, drawing contentedly on the pipe I'd just lit" [Je sortis me dégourdir les jambes. . . . On était en juillet. Il faisait bon. Un soleil tiède caressait le paysage aride. Il soufflait un doux vent du sud. Sur son mirador, la sentinelle allait et venait. Le canon de son arme brillait sous le soleil. Au bout d'un instant, je regagnai ma table, tirant avec satisfaction sur la pipe que je venais d'allumer] (11). In this moment of leisure, appreciation of nature—Chateaubriand contemplating heavy artillery rather than a babbling brook—distracts from the human-authored war. In the course of his rumination, the weapon shining in the sun also becomes part of the bucolic, sharing the same visual and phenomenological status as the "warm sun" and the "gentle breeze." In this scene, since the gun appears at the end of the sentence, it seems to put an end to the bucolic meditation: once it comes into the picture, the moment of leisure is over. And yet, silence about sentiment and emotional reaction, so fundamental to the hard-boiled, wanders by definition into morally problematic territory. The very blank slate that the silence produces, the absence of commentary, introduces the possibility that silence contains unconcern or, more disturbingly, actual pleasure, a possibility that has inspired much writing about the mutual exclusivities of aesthetics, morality, and violence.

Burma pushes the envelope of the ethical because his understatements, dismissals, and visual abstractions, although understandable or even touching considering his status as prisoner of war, are nonetheless rooted in the offhanded toughness of the American hard-boiled. The American counterpart was not conceived during an instance of American peril and so did not have to navigate the ethical in the way that the French did. Rendering heedless American toughness in the voice of a French prisoner of war lends that toughness an ethical complexity not present in the American version. More precisely, the rendering of aesthetic contemplation in the voice of a French prisoner of war raises the shade of a question about the dominant sentiment at hand—is it amoral coldness or victim's self-defense? Mackaman and Mays had written that "the course and outcome [of World War I] eradicated for poets, painters, and writers the right to follow a pastoral muse."[53] The insistence on nonetheless following a pastoral muse, which could be read as an

---

53. Mackaman and Mays, *World War I*, xviii.

act of resistance after World War I, came after World War II to read as an act of insensitivity or even perversion.

> The first war set adrift survivors who had lived too long "eye deep in Hell," young men wandering the streets of large cities and small towns physically maimed and, worse, psychically shattered, yet there still remained after 1918 a sense that some understanding of this horrible tragedy could eventually be gained. . . . Not even this miniscule consolation could endure the second war, however, after which survival itself became the question posed by such figures as Primo Levi, Tadeusz Borowski, and Bruno Bettelheim.[54]

It must be said that the wartime Paris of *120, rue de la Gare* is quite an anodyne version, as is the narrator's POW experience. Bureaucratic inconvenience presents a foil for narrative ingenuity, but as Platten rightly observes, real demoralization and physical threat are absent. The stakes for this narrator's contemplations of the pastoral muse are thus lowered, since he does not risk coming across as perverse or inhuman. And yet, because those stakes are sufficiently high for the narrator to use the wartime environment to question the ethical defensibility of retaining the "pastoral muse," that retention becomes the occupied French version of the toughness characteristic of the hard-boiled genre.

Turning now to another bucolic moment, I examine Burma's balancing the occupation victim's self-protective instinct to understate with the American hard-boiled's tough embrace of violence. This moment also questions the ethical resonance of understatement and, more precisely, the abstraction of violence into visual spectacle. In so doing, it constitutes the hard-boiled hero as a critical historian, able to tailor his words and actions to the present ethical landscape. In this scene Burma again enjoys a moment outside: "I knocked my pipe against the wooden steps. Sprinkling the ashes over the sparse heather bushes, I refilled the pipe with the Polish substance that the canteen called tobacco. It was a sort of stomach-turning dynamite, strong enough to bathe the landscape in a dusty and pleasantly bitter smoke" [Je cognai ma pipe contre les marches de bois. A la place des cendres que je venais de disperser sur les maigres bouquets de bruyère, je mis le produit polonais qu'on nous vendait à la cantine sous le nom de tabac. C'était une espèce de dynamite à ébranler les estomacs, très suffisante pour enfumer le paysage, répandre alentour une odeur poussiérieuse, agréablement âcre] (16). To pause a moment with one's pipe is a detective fiction standard: clas-

---

54. Ibid., xix.

sic Sherlock Holmes and classic Simenon. As for meditation on the coun-
tryside, the heather bushes, like the "gentle breeze" of the earlier citation,
are a romantic commonplace; Chateaubriand, for instance, describes such
a bouquet in the bosom of a woman he met harvesting tea leaves in Cap
d'Aigle. Maigret, a twentieth-century *promeneur solitaire,* contemplated the
landscape as he pondered the murder at hand.[55] But in this scene narrated
by "Dynamite Burma" in and about a war-torn landscape, the pastoral muse
relies upon—even as it distracts from—the vestiges of war. On the one
hand, it recounts simply the ironic ruminations of a disenchanted smoker
who dislikes wartime tobacco. At the same time, the image of a "stomach-
turning dynamite, strong enough to bathe the landscape in smoke," even as
it describes Burma's tobacco, evokes just as much bomb as pipe. "Dynamite"
points to an explosive, and the words "stomach-turning" (*ébranler les estomacs*), referring to the strength of the tobacco, in fact anticipate the French
néo-polar practice of turning figures of speech into gruesome anatomical
literalisms. What is more, "Dynamite Burma" is the narrator's own nick-
name, pointing both to his own explosiveness and to his admirable talents
for detection. To call something "dynamite" is to praise it, and to call this
detective "Dynamite" is to praise among other things his explosiveness. The
sentence thus floats the possibility of violence as a visual pleasure—indeed,
raises the possibility of participation in violence, but remains within the ethically anodyne parameters of pipe-smoking contemplation and the prisoner
of war perspective.

In addition to appreciating the shininess of accessories of war, Burma
presents several moments of actual violence abstracted into the performa-
tive. For instance, when Burma pushes an assailant into the Seine, the man's
tumble has something of the ballet to it: "I kneed him in the stomach and
caught him with an uppercut. His feet just missed hitting me in the face" [Je
lui plongeai mon genou dans le ventre et le redressai d'un uppercut. Ses pieds
manquèrent m'atteindre en pleine face] (73). When he knocks out Gerard Laf-
alaise in order to put him out of commission, the focus is once more on limbs
in motion rather than expression of sentiment: "My fist shot out and caught
him on the chin. He went down, joining his hat on the ground. I tossed a
scarf to Covet" [Mon poing partit et l'atteignit en plein menton. Il alla au sol,
rejoindre son chapeau. Je lançai une écharpe à Covet].[56] To render violence as
a sort of acrobatic art falls in line with classic American hard-boiled nonchalance, but it also approaches a morally vacant version of what philosophers

---

55. Simenon, *Les vacances de Maigret,* 17.
56. Malet, *120, rue de la Gare,* 80.

later in the century would call "an aesthetics of existence." As Richard Wolin writes of later Foucauldian aesthetics,

> Instead of an ethic of reciprocity or brotherliness, Foucault opts for what we might call a dramaturgical model of conduct, in which action becomes meaningful solely qua performative gesture. But this theory risks sanctioning an approach to ethics that is brazenly particularistic and elitist. Formally it remains only a hair's breadth removed from Nietzsche's rehabilitation of the right of the stronger. With Foucault, however, it is not necessarily the will of the strongest that is legitimated, but instead the "rights of the most beautiful."[57]

It could be argued that Burma raises ethical tension in order to dispel it— in other words, that he insinuates the possibility of an unethical use of the aesthetic in order to retreat from that possibility and maintain an "ethics of reciprocity or brotherliness." Ultimately, however, even when Burma is understating his own acts of violence, he maintains a consciousness of that ethics of reciprocity. The murder is reduced to the status of a somersault and the push to a voluntary recline; but because the murder is committed in defense of another—the assailant on the bridge has tried to kill Burma's friend Marc—the disembodiment of the recounting is balanced by the defensibility of the act. When Burma's friend and partner, Bob Colomer, is shot, on the other hand, the narrator focuses on the victim's face: "Suddenly, his face contorted as if in terrible pain" [Soudain, son visage se crispa, comme sous l'effet d'une intolérable douleur] (25). No humor and no lyricism intrude on this description.

Burma's instinct to give respect to the sentiments and sufferings of others marks him as ethical and kind. His long-standing friendships with Covet and his secretary, Hélène Chatelain, demonstrate his friendliness and even hark forward to the partnership-based hard-boiled model that will gain currency in the twenty-first century. It is worth noting that Hélène provides a crucial clue to the location of the mysterious address and maintains a decorous resistance when Burma wants to interrogate her, thus representing the strong and confident female interlocutor.[58]

---

57. Wolin, *Terms of Cultural Criticism*, 195.

58. The movie version, with Sophie Desmarets as Hélène, shows her as a rather girlish character, though still a smart one. At the end of the movie, it is she (rather than the daughter of Georges Parry, also named Hélène) who becomes Burma's romantic interest.

FIAT LUX

The hard-boiled subject as Burma embodies him makes an ethical sense of the aesthetic a cornerstone of conscience: this particular sensibility is suited to French cultural and historical circumstances. In examining Burma's sensibilities, I mean to underscore the notion of the hard-boiled character as a first responder (in these first novels, literally a first responder) to a diverse series of cultural crises—an individual who holds himself accountable for the actions that his cultural circumstances demand. Even when the idea of virtue as such is absent, which it is here, the value of a subject conscious of himself and his responsibility to others remains at a premium; part of this responsibility is an instinctive historicocultural sense of individual and social needs. The model of accountability "without thought of it" perseveres relatively unchanged, but the particular sensitivities, words, and actions called for do change over time and place.

Where Race Williams was ethical without being interested in ethics, Burma's French version of that hard-boiled distinction is in maintaining an ethical stance through words and actions—here, his fusion of the pastoral and the explosive—that would seem to threaten it. Fiat Lux, the biblical name of Burma's prewar detective agency, constitutes another instance of that fusion. The novel abounds with objects—weapons, flashlights, sun, fire, pipes—that shimmer, shine, and glow. Some of these shine in the service of investigative illumination, either as practical instruments of perception (the flashlights in the darkened house at the titular address, for instance) or as evidence ("the glint of burnished steel" [l'acier bruni scintillait]). Others shine in the sun as attractive articles somewhat removed from their actual function ("the barrel of his gun shone in the sun"), objects one could ponder while smoking a pipe. When Burma introduces himself it is clear that his preferred illumination is the symbolic sort: "'My name is Nestor Burma,' I said, trembling all over at the idea of casting light on this poor man's identity. 'In civilian life, I'm a private detective.'" [Je m'appelle Nestor Burma, dis-je, frémissant de tout mon être à l'idée d'élucider le mystère de la personnalité de ce malheureux. Dans le civil, je suis détective privé] (17). Much of what lights up this novel, however, is not symbolic elucidation in the form of truth, or flashlights used for investigation, but explosions in the form of gunshots or fire. These two sorts of clarification are closely intertwined, but Burma is careful to maintain the distinction between light that illuminates and light that demolishes. When he arrives at 120, rue de la Gare, there is a citywide blackout so solid that he has to guess whether or not he has in fact passed the Lion de Belfort at Denfert-Rochereau. Because the chapter starts, "I'm starting to see clearly" [On commence à y voir clair], with the treasure to be found in the "Maison Blanche," this scene promises to set darkness against light, obscurity against clarity. When the chauffeur notices a light upstairs in the white house, "Sir . . . there's a light up there on the second floor" [Monsieur . . . de la lumière, là-haut, au premier . . .], Burma distinguishes between the "good" illumination of the torches and lamps and the "bad" illumination of the house on fire: "You call that light? Hurry, Faroux. It's a fire" [Vous appelez cela de la lumière? Vite, Faroux. Ça flambe] (169). This distinction parallels another, when the searchlights (*pinceaux lumineux de projecteurs*) light up the sky and the sirens start to wail. Burma, enlightened in matters historico-political as well as criminal, quips, "They're signing the peace treaty. Don't you hear the fireworks?" [C'est la signature de la Paix. Vous n'entendez pas le feu d'artifice?] (168). The lights and sounds of war remain distinguishable from the lights and sounds of celebration, the flashes of discovery from the flashes of destruction. Furthermore, the vocabulary of *lumière* rescues the idea of illumination from occupation discourse and so contradicts or denies a connection between fascism and enlightenment.

BURMA AS EMBODIMENT OF FRENCH NATIONAL INTACTNESS

In the French model, "individualisme" connotes self-containedness rather than a maverick tone. Burma's ethics endorse the values and needs of the republic. And yet, incarnation of the French character model is presented as a matter of individual taste and manner: a style of incarnation consistent with the idea of cultural values as instinctual. This latter notion is crucial to the wartime hard-boiled, since it implies that cultural values are able to survive the dismantling of cultural institutions. Burma's detective work in *120*—the methods he uses to expose the criminals—situates him at once as a self-contained individualist and as an occupation-era culture hero. In an early scene, Burma is meeting with Armand Bernier, the Lyon police *commissaire* investigating the murder of Bob Colomer. Bernier, as it turns out, was a con-spirator in that murder, although his involvement is not initially suggested. Burma has made a joke, and the following conversation ensues:

> —Let's not joke around, Mr. Burma. I'm trying to catch the man who mur-
> dered your employee, understand?
> —Collaborator.
> —What? Ah! Yes, if you like. So, you met him by chance?

—Ne plaisantons pas, monsieur Burma. J'essaie de venger votre employé, comprenez-vous?

—Collaborateur.

—Quoi? Ah! Oui . . . si vous voulez. Alors, vous vous êtes rencontrés par hasard?

This rapid dialogue first appears to be a provocative appropriation of language. "Collaborateur" at the time the novel was written was a loaded indictment no one would want to claim in public. For Burma then to declare that Bob had been his "collaborateur" is a way of shutting out the word's sinister connotations, reclaiming its positive associations with cooperation and partnership as though there were no other meaning of the word. The dialogue, however, has another function, which is to connect the indictment of the murderer with the maintenance of national integrity. When Burma states "Collaborateur," his interlocutor is taken aback. His reaction first seems one of surprise that Burma would use this word about his closest associate. But on second reading, and once we understand that Bernier did collaborate in the murder of Colomer, it suggests a nervous reaction to a name that, in the framework of the occupation, resonated most immediately and forcefully as an accusation.

This dialogue allies the uncovering of the "collaborateur" with the uncovering of the murderer, underscoring the similarities between life under the occupation and detective work. Julian Jackson writes, "One aim of German propaganda was to encourage a return to 'normal.'"[59] The practical threats of the occupation, including the menace of the French collaborator who blurs the line between friend and foe, are the realities that must be understood and navigated, for the occupation imposed at once an apparent order and an actual constant threat (what Gorrara had described as "the eruption of an alien order").[60] In the American model, in which the threat of war had passed into the domain of memory and was carried onto American soil in the minds and recollections of the soldiers rather than being inscribed on the land itself, the detective was menaced by—and showed his prowess by dominating—actual and metaphorical enemies from the past. In the French model, where the threat of the occupation remained present and ongoing, the detective's valor came from his ability to comprehend and narrate the sinister facts beneath apparent normality. Of course, in one sense, that precise ability is the

---

59. Jackson, *France: The Dark Years,* 239.

60. Gorrara, *Roman Noir,* 25. Jackson describes the nuances and variations among "collaborators," "attentistes," "functional collaborators," and "functional resisters," citing Cobb, *French and Germans.*

essence of all crime fiction. The murderer is generally someone the reader has seen from the start and whose guilt has been concealed. In this case, to have the first French hard-boiled detective—a former prisoner of war detecting under the occupation—unsettle a guilty party in an early scene by deadpanning the word "collaborator" is to link the work of hard-boiled detection to the conservation of moral, national, and cultural intactness.

Carroll John Daly, who, though a less subtle writer than Malet was in many ways the more overarching psychologist, ensures the accidental or "ex nihilo" nature of Race Williams's psychological health by rooting his childhood in an unfeeling orphanage. Nestor Burma, whose childhood is unknown, nonetheless follows the classically hard-boiled, never-married, no-children convention to emerge similarly untethered to bourgeois "Oughts," even without taking into consideration the fact of the occupation.[61] At the root of both Nestor Burma's and Race Williams's exemplarity—the one coming from a grim orphanage and the other from a POW camp—is their exemplarity as sufferers. The absence of a normalizing social frame and the presence of adversity conspire to underscore individual subjectivity. Individualism, or an empathic life intuitively lived, can be read here as an exceptional response to the absence of conventions rather than either a rebellious response to them or a mannered absorption. As such, Burma can claim sole credit for sustaining "regulated forms of civilized conduct" in the absence of regulation. Each detective discussed in this chapter faces pain (his own and that of others) in a way that resonates with the particular circumstances of the culture as a whole: Williams with the sequelae of postwar neuroses, Burma with the privations and deceits of the occupation. Moreover, each faces pain with behavior mechanisms reminiscent of specific cultural heroic models—Williams with tough but empathic independence, Burma with a witty aesthetic distanciation. The capacity to remain within the bounds of good taste—in the sense of being able to both retreat into the aesthetic and understand the limits of such a retreat—functions as an essential and historically particular element of the French hard-boiled character model.

---

61. "In these regulated forms of civilized conduct, a pervasive aestheticizing of social practices gets under way: moral-ideological imperatives no longer impose themselves with the leaden weight of some Kantian Ought but infiltrate the very textures of lived experience as tact and know-how, intuitive good sense or inbred decorum. Ethical ideology loses its unpleasantly coercive force and reappears as a principle of spontaneous consensus. The subject is accordingly aestheticized: like the work of art, the subject introjects the Law which governs it as the very principle of its free identity and so, in Althusserian phrase, comes to work 'all by itself' without need of political constraint." Eagleton, *Ideology of the Aesthetic*, 77.

THE USES OF LITERATURE

Another element in Burma's arsenal, one that marks him as French and as an epitome of French conceptions of virtue, is his use of literature to separate the population into those who care and those who do not, those who are decent and empathic and those who are not. In an early scene, Burma goes to visit Julien Montbrison, the lawyer he hopes will have information about Bob Colomer's murder. Montbrison was Colomer's lawyer, of a sort, and had seen him before he took off for the train station where he was murdered. When he enters Montbrison's office, Burma finds him reading "a lovely edition of the works of Edgar Allan Poe" [une belle édition des Œuvres d'Edgar Poe] (53). Later in the novel, Burma learns that an important private letter from another of Montbrison's clients had been opened and then resealed before arriving at its intended destination. That discovery reminds him of the Poe story "The Purloined Letter," which in turn leads him to two conclusions. One is that the treasure described in the opened and resealed letter, treasure stashed away at the titular address, would be hidden in that house in plain view, on the mantel. The second is that Montbrison is the guilty party: the one who intercepted and resealed his client's letter, who murdered Bob Colomer, and who found the treasure on the mantel and stole it. When explaining the crime to an assembled crowd, Burma says of Montbrison, "He thinks of Edgar Poe and a light goes on. 'The Purloined Letter,' to which everything points in this adventure, you must agree . . . the best hiding place is the simplest, the one in plain sight" [Il songe à Edgar Poe et un trait l'illumine. La 'Lettre volée' des *Histoires extraordinaires,* que tout semble désigner, vous en conviendrez, à marquer de son signe une telle aventure . . . La cachette la plus sûre est la plus simple, la plus visible] (200).

In their first meeting, Montbrison is presented as a well-fed, contented lawyer who smokes hard-to-find Philip Morris cigarettes instead of mediocre tobacco. As such, he is juxtaposed with the wry, postcamp Burma. During that meeting Burma recounts his captivity: "When I entered, he closed the book he was reading—a lovely edition of the works of Edgar Poe—and came toward me with a charming smile, his plump hand extended. I sat down and at his urging spoke about my imprisonment. Most people you talk to couldn't care less about it, but to be polite they pretend to 'feel your pain,' as they put it" [A mon entrée, il ferma le livre qu'il lisait—une belle édition des Œuvres d'Edgar Poe—et vint vers moi avec un charmant sourire, sa main grasse tendue. Je m'assis et, à son invitation, parlai de la captivité. Généralement vos interlocuteurs s'en foutent, mais ils croient poli de faire semblant de compatir à vos souffrances, comme ils disent] (53). The implication that

Montbrison is likely among those who "couldn't care less" places him in the ranks of those who have hardly suffered, and the evocation of "people you talk to" and "your pain" encourage reader alignment with the narrator/sufferer, the one about whom Montbrison "couldn't care less." Indeed, as Burma notices on first seeing him, "Montbrison did not appear to be suffering too much from [food] restrictions" [Montbrison ne paraissait pas souffrir outre mesure des restrictions] (52). Montbrison's contented distance from the camp experience—whether or not that distance is imagined by Burma—also corresponds to a particular representation of Montbrison as critical reader. A crucial function of this scene is to connect French cultural status to ethical intactness and to measure both of these according to one's response to other people's stories, whether fictional or real. In this way, response to literature functions as a measure of empathic capacity, and it is the hard-boiled character who takes that measure.

Even before Burma recounts his experience as a prisoner of war, the principal clue in this first meeting is the edition of Poe. At the end of the novel, the recollection of Poe proves crucial to the identification of Montbrison as the person who opened and resealed the letter locating the treasure and also as the person who found that treasure in plain sight in the house at the titular address. This intertextual interlude presents Montbrison and Burma as different species of reader, with that difference signaling an ethical, intellectual, and cultural division.

Montbrison reads Poe and steps into the role of purloiner, slipping then into the role of investigator—the one who finds treasure in plain sight—solely for his own gain. Burma reads Poe, reads Montbrison reading Poe, and steps into the role of detective, finding the treasure and understanding the criminal's relationship to it. The novel's detour through Poe matches the opposition of Burma to Montbrison, of detective to criminal, to the opposition of the reflecting reader to the mere collector or spinophile—which ultimately amounts to the opposition of one who can enter into and learn from the experience of others to the one who cannot or will not do so. Insofar as detective fiction recounts a series of widening circles of perspective—the criminal schemes while the detective watches the criminal scheming—the detective represents the greater volume or level of understanding. In "The Purloined Letter," that greater volume or scope of understanding is directly associated with a curiosity about human nature. Dupin describes to the narrator the police prefect's error regarding the purloiner D:

> They consider only their own ideas of ingenuity; and, in searching for anything hidden, advert only to the modes in which they would have hid-

den it. They are right in this much—that their own ingenuity is a faithful representative of that of the mass; but when the cunning of the individual felon is diverse in character from their own, the felon foils them, of course. This always happens when it is above their own, and very usually when it is below.[62]

Montbrison, in imitating the concealment mechanisms of the purloiner D, seems to have given the text a cursory once-over and thus been doomed to imitate the limitations of D, not his victories; to imitate his status as an actor and planner, foregoing the role of observer. Montbrison reading Poe seems to have stopped at Dupin's description of D as an exceptional thinker, which is enough to find him the treasure but not enough to evade detection. To cite Poe again:

> "I mean to say," continued Dupin, while I merely laughed at his last observations, "that if the Minister had been no more than a mathematician, the Prefect would have been under no necessity of giving me this check. I know him, however, as both mathematician and poet, and my measures were adapted to his capacity, with reference to the circumstances by which he was surrounded. I knew him as a courtier, too, and as a bold intrigant. Such a man, I considered, could not fail to be aware of the ordinary political modes of action."[63]

READING LIKE DUPIN

When Burma comes into Montbrison's office, he sees the volume of Poe but cannot know which story Montbrison is reading. And yet, at the end of the novel, he points with certainty to "The Purloined Letter" as the lawyer's source of inspiration. It is true that a letter has been opened and resealed. But so far, that is the only indication of the Poe story in this narrative. The container of pearls was hidden in plain view on the mantel, but that fact emerges much later in the narrative. The "everything" in "everything points" seems as connected to Montbrison the character as to the facts of the case: as the reader discovers at the end, Burma's conviction of Montbrison's guilt predated the discovery of the intercepted letter. The illumination, then—in "un trait l'illumine"—is double in nature: an idea inspires Montbrison and at the same

---

62. Poe, *Complete Tales*, 132.
63. Ibid., 134–35.

time a character trait of his own "illuminates" him, in the "Fiat Lux" sense of highlighting his guilt. That character trait, an absence of interest in others, an appurtenance to the class of interlocutors who couldn't care less, who smoke expensive cigarettes and wear flashy jewelry, makes of Montbrison a limited sort of reader: one who approaches Poe as a manual and a mirror and, more important, one who chooses a story that at some level invites such an approach—invites an egotistical reading and promises a self-serving inspiration. Burma's initial reference to the "lovely edition" points out the materiality of the volume, a materiality that obscures its content, its strata of meaning, its other extrapolatable morals. The treasure is hidden in plain view, but so is Montbrison, who all along has contacted Burma and acted in friendly fashion. "Burma! What a nice surprise! What are you doing within our walls?" [Burma! Que voilà donc une belle surprise! Que faites-vous dans nos murs?] (53). Of course, this question, "What are you doing in our walls?" brings to the reader's mind one of Poe's craziest narrators.[64] And yet, the notion of hiding in plain view resonates powerfully within the context of the occupation, during which the capacity to unearth the evil and criminal within the apparently normal was at a premium. As Burma later discloses, "It was when you recovered your bearings that I really got suspicious" [C'était au moment où vous recouvriez relativement votre tranquillité que mes soupçons se précisaient] (207).

Montbrison as criminal hides in plain view until the end, even as he uncovers treasures that others have hidden in plain view. In taking up the role of "mathematician and poet," "courtier," and "bold intrigant," Montbrison has suppressed the inevitable future moment of capture, and not to have grasped that possibility is inextricably intertwined with the role of intrigant. When Montbrison asks, "What are you doing within our walls?" the reference is not only to geographical location but also to his field of vision, the parameters of his own plan. The idea of being "within the walls" of another does not occur to him, for he has sufficiently compartmentalized his reading in an effort to remove the character from its nineteenth-century confines. Montbrison, himself closed within his self-image, does not see that his name is a near homophone of "my prison" (*mon prison*), which his subjectivity and readership constitute, and where these will ultimately lead him. Burma, on the other hand, comes at the volume as clue, as illustration of human nature, as a Rorschach-esque diagnostic instrument—as a story important not just for its

---

64. In "The Black Cat," the narrator hides his wife's body in the wall, but he is found out by the police when the cat—also in the wall—starts howling during their visit.

content but also for the telling and illuminating readings it might inspire in other narrative agents.

The entire Poe interlude within *120* serves to align Burma with intuition and literary appreciation, and to link both to the detective novel at hand. As Jacques Lacan and other psychoanalysts have noted, the detective who can evaluate the capacities and motives of various sorts of reasoners becomes the reasoner par excellence. The literature fan who can evaluate the capacities and motives of various sorts of readers becomes the reader par excellence as well as an exemplary denizen of French culture. In this novel as in most detective novels, the person clearly interested in the characters of others and the most able to forget his own story while listening to another's is the crime solver and cultural exemplar. That interest, embodied in Dupin and Burma, also coincides with a loyalty to literature as placeholder of French culture. And in a period that generates such urgency of listening and witnessing, it functions here as a critical element of twentieth-century hard-boiled subjectivity. The intertextual interlude allows Burma, making his debut in the twentieth-century *120*, to claim a connection with nineteenth-century Paris and prewar France. Of course, Poe's Paris-centered ratiocination tales, his admirable Parisian protagonist, his introduction into French culture through Baudelaire's translations, and his role as father of the much-loved-in-France detective genre have earned him an honorary French status in the world of the *roman policier.* Furthermore, as "one of the 'saints' of surrealism"[65] and as author whose detective could get into the mind of the criminal without turning into one, Poe embeds Burma in a literature-identified Paris: in which a reference to Crébillon could serve as calling card and in which political manipulation was understood by reader and criminal alike to resonate with the horrors of Greek tragedy, in which, in short, political manipulation became at one with Crébillon's "gruesome plan." André Breton cites both Poe and Sade as figures of black humor, which he calls "the mortal enemy of beleaguered sentimentality" [l'ennemi mortel de la sentimentalité à l'air perpétuellement aux abois].[66] Finally, with the reference to Crébillon at the end, which assigns radically varying levels of moral turpitude within the text,[67] the Poe interlude is not so much about who is the better thinker but who is the better person. Through Poe, love of literature and nostalgia for solid narrative

---

65. Hollier and Bloch, *New History of French Literature,* 723.

66. Breton, *L'anthologie de l'humour noir,* 16.

67. "So gruesome a plan, while not worthy of *Atrée,* is worthy of *Thyeste*" [Un dessein si funeste, s'il n'est digne d'Atrée, et digne de Thyeste]. Poe, *Complete Tales,* 202.

closures, a binding moral compass, and horror of atrocity become embedded in this occupation-era novel.[68]

THE LITERARY OUTSIDER

Although Nestor Burma seems to have little time to read, he embodies a cultural ideal through his fondness for literature. Michelle Emanuel writes, "It is the combination of streetwise abrasiveness and well-read refinement that makes Burma such a compelling character."[69] I would contest the reading of Burma as being refined, but being "well-read" was central to the French cultural tradition, especially in 1943.[70] To love literature is to be on the side of France, of art, and of ethics, an association that becomes apparent when the clue to the location of the treasure has to be deciphered. In the opening chapters of *120, rue de la Gare*, the title clue is whispered to Burma by a dying prisoner of war—the man who had sent the letter to the treacherous Montbrison—and then shouted to him by his detecting partner, Bob Colomer, just before the latter is shot dead in a train station. Its immediate accessibility to Burma and to the reader initially conceals the trouble that Colomer had taken to find it. As it turns out, the address was the solution to a puzzle in the intercepted letter: "Coming from the Lion, after meeting the divine and infernal Marquis, it's the most prodigious of his works. (*My mania for word games persists even after death . . .*)" [En venant du Lion, après avoir rencontré le divin et infernal marquis, c'est le livre le plus prodigieux de son œuvre. (*Je persiste dans ma manie des rébus jusqu'au delà de la mort . . .*)] (178). Deciphering the puzzle demands familiarity with literary history: one must understand that the "divine and infernal Marquis" is the Marquis de Sade and that *120* appears in the title of his best-known work. It also requires the ability to read "SADE" as an acronym: the street number without a street can

---

68. In one French version of *Murders in the Rue Morgue*, Dupin was renamed Bernier, which in Malet's novel will be the name of the corrupt policeman.

69. Emanuel, *From Surrealism to Less-Exquisite Cadavers*, 83. She also notes that Malet's use of dream sequences places Burma "in a realm already utilized by poetry, [which] risks a literariness not readily associated with the American genre" (67).

70. In another famous wartime text, Vercors's clandestine publication *Le silence de la mer* (1942), the German soldier notices the books in the French house he occupies: "Les Anglais, reprit-il, on pense aussitôt: Shakespeare. Les Italiens: Dante. L'Espagne: Cervantès. Et nous, tout de suite: Goethe. Après, il faut chercher. Mais si on dit: et la France? Alors, qui surgit à l'instant? Molière? Racine? Hugo? Voltaire? Rabelais? Ou quel autre? Ils se pressent, ils sont comme une foule à l'entrée d'un théâtre, on ne sait pas qui faire entrer d'abord." Vercors, *Le silence de la mer et autres récits*, 28.

only be found once one grasps that "SADE" refers to the city water authority. The bulk of detective interpretation is completed by Burma's colleagues: Bob Colomer's father had worked as night watchman at the SADE, and Burma's assistant mentions the place, enabling Burma to locate the address. Burma stands out in his present cohort because unlike Bob Colomer, who had to consult a journalist and visit the library in order to identify the Marquis, he knows who Sade is. Burma's journalist friend Marc Covet announces that he himself had had no idea: "I didn't know Sade had written anything. Don't look at me like that, Burma" [J'ignorais que Sade eût écrit quoi que ce fût. Ne me regardez pas comme cela, Burma] (38). Covet also remarks, remembering Colomer's sudden interest in Sade or in libraries in general, "He needed to do some library research. That gave me a good laugh" [Il en avait besoin pour effectuer des recherches à la bibliothèque. Cela m'a fait rigoler de plus belle] (39).

On the one hand, finding the solution to the mystery through the Marquis de Sade (as it was through Poe) is tantamount to reanimating or at least recalling a prewar culture in which French literature had a storied role, in which "collaborateurs" constituted no threat and criminals such as D. and Montbrison were caught in their own webs. As Claire Gorrara writes, "Burma's past as 'Dynamite Burma' . . . represents an assured and autonomous prewar identity that seems irrecoverable in 1941."[71] Sade is associated with the era of the French Revolution—in other words, with a time when modern France was coming into being—therefore in contrast to the occupation, which threatens the very existence of France as such. Sade and Poe both emblematize the value of literature to the solving of crime and to the reconstitution of a culture under assault. At the same time, both authors represent literature as a passcode to a transgressive, even criminal, mentality but also an ethical one. Jonathan Eburne writes that "Malet's crime novel is in many ways dedicated to [Sade's publisher and defender] Maurice Heine" and says of the latter, "As Heine argues . . . noir fictions render a stark contrast between the indifference and lack of awareness of those who take them literally and the analytical power available to those who are attentive to their atmosphere and structure."[72] Given Sade's aesthetic of violence and Poe's poeticization of death, to evoke these authors is to hint at French crime fiction's later moral dissolution, to its amoral use of the aesthetic, and to its deliberate fracturing of the accountable subject.[73] It is also to link the

---

71. Gorrara, *Roman Noir*, 31.
72. Eburne, *Surrealism and the Art of Crime*, 251, 194.
73. See discussion of violent aestheticism in Sheehan, *Modernism and the Aesthetics of Vio-*

roman noir, as Eburne points out, to reading and writing as ethical practices and to cast the ethical reader (Burma) as a national treasure. In one sense, had the novel wanted to evoke canonical French culture, it could have based its cryptograms on Balzac or Hugo rather than on surrealist darlings Sade and Poe. In raising Sade's name, and in knowing him when others did not, Burma at once stands up for his nation and sneaks in (the French version of hard-boiled maverick subversion) the homespun literary outsider. The point of this chapter has been to examine how the first hard-boiled novels of France and the United States, respectively, reconstitute early nineteenth-century models of spiritual authority and exemplary character. It has also been to demonstrate how the outlines of such character, each associated with national intactness and patriotic morale, function as modern markers of psychic fortitude and social accountability. Finally, it has been to point out how these first hard-boiled personages introduce the menace of moral devolution, then ultimately avoid it. The American detective responds to violence, murder, and another's pain with an ethic "of his own" that, coincidentally, is intelligible rather than bizarre or menacing to others. The French detective responds with a seemingly instinctual balance of the ethical and the artistic, the empathic and the sardonic. To some extent the downside to both these balancing acts might seem to be the inauthenticity of the individualism at hand—the too-marvelous nature of its coincidence, the too-intelligible or too-classic nature of an ethics that are purportedly "of one's own." In other words, the congruence of moral-ideological imperatives and one's own instinctual ethics could paint the very idea of that autonomy as illusory. But the hard-boiled as a genre, throughout its history and most particularly in these initial texts, has taken considerable pains to preserve the individual as a phenomenon by separating him from a bourgeois world and by underscoring the experiential, personal, and organic foundations of his conduct. In so doing, it insists on the existence of individual subjectivity as independent from social strictures.

Twentieth-century constitution of individual conscience is distinct from that of nineteenth-century romanticism, which represented character attributes without such concern that those attributes be independent of hegemonic bourgeois values. Daly and Malet do contend with that concern. And yet they imitate the romantics by creating a space in which personality features can arise—in their own culturally and historically specific ways— from nothing, devoid of any larger frame that could force those aims with

lence; Sanyal, *Violence of Modernity;* Bronfen, *Over Her Dead Body;* Matthews, "Right Person for Surrealism."

"immediate obviousness." Those personality features have a social and political resonance, but like the character attributes of the romantic characters, they ultimately represent only themselves, their effects, and the very force of conscience.

THE PRECARITY OF MORAL AUTHORITY

The principal menace to the future hard-boiled will not be an individualism insufficiently realized or overly allegorical but an individualism squandered. In its initial incarnations, the character generates—not just incarnates but generates, creating against a negative and adverse background—positive ideals. As Sean McCann demonstrated in *Gumshoe America,* the hard-boiled genre celebrated the individual as a phenomenon not just valid and possible but salutary. What "society" as a whole could no longer provide or exemplify, the individual could. What happens as the hard-boiled evolves is that the notions of ethics and principle, and by extension the very nature of ideals, come to be reconstituted as essentially, fundamentally embodied. They live in the mind and instinct of the character rather than being rooted in an "elsewhere." Mikhail Bakhtin had written of Dostoevsky's fiction, "Living an idea is somehow synonymous with unselfishness."[74] "My ethics are my own," however, does not mean living an idea in the Bakhtinian sense, which amounts to dedicating oneself to an idea rooted outside. Rather, it means dominating an idea, appropriating an idea. When a character claims that his ethics are his own, and when no other individual or institution even mentions ethics, much less presents an alternate ethical voice, then each individual version of the ethical is on the road to becoming the living embodiment of the idea.[75] In this sense, the individual version of the ethical resembles the individual theism that went some distance toward preserving religion in the face of the nineteenth-century process of secularization.[76] And yet, as the hard-boiled evolves, the *idea* as such ceases to be the force or model that ennobles, that saves one from self-absorption. Rather, the idea becomes sublimated to a

---

74. Bakhtin, *Problems of Dostoevsky's Poetics,* 71.

75. Much as Homais's "my religion" was in many ways a reasonable phenomenon, given the steady secularization of the mid-nineteenth century.

76. As Don Cupitt writes, "[Theological realists] declare their unshakable allegiance to a vanished world in which the prevailing cultural conditions made it possible really to believe in objective theism. We do not have that particular mode of consciousness any longer because we do not live in that world any more. Theological realism can only actually be *true* for a heteronomous consciousness such as no normal person ought now to have." Cupitt, *Taking Leave of God,* 12.

voice, a character, and an attitude. That sublimation has its perils, all of which are outlined in schematic form in these first hard-boiled novels.

I claimed that each of these novels is the almost entirely undisputed foundation for hard-boiled novels that followed: the outlines that Daly created in *Snarl* are repeated in Raymond Chandler, Dashiell Hammett, James Cain, and others.[77] Each hard-boiled character examined here functions as a culturally specific respondent to the modern world, but each is also significantly different from its successors. These initial incarnations of the hard-boiled present an ideal of sorts, a high point of character solidity that engenders subsequent iterations. Not, as Robert Skinner proposed, because these first examples provide the raw-ish material of what will later be made fuller and more eloquent, but because they provide an ideal, if rather schematic, rendition of what will later, indeed almost immediately, become diluted and disappointing. Hammett's *Red Harvest,* published three years after *The Snarl of the Beast,* and *La mort et l'ange,* published five years after *120, rue de la Gare,* represent steps toward that devolution of accountable subjectivity. Tolstoy famously wrote that whereas all happy families are alike, every unhappy family is unhappy in its own way. In the hard-boiled, heroes are similar to one another in their heroic function, yet each culturally specific heroic model is contaminated in its own way. In the American post–hard-boiled, traumatic memory and stifling social pressure return to destroy both accountability and a sense of self. In the French post–hard-boiled, or *néo-polar,* contemplations of the self and its parameters will create a parody of introspection that invites rumination on complicated ideological models even as it steadily dismantles character (and Character) as such. In the American post–hard-boiled, "plainspeaking" anti-intellectualism and instinctive sense of right will escalate to sociopathic proportions. In the French, the capacity for aesthetic contemplation in the midst of violence will morph into a *Clockwork Orange*-style pleasure in destruction. In the post–hard-boiled literature of each nation, ideals deteriorate precisely because they are founded, embodied, incarnated in a too-volatile individual who abdicates conscience and accountability. The individual has become volatile precisely because the forces of corruption, trauma, or deadening convention are exploited to such sinister narrative effect as to evacuate character as such. The history of twentieth-century crime fiction thus becomes the history of the dismantling of the canonical culture hero and also of accountability itself, that foundation of self and of moral authority.

---

77. Schwartz, *Nice and Noir,* 156. Geoffrey O'Brien writes: "Hammett was in every way the pivotal writer. . . . The hardboiled novel was born complete in *Red Harvest* in 1929, after a decade of experiments in the pages of *Black Mask.*" O'Brien, *Hardboiled America,* 63.

CHAPTER 3

JIM THOMPSON

"Don't You Say I Killed Her!"

THE HARD-BOILED GENRE is inextricably intertwined with the idea of conscience as a continual achievement and with restoration of individual moral choice in the midst of circumstances that could dilute it. Essential to the tension of the hard-boiled is the sense that encroaching social contamination threatens the individual's autonomy. Indeed, the dominant narrative theme of the hard-boiled has most often been read as one of society against the individual. Jim Thompson's novels dismantle that opposition, provoking critical questions of whether the faltering individual merely responds to a corrupt environment or is in fact amoral to start with. I contend that that entire question, which foregrounds social criticism even as it puts individual psychosis on display, is the wrong one to ask. In Thompson's work, the individual is as much the problem as it is the solution, and the notion of the individual crushed by outside forces becomes a strategy for avoiding accountability.

Before focusing on Jim Thompson, I should say a word about the roads not taken in this chapter. In the aftermath of Carroll John Daly, Dashiell Hammett and Raymond Chandler created characters that are for the most part functional embodiments of the Race Williams dynamic. Sam Spade and Philip Marlowe join an individualistic manner of being with an incarnation of spiritual values—a freedom of agency together with a traditional, if accidental, ethics of reciprocity and community. And when those ethics waver, as they inevitably do, Chandler and Hammett nonetheless maintain a space for the accountable subject. This is even the case in Hammett's famously bloody *Red Harvest,* in which corruption and violence are as encompassing as possible. In that 1929 novel, the Continental Op has been called to Personville to "clean up" the town. Not much is personal about the characters who populate Personville, which Sean McCann calls a "fantastically cosmopolitan underworld"; almost all the characters are perpetrators, victims, or witnesses to the novel's numerous murders.[1] In the course of the novel, the Op acknowledges—not surprisingly given the sixteen murders committed at that point—that the town is getting to him: "This damned burg's getting me. If I don't get away soon I'll be going blood-simple like the natives. . . . This is the first time I've ever got the fever. It's this damned burg. You can't go straight here."[2] With these statements, the Op's narrative describes more communal and political decline than individual corruption.[3] John Whitley writes, "In *Red Harvest* the question of individual guilt becomes submerged in a wider view of social guilt."[4] This view of guilt is so vast, in fact, as to consume the conventional structures and vocabulary of morality; "fever" and the neologism "blood-simple" disconnect the novel's violence from conventional moral discourse and situate violence at a cellular level. As Christopher Breu incisively puts it, "While placing the Op at the center of the violence (and of the critique of this violence), the text resists making him its cause. Instead, his increasingly brutal tactics are presented as one more symptom of the town's (always already) 'fallen' condition."[5] The "always already" nature of the "fallen" condition amounts to an utter absence, rather than loss or abandonment, of moral and spiritual standards. Indeed, the earlier-cited description of Fichtean philosophies of history as "mak[ing] a negative judgment on the present without basing it explicitly on a value judgment" comes to mind here, since as Breu and others note, the town radiates an amorality that is totalizing and irreversible.[6]

---

1. McCann, *Gumshoe America,* 80.

2. Hammett, *Red Harvest,* 584.

3. Indeed, the novel constructs a continuous loop that erases the accountable (or even conscious) subject before it is even postulated. For instance, shortly before telling his colleagues, "Don't kid yourselves that there's any law in Poisonville except what you make for yourself" (551), the Op declares that "anybody that brings any ethics to Poisonville is going to get them all rusty" (549). That initial disclaimer weakens the subsequent "you" as a meaningful maker of laws; the subsequent mention of "laws you make for yourself" rings hollow.

4. Whitley, "Stirring Things Up," 452.

5. Breu, *Hard-Boiled Masculinities,* 66. Some critics do see the Op as responsible for his "blood-simple" condition. Heise writes, "The line between law and crime is deliberately rubbed out by Hammett, who consistently figures the detective as the most violent, bloodthirsty presence in a city where municipal reform is made synonymous with the expunging of immigrants and criminalized working-class culture." Heise, "Going Blood-Simple," 490.

6. Romantic heroism is conspicuously absent here. Even Cooper's description of Hawkeye's "expression of sturdy honesty" gets retroactively undercut as the Op comments: "I looked

The 1802 Baptist minister cited in the first chapter of this book had described American religious revivals—themselves a sort of cleaning up and reconstruction—in which "hot-headed young men, intoxicated with the prevailing element of excitement" "assumed the office of public exhorters and instructors." In that formulation, the excitement of being the cleaner turns into an excitement that impedes the cleaning. And indeed, the dominant legacy of religious revivals is precisely that excitement, that fervor, which finds a sort of counterpart in the Op's blood-simple "fever." Excitement drives the "assumption of office" and the devolution into ego, much as the Op's "fever" drives the enthusiasm and then the degeneracy of the cleanup. In both cases, excitement for the job devolves into corruption and domination. Despite the force of exhilaration, though, Hammett's novel does nonetheless remind us that the flow of ideas between the individual and the outside world is neither automatic nor unconscious, and that moments of conscience stand in the midst of that motion. When the Op tells Dinah Brand that he fears going "blood-simple," she observes, "Your nerves are shot. You've been through too much excitement in the last few days. Keep it up and you're going to have the heebie-jeebies for fair, a nervous breakdown." The Op then holds up his hand to display its steadiness, and Dinah says, "That doesn't mean anything. It's inside you. Why don't you sneak off for a couple of days' rest?" To which the Op answers, "Can't, sister. Somebody's got to stay here to count the dead. Besides, the whole program is based on the present combination of people and events. Our going out of town would change that, and the chances are the whole thing would have to be gone over again."[7] This dialogue creates a moment of subjectivity wherein the Op's emotional response to his surroundings meets his accountability as an actor within those surroundings. In one sense, the excitement that Dinah cites aligns with the term "blood-simple" that implies biological resistance to understanding.[8] At the same time, Dinah's warning not to "keep it up" makes the Op responsible for perpetuating the excitement and thus for continuing the narrative. Also, crucially, it is when she notes that "it's inside you" that the Op declares the whole program "based on the present combination of people and events." That moment interrupts the continuous diffusion of responsibility and places emphasis, as in Saussure's linguistic chessboard, on the world as it presently is. It acknowl-

---

most honest when I was lying." Hammett, *Red Harvest*, 598.

7. Ibid., 588.

8. John Walker writes that the Op "internalizes and replicates the violence of his environment in the manner of a machine, yet his delirium precipitates a regression to animal instincts." Walker, "City Jungles," 126.

edges that individual people have a distinct role in that world and that the Op knows it.

Most of Chandler's and Hammett's characters make pointed admissions of halfheartedness, even corruption, that point to an environmental undertow but maintain conscious subjectivity. One such gesture is Philip Marlowe's admission at the end of *The Big Sleep* (1939): "I was part of the nastiness now," an admission that casts the individual as an astute if fading beacon in a spiritual night.[9] But as Johanna Smith writes of that admission, "While it would appear that Marlowe is now tarnished by the corruption around him, his statement actually attests to his continuing purity. That is, simply by knowing that he is 'part of the nastiness,' Marlowe in effect testifies to a moral discrimination so fine as to negate his self-condemnation."[10] In a similar vein, Hammett's third-person *Maltese Falcon* (1930) describes Sam Spade—and here one need not be concentrating on the spiritual resonances of hard-boiled heroism to read this as a symbolic provocation—as looking "rather pleasantly like a blond satan."[11] And yet, Sam Spade's insistence that "I won't play the sap for you," as he turns Brigid over to the police at the end of *The Maltese Falcon,* is often read as a declaration of independence from corruption.[12]

In their relationships with women, such characters slip from Race Williams's "Victorian" attitude to an abiding mistrust—of women and of people in general—that turns individualism into self-absorption. John Irwin had written that Sam Spade's decision to turn Brigid in has to do with a typically American privileging of who one *is* over relationships one *has,* and he also notes "the recurring situation . . . of Spade telling parabolic stories or giving explanations . . . only to have those not be understood by the women who hear them."[13] Philip Marlowe avoids romantic entanglements, and John Paul Athanasourelis proposes that this avoidance might amount to "downright misogyny."[14] LeRoy Panek contests that reading, proposing instead that the detective of the twenties and thirties merely "wants what he cannot find in this world."[15]

9. Chandler, *The Big Sleep,* 197.

10. Johanna M. Smith, "Raymond Chandler," 596.

11. Hammett, *Maltese Falcon,* 5.

12. Deming, *Running Away from Myself,* 30. As Ross Macdonald has written, "the classless, restless man of American democracy, who spoke the language of the street . . . [Sam Spade] possesses the virtues and follows the code of a frontier male." Macdonald, *On Crime Writing,* 15–16.

13. Irwin, *Threat of Death,* 28, 26. John Cawelti has written of hard-boiled misogyny in *Adventure, Mystery, and Romance,* as has, more recently, Erin Smith in *Hard-Boiled.*

14. Athanasourelis, *Raymond Chandler's Philip Marlowe,* 72.

15. Panek, *Introduction to the Detective Story,* 163.

A similar compendium of violence and sentimentality, empathy and distance, stoicism and sensitivity emerges in Mickey Spillane. Spillane is sometimes grouped with Jim Thompson under the heading of pathological aggression, and his name has become shorthand for literature made to please an unthinking public. Frank McConnell calls Mike Hammer "hyperviolent," and E. M. Beekman finds in him a "savage delight in blood and guts."[16] To cite an account from a critic of Spillane's own time, Frank Leonard writes, "The sex content of such works as Spillane's is of an unreal nature, in no way comparable to the experiences of readers in their own lives; Spillane seeks to challenge no commonly held ideas, to discuss no real human problems, and is therefore free to write on the subject more or less as he pleases."[17] At the same time, Mike Hammer is often read as an embodiment of the national mood, particularly with respect to communism and the Cold War. Although he can be read as a character driven by aggression, he belongs in fact to the classic hard-boiled school. An examination of Spillane demonstrates that what marks the real deterioration of the hard-boiled hero is neither violence nor crudeness but rather an abandonment of self-appraisal.

In *I the Jury* (1947), Mike Hammer's close friend and army buddy, Jack Williams, has been murdered. He promises his dead friend that his killer will die the same way he did, "with a .45 slug in the gut." In the course of his investigation, Hammer meets and falls in love with Charlotte Manning. In the end, he finds out that she is in fact the murderer, and he shoots her in the stomach. The novel ends thus: "'How c-could you?' she gasped. I only had a moment before talking to a corpse, but I got it in. 'It was easy,' I said."[18] This ending recalls Hammett's *The Maltese Falcon*, which ended with Sam Spade handing over to the police the woman who had murdered his partner. *The Maltese Falcon*, however, ended with a turn to the police rather than to an eye-for-an-eye revenge killing; John Cawelti has cited Hammer's "It was easy" as evidence of Hammer's misogyny as well as of the hardening of the hard-boiled hero.[19] But in spite of a "kill-crazy" public persona, he falls into conventional ethical parameters. The contrast between Hammer's minimal reaction to violence done to him, and his empathic response when violence is done to others, shows him to be the descendant of Race Williams and Nestor Burma.

---

16. McConnell, "Detecting Order," 183; Beekman, "Raymond Chandler," 155.

17. Leonard, "Cozzens without Sex," 216.

18. Spillane, *Mike Hammer Collection*, 1:7, 147.

19. "Here the killing of the evil one is obviously a matter of self-defense, vengeance, and the righteous execution of a vicious killer who endangers society. But the killing is given further moral overtones as an appropriate response to an immoral use of feminine sexuality for the purpose of betrayal. It becomes a purification of the obscene as well as the destruction of a killer." Cawelti, "Myths of Violence," 527.

One of the most striking elements of the Hammer series is the spiritual import given to another person's moral evaluation of him—to the combination of empathic connection and self-appraisal. In Spillane's fourth Mike Hammer novel, *One Lonely Night* (1951), Hammer is leaving a courtroom where a judge has reluctantly acquitted him of murder. Hammer is tormented at recalling the judge's lecture, which accused him of having developed a taste for blood during the Second World War. That lecture, in Hammer's mind, resonates not just as another person's moral evaluation of his character but also as a sort of divinely significant indictment. "He had a voice like an avenging angel. The dignity and knowledge behind his face gave him the stature of a giant, the poise of Gabriel reading your sins aloud from the Great Book and condemning you to your fate. . . . He prophesied a rain of purity that was going to wash me into the sewer with the other scum leaving only the good and the meek to walk in the cleanliness of law and justice."[20] The judge's words to Hammer, as well as their overtones of fire and brimstone, echo throughout the book. "So the judge was right all the while. I could feel the madness in my brain . . ."[21] Although the character's ideas can be seen through the lens of national mood, it is the individual rather than the national mood who acts within the world of the hard-boiled, which, particularly in Spillane, is invariably a microworld of individual characters. Alternating between vituperative indictments of society and claims to want to stand up for it, Hammer's focus is on society's problems and the insufficiency of its institutions. And yet, the character's own most compelling problems are not with society but with himself and other people. It is striking that this novel, which gives an almost anthemic voice to national concerns about communism, also reveals Hammer engaged in his most insistently personal moral inventory. The events of the novel, coming on the heels of the judge's lecture, pushes him not only to an investigation into the identities of others but to self-examination as well.

Prominent in the judge's discourse and in Hammer's endless recollections of it is the claim that Hammer found pleasure in war's violence: "He had to go back five years to a time he knew of only secondhand and tell me how it took a war to show me the power of the gun and the obscene pleasure that was brutality and force, the spicy sweetness of murder sanctified by law." Hammer subsequently goes into a sort of moral tailspin, concerned that he "would be washed down the sewer with the rest of all the rottenness sometime."[22] Implicit in his concern is that the experience "over there"

20. Spillane, *Mike Hammer Collection*, 2:6, 7.
21. Ibid., 2:6, 158.
22. Ibid., 2:6, 8.

was incidental and that the "taste for death" was innate. His recollections take on an obsessional, apocalyptic cast. In a dream, for instance, remembering a suicide he witnessed, "I saw the bridge again, and two people die while the stern face of the judge looked on disapproving, uttering solemn words of condemnation. I saw flashes of fire, and men fall."[23] What is significant about these ruminations and remembrances is their representation of postwar mental intactness in spiritual terms as well as of postwar mental aftermath—a collective experience—as they relate to individual moral assessment. His violent memories echo Lyman Beecher's nineteenth-century warnings against sin. Benoît Tadié points out the potential dangers in Hammer's quasi-admission of a "taste for death," but also his ultimate avoidance of that peril: "The author brings his narrator to the dangerous point of knowing his own cruelty, which imperils his own existence as protagonist: the reader who is not aberrant will have trouble identifying with a character who enjoys cutting prisoners of war into little pieces. But the plot of the novel allows the violence to be justified. . . . Violence and the taste for murder prove useful to the community" [L'auteur conduit son narrateur jusqu'à cette limite dangereuse où il reconnaît sa propre cruauté, mettant en péril ses conditions d'existence comme héros de roman: le lecteur, à moins d'être un pervers, aura du mal à s'identifier à un personnage qui découpe en rondelles des prisonniers de guerre et aime ça. Mais l'intrigue du roman permettra de justifier la violence du héros. . . . La violence et le goût du meurtre s'avèrent finalement utiles à la collectivité].[24] It is true that Hammer's violence has become useful to the collective, but what really prevents him from coming across as an out-of-control psychopath is precisely his ruminations, his admissions of perversity. In his moments of introspection he turns to his secretary, confiding, "I want to find out about myself, Velda."[25] These ruminations protect Hammer in part because the American heroic tradition is much more welcoming than the French to admissions and redemptions but also because those admissions underscore accountability, the point being that an individual conscious and critical of his own actions is inherently more likely to be helpful to society.

JIM THOMPSON

Criticism of hard-boiled fiction often uses a vocabulary of ethical pollution—submersion, repetition, desensitization, internalization—that represents the

---

23. Ibid., 2:138.
24. Tadié, *Le polar américain*, 20.
25. Spillane, *Mike Hammer Collection*, 2:16.

individual as ceding to the outside. As long as his principal battle is against the outside world and his own "internalizations" of it, as long as there is a "self" to wage that battle, the character can maintain an ontological separation from the outside world and preserve his status as repository of moral authority. With Jim Thompson, though, the hard-boiled genre made a radical turn from that tension. Departing from the well-trodden opposition of the good or trying-to-be-good individual to a problematic environment, even a problematic internal environment, it veered into the individual as problematic in and of himself, on his own steam. This sharp break altered the history of the hard-boiled, not because there were no more novels published about classically heroic characters but because autonomy and accountability became optional. The very notions of character and self and conscience, solid in the classic hard-boiled, began to splinter, or rather to be splintered by the narrating character himself. The deliberate nature of this dismantling is crucial, since otherwise the distinction between an individual who is the source of contamination and one who merely succumbs to it might seem purely academic or semantic. If corruption is so extensive that even the best-intentioned individual ends up being a relatively active part of it, and if the individual turns out inevitably to perpetrate or perpetuate structural and institutional corruption, then what is the use of talking about the individual *qua* individual at all? And yet Jim Thompson demonstrates that the dilution or truncation of individual autonomy is less an external reality than a demoralizing narrative strategy.

In a sense, the contamination or corruption of the individual in Thompson's fiction mirrors the suppression of meaningful individualism by totalizing bourgeois structures. Carl Freedman and Christopher Kendrick, for instance, frame Hammett's Continental Op in terms of "bourgeois legality": "Though he is on one level independent of the police—and hence free of certain statist constraints on the individualist or 'whole man'—his entire position as a respectable entrepreneur (or an entrepreneur's loyal employee) ties him to the state and makes him function, in the last analysis, as an adjunct to the official forces of law and order."[26] Bourgeois legality focuses on social responsibility and the ethics of reciprocity, whereas post–hard-boiled representations of contamination underscore meanness, carelessness, and violence. The first focuses on social function and the latter on social dysfunction, but the essential problem remains the same: what is the point of the individual? Is talking about individual autonomy in some sense always tantamount to reanimating a useless fantasy of free subjectivity?

---

26. Freedman and Kendrick, "Forms of Labor," 214.

Jim Thompson's momentous contribution to that conversation lies in showcasing an individual cannily manipulating the apparent bounds of autonomy. What appears to be structural or institutional corruption is in fact the work of an individual or individuals. That work may be represented as careless and nearly automatic in nature, or at times as inevitable (as in post-Foucauldian examinations of ethics and motivation), but automation and inevitability in Thompson's fiction are in fact a narrative ruse intended to blur the lines of accountability. What is more, such a ruse serves to mock the blame-diffusing effect of twentieth-century theories of subjectivity. The reason these mockeries merit examination is that, paradoxically enough, hard-boiled representations of the individual as intensely, dramatically, and creatively bad and unethical—and these are numerous as the twentieth century evolves and as the bar of unacceptable conduct falls lower—are the best road to a constructive critical conversation about moral authority and the possibility of an ethical collective. To put it another way: the opposition, even the eventually failed opposition, of the individual and the collective may make for a compelling dramatic line. But discussions of contamination, corruption, pollution, and deterioration—all of which appear in the traditional hard-boiled—can also be powerful instruments for distracting attention from the individual. In *The Killer Inside Me*, Thompson's most famous novel, the narrator puts the idea of limited autonomy and accountability to great use. Provocatively, he manipulates the discourse of traumatic repetition, mental illness, and overbearing social control to create these limitations by painting a broad and sinister picture of the self as hopelessly porous social product. But he also reveals that porous mass to be something of an illusion, since every individual is a narrative actor.

NOIR AND THE MID-CENTURY HARD-BOILED

Jim Thompson's name functions as veritable shorthand for the post–hard-boiled of the postwar period. Two of his most popular novels, *The Killer Inside Me* and *Pop. 1280*, feature sheriffs as characters and thus maintain a tenuous connection with the idea of law enforcement, but these are not crime fighters in the usual sense, nor were his novels murder mysteries. The unknowns in Thompson's novels focus on who will be killed next and what pathologies revealed, rather than the traditional hard-boiled questions of who has done the killing and what the detective can do about it. Resolving unknowns is thus disconnected from either social restoration or redemption and resembles watching a train crash. Given these sharp structural and tonal departures from the hard-boiled formula, as well as Thompson's relentless ridicule of Chandler's "man of honor" and "man who is not himself mean," including Thompson in the hard-boiled school may not be immediately comprehensible. Indeed, it is somewhat surprising to find him in the pantheon of hard-boiled crime fiction authors at all; and yet, not only is he there, he is the quintessence of the postwar hard-boiled. It is in that capacity that he so radically transfers responsibility to the main character and ushers in the problematic individual.

One oft-mentioned explanation for such inclusion in—not to mention position atop—the hard-boiled pantheon is the rise of *noir* as a generic and critical term. J. Madison Davis writes of Thompson: "A tiny number of grumblers might argue he doesn't deserve to be a household name, dismissing him as a pulp writer, but thanks to the French critics who recognized the underlying power of a certain kind of film and novel and dubbed it *noir,* as well as the breakdown of artistic hierarchies among critics in general, pulp fiction is no longer immediately dismissible."[27] Because Thompson's popularity coincides with a distillation of hard-boiled into *noir,* it is worth a moment to parse this coincidence and point out that Thompson's contribution to the hard-boiled school depends essentially on its basis in individualism, not its dissolution into *noir* despair. As generic descriptors, "hard-boiled" aligns more with fiction and *noir* with film; as critical terminology, it emphasizes narrative form and attitude, whereas *noir* looks at ambiance, atmosphere, and existential worldview. Alistair Rolls and Deborah Walker write: "To noir is not to remember the past with longing or to harbour delusions as to the way life used to be; instead, it is to act in the present with no idea of what is to come and in full (if suppressed) knowledge that our memories of the past are longings and not more than that."[28] For Christopher Breu, "What emerges from [*noir* stories] is a resolutely negative fantasy space, in which the reader has no stable site of identification and in which no larger social collectivity or unproblematic social or moral position can be imagined."[29] In these and other interpretations, *noir* is an absence—of technicolor, heroism, idealism, redemption, transcendence, order, the absolute.[30] It is not a coincidence that Jim Thompson found great critical and commercial success in France, where film noir was born and where his books were made into movies. *A Hell of a*

27. Davis, "No Man Is a Prophet," 39–40.
28. Rolls and Walker, *French and American Noir,* 7.
29. Breu, *Hard-Boiled Masculinities,* 43.
30. *Noir* is also a common term to use when referencing French interactions with—interpretations of or influences on—the American hard-boiled. The closest French translation of hard-boiled is *roman noir,* for the more literal *dur à cuire* usually has a somewhat parodic resonance.

Woman (1954) became Alain Corneau's 1979 film *Série noire,* and *Pop. 1280* (1964) became Bertrand Tavernier's 1981 *Coup de torchon,* set in 1930s West Africa.

The transition from 1930s and 1940s hard-boiled fiction into *noir* fiction and film, or from urban wasteland into negative fantasy space, coincides with the publication of Jim Thompson's work, that in criticism is often read as evidence of those precise absences. In other words, he is a writer often associated with what has gone missing from society, and virtually every critic who studies him employs the vocabulary of disappearance or deterioration. Peter Prescott, in a review for *Newsweek,* finds in Thompson's novels "the absence of any moral center at all."[31] This absence is situated in the principal character but is most often read as emblematic of a contaminated world. So it is for Kenneth Payne, who sees the "world gone wrong" as emblematic of the postmodern condition: "There is a place for Thompson in the postmodern. . . . His discourse of disintegration undermines the illusions of American community, exceptionalism, and moral order."[32] Joel Black writes, "Stories of serial violence are inherently episodic and lack any definite beginning, middle, or end. . . . Such 'promiscuous analogism' flourishes in the absence of narrative structures informed by cause, intention, and motive."[33] These readings furnish incisive descriptions of his novels' bleakness but are persistently wrong about its cause. Like the transition to secularism in the nineteenth century, the mid-century dissolution of the individual subject is as much a story as it is a historical phenomenon. Historical circumstances such as the McCarthy witch hunts, the development of the hydrogen bomb, and increased social conformity contributed to the material generation of that story, in which the principal character was precisely the absence of individual character. But Thompson nonetheless places individual moral choice in the foreground, insisting that individuals acting upon one another combine to generate the stories that become master narratives.

The advent of *noir,* with its focus on ambiance and atmosphere, encouraged discourse around the hard-boiled to focus with respect to individual characters on mental condition rather than thought. If hard-boiled is a persona and a series of decisions, *noir* is a diagnosis, and one that seems to underscore the hopelessness of worlds inside and out. Furthermore, since the early hard-boiled foregrounded (and criticism of it studied) the tension between the individual and a spreading corrupt environment, both *noir* and the mid-century hard-boiled read as symptomatic of that encroachment.

---

31. Prescott, "Cirrhosis of the Soul," 90.
32. Kenneth Payne, "Pottsville, USA," 127.
33. Black, "Murder," 790.

Biographer Michael McCauley writes of Thompson: "His criminals and their actions are only the most extreme examples of a whole world gone wrong." Biographer Robert Polito writes that the vision in *Pop. 1280* "wriggles past private madness, or American rot, to universal horror."[34] In these readings, the myriad wrongs in Jim Thompson's world find reflection in the individual but do not necessarily have their source in him—the atmosphere seems too grim to be reducible to one individual. And yet, the elephant in the room, the element that renders Thompson's fiction hard-boiled, and that renders his name synonymous with a hard-boiled turn toward hopelessness and away from exemplarity, is not just its dark mood and anti-idealistic characters, but its maintenance—ironic but nonetheless insistent and consistent—of the individual as beacon and center of the narrative. When Race Williams declared, "My ethics are my own," he placed himself at the moral and narrative center of the novel, refusing to cede ground to the forces of meanness and destruction around him, and refusing as well to cede to other perspectives, other voices. Philip Marlowe made small gestures in the direction of some such surrender at the end of *The Big Sleep*, musing, "I was part of the nastiness now." Mickey Spillane's Mike Hammer also wondered about his role in the world's nastiness, though he viewed his own nastiness as standing hand in hand with the world's, not subordinate to it. Jim Thompson's main characters combine these stances, switching shrewdly between determined centrality and gestures of hopelessness. The result is not existential torment but an ersatz nihilistic powerlessness. There is much more drive than pessimism in Thompson's fiction, for hard-boiled individualism and behavioral consistency—in the vein of Race Williams's "my ethics are my own"—are alive and well in Lou Ford. He perpetuates the cult of personality and of individualism that Race Williams had inaugurated. What is missing, of course, is the continuity of this individualism with received historic models of heroic conduct—models discursive and behavioral—for the man is a point-by-point rewriting of the hard-boiled American model of spiritual exemplarity.

THE KILLER INSIDE ME

The Killer Inside Me, published in 1952, one year after Spillane's *One Lonely Night*, is Thompson's best-known novel. Lou Ford, the twenty-nine-year-old sheriff of Central City, pretends to be a bland and boring rube though in fact committing every murder in the novel. He recounts memories of his child-

---

34. McCauley, *Jim Thompson*, 242; Polito, *Savage Art*, 456.

hood, his tendency to violence, his overbearing father, his sexual relationship with the housekeeper, and his early awareness of his own mental illness. In some ways he comes across as a descendant of Spillane's Mike Hammer, who wanted to "find out about myself." Lou Ford seems at numerous points to want to find out about himself, describing his present behavior in relation to past experiences, searching his father's collection of psychiatric literature for accounts of his diagnosis, remaining on the lookout for circumstances that could reactivate his sublimated—and italicized—*sickness*. Dorothy Clark writes, "He is a constant, self-consuming commentator on his own character, a kind of literary critic of his own life narrative." This is quite true, though it is essential to note that he is also the author of his life narrative. Ford's gestures of introspective curiosity are misleading, in part because, as Clark notes, he subverts the "traditional, modern, and postmodern explanatory models of evil" even as he proposes them.[35] Beyond this, though, much of what is demoralizing about this character—for it is a character-centered narrative, not a philosophical one—is Ford's subversion of the standards of heroism laid down in the nineteenth century and solidified in the classic hard-boiled. Ford turns simplicity into stupidity, intelligence into calculation, guilelessness into cluelessness—not to mention a consistent narrative voice and point of view into a disorienting series of contradictions. Virtually every feature of the Western or hard-boiled hero, including steadiness of vision, point of view, and critical distance from the outside world is undone, and so the crucial character connections among intelligence, simplicity, and moral uprightness—connections central to the American hero for more than a century—are broken.

First, Ford eschews any humble or practical distance from the intellectual: while Race Williams avoided "long-winded professors," Lou Ford quotes Wordsworth and then states, "I reckon I should have been a college professor or something like that."[36] He also mentions his capacity to read German, French, Spanish, and Italian, noting, "I'd just picked 'em up with Dad's help, just like I'd picked up some higher mathematics and physical chemistry and half a dozen other subjects" (27).

Second, he embraces rather than demurs the claim of spiritual authority: he declaims Bible verses before murdering Johnnie Pappas, who had looked up to him and trusted him. This reversal is still stronger in the 1964 *Pop. 1280*, where Nick Corey exults in messianic delusion: "I said I meant I was just doing my job, followin' the holy precepts laid down in the Bible. It's what I'm

35. Clark, "Being's Wound," 52, 54.

36. Thompson, *The Killer Inside Me*, 5. Subsequent references to this work are given parenthetically.

supposed to do, you know, to punish the heck out of people for bein' people. To coax 'em into revealin' theirselves, an' them kick the crap out of 'em."[37] Kenneth Payne describes Corey's messianic fantasies as "futile gestures in the face of his overriding sense of the vacuum at the center of things."[38] But futility is the character's very aim, for Corey is the source of the vacuum, its narrator, and its most enthusiastic fan. His ironic abdication, "You can't fault a jug for being twisted because the hand of the potter slipped,"[39] reminiscent of Chandler's rueful "I was part of the nastiness now," taunts the reader who is accustomed to blaming character on culture.

Third, Ford abandons all claims of responsibility. He explains that his affair with Amy "hadn't started anywhere. We'd just drifted together like straws in a puddle. . . We hadn't needed to do anything. It was all done for us" (30). When he murders Joyce, he tells the man he intends to frame, "Don't you say I killed her. SHE KILLED HERSELF!" (52). And when he finds out Joyce is not in fact dead, he complains that "things shouldn't have turned out this way. It was just plumb unreasonable" (55).

Fourth, he abandons the physical initiative of the pioneer wanderer: On his visit to Fort Worth, Ford remains in the hotel, musing that "I had to stay here by myself, doing nothing, seeing nothing, thinking the same old thoughts" (78). A sense of limited possibilities accompanies his sedentariness, as does a sense of limited perspective. On the plane to Fort Worth he sleeps through the flight, missing the bird's-eye view, and he "felt kind of disappointed. I'd never been out of the county before, and now that I was sure Joyce wasn't going to live I could have enjoyed seeing the sights. As it was I hadn't seen anything. I'd wasted all my time sleeping" (74). And in contrast with Hammett's Continental Op, who plowed though *Red Harvest* on large quantities of alcohol and almost no sleep, Ford declares: "I can sleep eighteen hours and still not feel rested. Well, I'm not tired, exactly, but I hate to get up" (94).[40]

Fifth, he mocks the former soldier, declaring of Howard Hendricks, the county attorney: "I hoped that chunk of shrapnel under his ribs had punc-

---

37. Thompson, *Pop. 1280*, 206. And, "I'm the savior himself, Christ on the Cross come right here to Potts County, because God knows I was needed here" (179).

38. Payne, "Pottsville, USA," 56.

39. Thompson, *Pop. 1280*, 179.

40. So too in *Pop. 1280*, whose principal character, small-town sheriff Corey, eats and sleeps a lot: "I'd sit down to a meal of maybe half a dozen pork chops and a few fried eggs and a pan of hot biscuits with grits and gravy, and I couldn't eat it. Not all of it" (3). "It was the same way with sleeping. I'd climb in bed. . . . And then, no more than eight or nine hours later, I'd wake up. Wide awake" (4).

tured a lung. That chunk of shrapnel had cost the taxpayers a hell of a pile of dough. He'd got elected to office talking about that shrapnel" (100).

Sixth, he disposes of the ethics of amusement: Nestor Burma was able to deride his own misfortune, but he was careful not to mock the troubles of others. Ford's sense of the comic is strongest when others suffer. "I've stood like that, looking nice and friendly and stupid, like I wouldn't piss if my pants were on fire. And all the time I'm laughing myself sick inside. Just watching the people" (121). When the body of his murder victim is discovered by the man he intends to frame for that murder (this occurs twice), he laughs (187). He deadpans about the women he has pummeled, calling them cases of suicide (182).

Seventh, he twists the populist resonances of plainspokenness. As Erin Smith writes about the language of advertisements published in *Black Mask*:

> Rather than employing learned terms, the language of these [advertised educational] programs was like the speech of working men addressing each other. One advertised training method was "so simple, thorough, and up-to-date that you can easily understand and apply every line of it—no big words, no useless theory, no higher mathematics—just plain, every-day, straight-from-the-shoulder, man-to-man English-the kind you and I use everyday." . . . Not coincidentally, both autonomous work and plain-speaking were deeply enmeshed with "manliness" in the phenomenal world of *Black Mask*.[41]

As discussed in earlier chapters, "plain-speaking" in this sense means a populist avoidance of elaborate language and unnecessary verbosity. Lou Ford's plainspokenness, however, takes the term to another conclusion: rather than speech that avoids ornamentation and intellectualism and facilitates communication, it is speech so bland and uninteresting as not to constitute communication at all. As David Anshen writes, "Thompson's novel represents clichés as both a key feature of commodified social existence and emblematic of the way late capitalist society presents itself as stagnant, timeless, and beyond challenge."[42] If the environment at hand is stagnant and timeless, then a subject that "is its travels" could not be blamed for clichéd noncommunication. This novel seems to capitalize on the idea that in the absence of aims given to the character, either with "immediate obviousness" or not, there is no hope for conscious subjectivity and expression. For Anshen, the cliché

---

41. Erin A. Smith, "How the Other Half Read," 215.
42. Anshen, "Clichés and Commodity Fetishism," 402.

resonates with postmodern alienation: "The novel also stages a fictional individual's relationship to his own language which can, usefully, be taken as an allegory for the relationship between labor and commodity production that exists in modern and postmodern society under conditions of generalized reification."[43] This reading can be expanded to indicate a general elision of the subject, which is the novel's point, albeit an ironic one.

Numerous speaking moments in the novel are also constructed to this elision. In the novel's opening scene, a waitress from Dallas is surprised that Lou carries no gun, and his response is a model of disarmed and disarming blandness. "'No,' I smiled. 'No gun, no blackjack, nothing like that. Why should I? . . . People are people, even when they're a little misguided. You don't hurt them, they won't hurt you. They'll listen to reason'" (3). The refusal of weapons suggests a personal (as opposed to impersonal) approach to policing, but what is more remarkable is the use of "smiled" that obscures or erases the act of speech. As clichéd as Homais and as bland as Charles Bovary, Lou Ford's entrance into speech is notable for the elision of the speaker. The same erasure appears in conversation with Joe Rothman, who will eventually accuse him: "'Sure,' I smiled stupidly. 'You just haven't thought this deal through, Joe'" (22), and with Joyce Lakeland, as he launches into the novel's first act of violence. "'Sure,' I grinned. My vision was clearing and I found my voice again. 'Sure, ma'am, I know how it was. Used to get that way myself'" (75).

DEMENTIA PRAECOX

When the hard-boiled switches directly from accidental or unintentional heroism to exclusion of the subject, it appears to let the individual abandon center stage—to turn the critical conversation from psychology to social contamination, from character to culture. But Lou Ford's particular reversals of the nineteenth-century model in fact serve to usher in a new sort of individual—the one who seems to blend into his surroundings, to cede to the atmosphere, to blend into an overweening "nastiness," but who nonetheless thinks, acts, and speaks with as much autonomy as his more reassuring predecessors.

Lou Ford's most detailed and provocative reversals of the classic hard-boiled concern his perspective on his own shortcomings and his dealings with his own traumatic past. The original hard-boiled character practiced either a perspicacious self-deprecation or an admission of fault that actually belied moral intactness. In contrast with Race Williams and his descendants,

---

43. Ibid., 403–4.

who held themselves to higher standards than other characters and seemed to reveal an organic American fortitude, Lou Ford perverts or inverts that formula. He demonstrates a consciousness, even a wariness of his own shortcomings, but that awareness changes nothing.

When Ford sees a picture of his father's former housekeeper, the woman who had abused him: "I was only like that for a few minutes, sitting there and staring, but a world of things, most of my kid life, came back to me in that time" (106). "So nothing had changed; I was still looking for *her*. And any woman who'd done what she had would be *her*" (216). This account perpetuates his imprisonment within the bounds of the past and ensures his continuing destructiveness. As narrator, he orchestrates this slide and, to harden the overdetermining force of his past, casts himself as a diagnostic study:

> I've read a lot of stuff by a guy—name of Kraepelin, I believe—and I can't remember all of it. I remember the high points of some, the most important stuff, and I think it goes something like this ". . . difficult to study because so seldom detected. The condition usually begins around the period of puberty, and is often precipitated by a severe shock . . ." That was written about a disease, or a condition, rather, called dementia praecox. Schizophrenia, paranoid type. Acute, recurrent, advanced. Incurable. (219)

This citation is remarkable for several reasons. For one, it is not a quotation from Emil Kraepelin, though it does sample a smattering of ideas about dementia praecox that were published by Kraepelin and others. However, the element of incurability—given dramatic prominence in Ford's citation—had already been abandoned or at least partially discredited in subsequent research on the illness. Eugen Bleuler, another researcher into "morbid psychology" cited earlier in the novel, stated that progressive decline was not inevitable and that partial or near-complete remission was possible. The reference to Kraepelin rather than to Bleuler produces a Ford impervious to treatment, as overdetermined by his "sickness" as the *noir* character is by a nihilistic outside atmosphere. He is thus reaching for a dramatic anachronism, an accountability-erasing diagnosis that would dovetail with received notions of traumatic repetition. What is most important about the references to Kraepelin, however, is that the precise pathology that Ford describes, cobbled together with ellipses and selected references to shrewdness, soundness of reason, and apparent logic, is nowhere close to clinical dementia praecox. It is true that *some* early research into the disease corresponds to *some* of Ford's citations. Early writings about it include this account: "Some special physical or mental stress occurred at the critical period of adolescence. Other exciting causes may be severe illness, the puerperium, especially an illegitimate confinement, fright, or any *severe shock*."[44] Or: "It is not uncommon to have dementia praecox follow relatively slight psychic shocks."[45] As for the idea of being "seldom detected," Kraepelin and Diefendorf write of a "'moral imbecility,' in which patients show a certain *shrewdness* in the attainment of selfish advantages which often conceals the real severity of the disease."[46] These citations do not, however, establish an accurate portrait of dementia praecox (later called schizophrenia). Schizophrenia is not "seldom detected," nor does the schizophrenic (or dementiac) "appear logical" or "reason soundly, even shrewdly." On the contrary, schizophrenia, particularly in the case of pubescent onset (hebephrenia), which Ford claims to have, is characterized by thoughts and actions that do not make sense to the outside world; according to the *DSM IV*, "The most restrictive definition of psychosis requires a break in reality testing that is manifested by delusions or hallucinations about which the individual has no insight."[47]

The deceptively logical surface that Ford creates in the fictitious Kraepelin blurb in fact corresponds not to schizophrenia but to psychopathy. Psychopathy, not psychosis and not schizophrenia, is associated with "superficial charm, unreliability, poor judgment, and a lack of social responsibility, guilt, anxiety, and remorse."[48] The emotional component of morality is absent in the psychopath, though there are no cognitive impediments to its articulation. As to the effects on narrative coherence, Gerald Prince writes: "Incoherent commentaries expressed by the narrating voice, as well as deceptive or erroneous explanations and illogical conclusions . . . cast doubt on the interpretive powers of the narrator; they do not necessarily deprive him or her of other powers. Lou Ford is a psychopath, but the geographical information he gives us about Central City is no less true."[49] Psychopathy, unlike psychosis, does not impede factual reporting but rather alters or eliminates its emotional tenor. Not every psychopath, of course, is a murderer. But the emptying of the emotional component threatens the substance of the hard-boiled character—threatens the outlines of character in general—by introducing the

---

44. Perkins, "The Nurse and the Mental Patient," 175.

45. Bartschinger, "Causation of Schizophrenia," 227.

46. Kraepelin and Diefendorf, *Clinical Psychiatry*, 63. Zane and Reid mention a class of criminal reformers who applied the term "dementia praecox" to any criminal. "They assert . . . that the victim of dementia praecox will not be cured by segregation and that he must be prevented from multiplying, for having inherited his condition he will transmit it." Zane and Reid, *Story of Law*, 348. These authors, however, discredit the idea of dementia praecox as coterminous with criminality.

47. Allen et al., *DSM-IV Guidebook*, 166.

48. Sperry, *DSM-IV-TR Personality Disorders*, 37.

49. Prince, "Narratology," 548–49.

specter of pure automation and pretense and destroying what Cassuto convincingly described as his sentimentality. In light of this destruction, critical readings that see Lou Ford as embodiment of broad modern disillusion seem excessively apocalyptic. To cast psychopathic "lack of social responsibility, guilt, anxiety, and remorse" as continuous with the outside world is to paint a grim picture of that world. It is also to paint a startlingly pessimistic picture of the modern individual status quo. Elision of the accountable individual is part of the story of mid-century alienation, but it is nonetheless a story, a narrative invention. The actions and choices that Ford conceals under discussions of dementia praecox create that story, constituting the central facts and dominant events of this novel.

David Anshen distinguishes between Ford as narrator and Ford as character. "At the beginning of the novel, he seems a reliable narrator and an unreliable character but by the end as the character tries to master events his descriptive coherence breaks apart, spilling over into the narrative."[50] Anshen discusses this breaking apart in postmodern terms of words "losing referential character," but the character's unreliability is choreographed. It is striking that in this iconic tale of madness, the madness is so visibly fictitious. The misleading specter of dementia praecox, combined with moments of clarity that are inevitably washed over by further violent action, produces a doomed analytical process. Does Ford know something, or does he not know it? Does he actually believe something, or does he only pretend to believe it? But once the fact of his psychopathy emerges, once the "nastiness" of his being is shown to be a foundational part of the entire narration rather than an italicized adversary he must combat, then the story emerges as a dark satire of individualism. Once he is understood to be psychopathic rather than psychotic, and once cognition is separated from emotion, his apparent "trying," "believing," and "knowing" cease to function in the service of an ethical *telos*, and his gestures at the *sickness* read as parodies of the sort of jaundiced clarity for which the hard-boiled is famous.

DANIEL PAUL SCHREBER

The mention of dementia praecox, by then a thoroughly outdated term for schizophrenia, exposes an intertextual reference that highlights Thompson's satire of hard-boiled individualism. There is a moment in the narrator's reminiscences when he recalls a conversation between his father and the family housekeeper, who had seduced Lou when he was a young teenager. "A mere

---

50. Anshen, "Clichés and Commodity Fetishism," 418.

child. Why not remember that? Listen to me, Daniel" (107). This is the sole mention of the name of Lou Ford's father, but it calls to mind another father named Daniel, whose son, the famous real-life dementia praecox patient Daniel Paul Schreber, wrote memoirs about his illness in which his controlling father loomed large. Lou Ford's references to dementia praecox, combined with the schematic similarities between the Ford and Schreber families, encourage an intertextual association with Schreber. Like Lou Ford, Schreber was raised by a physician (Daniel Moritz Schreber) who was deeply mistrustful of his own children. Like Lou Ford, Schreber had an older brother who died. Like Lou Ford, he worked in the domain of the law (as a lawyer and then a judge) until madness derailed him. Lou Ford's mother was dead, and Schreber's mother receded to the point of complete absence. Daniel Paul Schreber had by numerous accounts been irrevocably warped by his father's catastrophically intrusive child-rearing practices. Furthermore, and unlike Lou Ford, Schreber actually *was* diagnosed with dementia praecox, and also unlike Ford, Schreber did not kill anyone. The connection is a shrewd red herring that parodies the hard-boiled traditions of humility and personal accountability.

Daniel Paul Schreber (1842–1911), author of *Memoirs of My Nervous Illness,* was at the same time one of the most studied psychiatric patients in the world and also one of the most famous victims of an authoritarian, arguably sadistic father. As Rosemary Dinnage writes in the introduction to Schreber's *Memoirs,* Schreber's father "had a system and a manual for everything."[51] He invented the *Geradehalter,* a contraption to make children sit up straight, and a *Kopfhalter,* to keep the head straight. He wrote a number of books on children, including *Peculiarities of the Child's Organism in Health and Illness* and *Medical Indoor Gymnastics.* In an aside perversely relevant to Lou Ford's sexual memories of his family housekeeper, Schreber also authored *The Friend of the Family [Der Hausfreund] as an Educator and Leader to Family Happiness and Human Refinement* (1861). He had written of the need to rid a child of "that vestige of innate barbarity," wanting, as Morton Schatzman puts it, to "curtail their children's freedom by harsh disciplines" or as Louis Sass writes, to "root out and suppress much of the child's natural spontaneity, willfulness, and independence." Schatzman, in *Soul Murder,* intuits "a possible link between micro-social despotism in the Schreber family and the macro-social despotism of Nazi Germany."[52] Schreber's *Memoirs* articulates an intense

---

51. Schreber, *Memoirs,* xii.
52. Sass, *Paradoxes of Delusion,* 119; Schatzman, *Soul Murder,* 170. Schatzman also cites Elias Canetti, who did not speak of the father, but who found echoes of totalitarianism in Schreber's delusions of God's power.

sense of persecution, of being watched and corrected, a sense readers have associated with his father's relentless and disastrous parenting.

Ford's use of cliché and his suppression of the subject are also reminiscent of the detachment characteristic of Schreber. As Louis Sass writes about mental illness and alienation from language:

> The linguistic experience of the young child . . . seems to be vibrant and magical, with meanings proliferating wildly and sound and sense bleeding into each other. In Schreber's experience, by contrast, language seems to be progressively stripped of significance: words stand forth with a quasi-materiality nearly devoid of all emotional or semantic charge. It seems more accurate, and more consistent with the overall character of his panoptical world, to understand this linguistic opacity (and also the passivization) as resulting from an intense and disengaged introspection, from an alienated mode in which one does not live within language but contemplates it as a thing apart.[53]

But whereas Schreber's relationship to language was informed by his schizophrenia, Lou Ford's relationship to language seems choreographed to eliminate the subject when the narrator finds it necessary.

Another point of intersection between Daniel Ford and Schreber *père* lies in the two fathers' opinions of religion. Lou Ford said of his father, "Dad always said that he had enough trouble sorting the fiction out of so-called facts, without reading fiction. He always said that science was already too muddled without trying to make it jibe with religion. He said those things, but he also said that science in itself could be a religion, that a broad mind was always in danger of becoming narrow" (104). The idea of the broad mind becoming narrow can read as a grotesque figuration of the *Kopfhalter*, or "head compressing machine" that Daniel Moritz Schreber invented. The notion that religion *qua* religion—the doctrinal nature of religion—can narrow the mind does correspond to what is known of his opinions. Eric Santner notes that Daniel Moritz Schreber advocated protecting children from religion until the age of twelve, since otherwise "the child is in danger of forever confusing the dead letter of religious doctrine . . . with the voice of authentic spiritual authority."[54]

The parallels between the Ford and Schreber father-son pairs, though schematic, are too numerous to be coincidental. Although there is no evi-

---

53. Sass, *Madness and Modernism*, 137.
54. Santner, *My Own Private Germany*, 90.

dence that Jim Thompson researched the Schreber case, the team of doctors of morbid psychology on Lou Ford's reading list—Jung, Freud, Bleuler, Meyer, Kretschmer—all wrote about and studied Schreber, and it would be difficult to read about dementia praecox in even a cursory manner without encountering its most famous patient. These parallels, combined with Lou Ford's disingenuous mention of dementia praecox as his own diagnosis, link him to a dramatic case of childhood trauma and, more to the point, of well-documented, insurmountable parental fault.[55]

Lou Ford declares that his trouble—the *sickness* he calls dementia praecox but that more resembles psychopathy—resulted from his father's discovery of Lou's relationship with the housekeeper:

> My [trouble] had started back with the housekeeper; with Dad finding out about us. All kids pull some pretty sorry stunts, particularly if an older person edges 'em along, so it hadn't needed to mean a thing. But Dad had made it mean something. I'd been made to feel that I'd done something that couldn't ever be forgiven—that would always lie between him and me, the only kin I had. And there wasn't anything I could do or say that would change things. I had a burden of fear and shame put on me that I could never get shed of. (215)

The idea that Lou had a burden of shame "put on" him corresponds to Schreber's delusion of forces at once within and without. Indeed, this sense of a burden or force exerted both from within and without is borne out by Daniel Moritz Schreber's pedagogical design.

The points of intersection between Daniel Moritz Schreber and Daniel Ford contribute to the representation of Lou Ford as a manipulated and confused victim of bad parenting and to his own endeavors to attenuate his accountability. Lou Ford writes that his father was subsequently conscious of his son's pathology—a pathology for which at some level he seems to blame his father: "Dad had wanted me to be a doctor, but he was afraid to have me go away to school, so he'd done what he could for me at home" (27–28). Doing "what he could for me at home" meant arranging a job and a place to live. It meant encouraging his son to "talk and act like any other rube around town"

---

55. Theodore Dorpat opens a chapter titled "The Childhood Roots of Paranoid Psychopathology" with an examination of the Schreber case, writing that "childhood traumas, including corporal punishment and emotional and physical abuse, may play an important causal role in the etiology of paranoia and paranoid symptoms. One of the best-known cases of a patient with paranoid symptoms is that of Dr. Daniel Paul Schreber." Dorpat, *Crimes of Punishment,* 26.

in order to conceal his madness. It also meant arranging for his son to be sterilized, a procedure some of the psychiatrists cited on Lou Ford's reading list recommended for patients with dementia praecox.[56] He relaxes and eats his meals in his father's office:

> I sat in his big old leather chair, sipping coffee and smoking, and gradually the tension began to leave me. It had always made me feel better to come here, back from the time I was kneehigh to a grasshopper. It was like coming out of the darkness into sunlight, out of a storm into calm. Like being lost and found again. I got up and walked along the bookcases, and endless files of psychiatric literature, the bulky volumes of morbid psychology . . . all the answers were here. (27)

Schreber's memoirs also complain of the darkness: "Light, necessary for every human occupation, had become almost more essential for me than my daily bread in my allotted task of at all times convincing God, Who does not know the living human being, of my undiminished powers of reason." Noting that "rays have the capacity to calm nerves and bring sleep," he remarks that patients with nervous illnesses are calmer in the late morning "after the influence of a few hours of sunlight. The result is increased immensely if, as in my case, the body receives divine rays direct."[57]

TRAUMATIC PANOPTICON

The intertextual shades of Schreber—the sympathetic specter of a damaged son—amounts to a subtle satire of accountability and a subversion of the classic hard-boiled profile. More than this, however, the Schreber case, with its implications of insurmountable trauma, raises the question of accountability in a way that corresponds to mid-twentieth-century *noir* nihilism. The hard-boiled, as we remember, has to do with psychic fortitude and character intactness in the midst of a contaminated atmosphere—with the ability to transcend or compartmentalize a traumatic past. Moritz Schreber was notable for a "poisonous pedagogy" that made transcendence impossible

---

56. For Schreber, part of his pathology seems to have centered on the desire to have children. Writes Ida Macalpine, Schreber's translator: "Schreber fell ill when a fantasy that he could, would or should have children became pathogenic. Simultaneously he became doubtful of his own sex" (Schreber, *Memoirs*, 385). Schreber and his wife had wanted children but had several stillbirths and no living biological children. They adopted a little girl.

57. Schreber, *Memoirs*, 161, 92.

precisely because it encompassed the child so completely.[58] Not surprisingly, late twentieth-century analyses of his parenting and parenting philosophy focus on their wider resonances, or the ways in which his philosophy echoes an impersonal and inhumanly structured society. Sass, in an article titled "Schreber's Panopticism," wrote that Moritz Schreber's child-rearing practices bore "an almost uncanny resemblance to the modern penal procedures of *Discipline and Punish*. His techniques can, in fact, be said to involve the two great bulwarks of the modern disciplinary order of power/knowledge described by Foucault: 'exercise,' whose goal is the creation of docile bodies; and 'the examination,' whose purpose is the monitoring—ultimately, the self-monitoring—of action and thought."[59] Some of the son's delusions echoed his actual experiences at the hands of his father, though in his madness he attributed persecution and surveillance not to his father but to other individuals and to outside forces, notably, the "rays." As Leonard Cassuto writes, "Thompson's unsettling play with the reader's expectations invokes what sociologist Philip Rieff later called 'the triumph of the therapeutic.' In Rieff's influential 1966 argument, the rise of psychoanalysis—or more accurately, the psychoanalytic worldview—reduces the social to an analogy for the workings of the individual psyche."[60]

I would contend that Thompson's more disconcerting achievement is a reduction of the individual psyche to an analogy for the workings of the social, the result being a double reduction or endless transferral of reference that places responsibility nowhere. When we recall Christopher Breu's statement about Hammett's *Red Harvest* that the Op's "increasingly brutal tactics are presented as one more symptom of the town's (always already) "fallen" condition,"[61] it becomes clear that subsequent interpretation of the social as analogy for the individual psyche sets up ethics as a perpetual moving target, one that undercuts the idea of origination in individual choice. Much has been written about the parallels between Schreber *père*'s parenting and totalitarian political regimes, with some claiming that he was a proto-Nazi and others that he was not. But in either case, the parallels between Moritz Schreber's poisonous and "panoptical" parenting and Foucault's panoptical culture hint at an overbearing structure that the child has no hope of escaping. Thompson's novel predated Foucault, but the undercurrent of Schreber in Thompson conveys both the insurmountable and all-encompassing nature of the *sickness* and its congruence with a worldview that pushes against the

58. Miller, *For Your Own Good*.
59. Sass, "Schreber's Panopticism," 112.
60. Cassuto, *Hard-Boiled Sentimentality*, 132.
61. Breu, *Hard-Boiled Masculinities*, 66.

idea of the autonomous individual. A sort of über-parent, Moritz Schreber both advocated and embodied the inescapably intrusive force of the father-as-dominant-order. His style of parenting created an atmosphere in which the very notion of the subject becomes radically hopeless. Hopelessness, as trope and as social diagnosis, becomes the foundation of *noir*. In sum, the parallels between Ford and Schreber play with the notion of surroundings devouring the individual by introducing the storied, and genuinely tragic, specter of Schreber's helplessness and hopelessness.

I have examined the Schreber parallel in order to show how Thompson conjures two major threats to hard-boiled individualism and even to the idea of the "individual" as such. One is the specter of psychic trauma, an experience that resists and derails narrativization and results in a splintered self, the other the presence of overwhelming and insurmountable social control. Evoking dementia praecox and the overbearing father combines both, locating internal and external enemies of psychic coherence. In this sense, dementia praecox becomes a metaphor for the character's autodeconstruction. And the image of Schreber *père*-as-panopticon widens the scope of the menace to subjecthood. Schizophrenia, being a pathology, can constitute a departure from what Clifford Geertz called the "Western conception of the person as a bounded, unique, more or less integrated motivational and cognitive universe, a dynamic center of awareness, emotion, judgment, and action organized into a distinctive whole" without threatening the normative status of that conception.[62] But schizophrenia-become-social-phenomenon turns that departure into an atmospheric condition.

PARANOID READING

It is also worth noting that Schreber's paranoid sense of being controlled by outside forces finds an echo in many critical responses to the late hard-boiled and to Thompson in particular. In her 2003 essay contrasting "paranoid" to "reparative" readings, Eve Sedgwick points out Freud's comparison of Schreber's paranoia to his own theories and to theory in general: "In the last paragraphs of Freud's essay on the paranoid Dr. Schreber, there is discussion of what Freud calls a 'striking similarity' between Schreber's systematic persecutory delusion and Freud's own theory. Freud was indeed later to generalize, famously, that 'the delusions of paranoiacs have an unpalatable external similarity and internal kinship to the systems of our philosophers'—among whom

---

62. Geertz, *Local Knowledge*, 59.

he included himself." Sedgwick's critique of what she calls paranoid readings is based on the sense that a "view of large and genuinely systemic oppressions does not intrinsically or necessarily enjoin that person to any specific train of epistemological or narrative consequences."[63] In other words, to know that the outside world is incontrovertibly iniquitous does not necessarily amount to meaningful understanding. Paranoid reading, similar to *noir*, constitutes a diagnosis. In a paranoid reading, the absence or ultimate uselessness of individual moral choice—and the positioning of individual characters relative to that uselessness—seems a historical fact, whereas in reality it is as much an epistemological framework as the nineteenth-century idea of sacred frames. A complete examination of Sedgwick's argument is of course outside the scope of this chapter; however, she argues for "reparative" reading in a passage that I will quote in its entirety because it comes close to the aim of the present study:

> To read from a reparative position is to surrender the knowing, anxious paranoid determination that no horror, however apparently unthinkable, shall ever come to the reader as new; to a reparatively positioned reader, it can seem realistic and necessary to experience surprise. Because there can be terrible surprises, however, there can also be good ones. Hope, often a fracturing, even a traumatic thing to experience, is among the energies by which the reparatively positioned reader tries to organize the fragments and part-objects she encounters or creates.[64]

To argue for the importance of individual moral choice and for the centrality of conscience to the hard-boiled genre is not to deny the broad cultural currents that make that choice seem compromised or even futile. My focus here is on the ways in which such cultural currents in fact renew, again and again, emphases on the accountable subject as site of narrative originality. To reduce Ford's psychopathy to a symptom of broad cultural devolution, as many critics do, is to imitate Ford in his evocations of Schreber and concur with him in an overweening pessimism. It is also to concur with him in the elision of individual subjectivity—the very subjectivity that romantics participated in creating and that Race Williams buoyed when he insisted that his ethics were "his own." It is true that *The Killer Inside Me* pushes for that elision, but with such insistence as to reveal its fictitiousness, its disingenuousness. Again, this is not to say that the accountable individual represents an ideal or can

---

63. Sedgwick, *Touching Feeling*, 125.
64. Ibid., 146.

reverse systemic oppression. Such a proposition would constitute a paranoid reading of its own, since dreaming of an ideal individualist would be almost as futile as declaring its nonexistence. And yet, in historically and culturally specific ways, the hard-boiled's focus on individual moral choice continues to emerge and to counteract the very modern master narratives that would seem to attenuate it.

Several chapters before the end of Stendhal's *Le rouge et le noir* (1830), Julien Sorel declares, "My novel is finished, and the credit is all mine" [Mon roman est fini, et à moi seul tout le mérite].[65] He is wrong, on the one hand because his novel is not finished but more importantly because the credit is not his alone: it belongs also to others. Lou Ford's conundrum is of a completely other kind: rather than pretending to invent a life and a self that have in fact already been invented, he evokes reasons why self-invention is impracticable from the start. "Dad had made it mean something. I'd been made to feel that I'd done something that couldn't ever be forgiven" (215). From the insurmountable parent to the incoherence within, Ford abdicates control of his person in ways that gesture at modern trauma theory. And yet, for all his complaints of a severely wilted individual*ism,* Ford is nonetheless an individual, remarkably articulate, active, and consistent.

The philosophical question of whether or not "character" is a legitimate idea has been as much examined in philosophy as in literature. Gregory Currie writes, "Character must be displayed through the representation of regularities of behavior that are robust under variation of circumstance," but the version of circumstance, as various studies reveal, has a substantial effect on behavior.[66] "Character" may not be a robust entity, which becomes problematic if, as Currie claims, "Strong character is a necessary but insufficient condition for being morally good." Studies that demonstrate the force of outside circumstances complicate the issue of accountability without solving it. In essence, Lou Ford has anticipated these studies and run them to their most provocative conclusion, namely, that the individual cannot be pinned down enough, psychologically or conceptually, even to discuss accountability in a meaningful way. To say that the character cannot be pinned down is not the same as to say that the character is not "readable," in the sense that Steven Cohan uses the term when he locates character readability "not in the psychological grounding of realism (representationalism) or in the aesthetic grounding of modernism (self-reflexivity), but in that crucial space between text and reader. For it is here that the coherence of character as a virtual exis-

65. Stendhal, *Le rouge et le noir,* 585.
66. Currie, "Narrative and the Psychology of Character," 61–62.

tent comes into play."[67] Ford's mention of defining past experiences ("I had a burden of fear and shame put on me that I could never get shed of") are less about undercutting the coherence of character as a concept, as Cohan points out when he refers to poststructuralist critics for whom "character functions as a psychological microcosm of the text itself as representation"[68] than about derailing accountability. In other words, in discussing Ford's narrative and his evocation of outside forces, I do not mean to enter into the discussion of character as reliant on psychological determinism (Todorov) vs. character as phenomenological (Price)—a discussion that Cohan resolves by insisting that "to understand character as a readable figure we need to distinguish between its psychological attributes as a representational figure and its phenomenological identity as an imagined figure"[69]—but only to measure the character as someone who acts toward others and is conscious of those actions. Ford as narrative actor is remarkably consistent, and perhaps his most impressive accomplishment as such is to convey the sense of an atmospheric pollution that cannot be changed, that trumps or derails psychology.

AUTHORSHIP AND ACTION

Robert Polito writes, "During his dance around Stanton's death, Ford styles himself a novelist."[70] Indeed, in one of his more exuberant moments, Ford promises a thorough narration: "In a lot of books I read, the writer seems to go haywire every time he reaches a high point. He'll start leaving out punctuation and running his words together. . . . But the way I see it is, the writer is just too goddam lazy to do his job. And I'm not lazy, whatever else I am. I'll tell you everything" (180). The idea of Lou Ford as a novelist or narrator prepared to "tell you everything" generates—and then undercuts—a number of assumptions about reliable narrators and the value of "telling everything." One assumption is that "everything" amounts to a coherent whole. Lou Ford as narrator-novelist puts out a rather jumbled "everything," including false citations and fictitious diagnoses. As for point of view, the novel's narratology becomes perplexing when Ford narrates from within an exploding building. As Polito writes, "The logic of the endings of *The Killer Inside Me* and *A Hell of a Woman* requires that we believe that their narrators have been speaking

---

67. Cohan, "Figures beyond the Text," 9.
68. Ibid., 7.
69. Ibid., 15.
70. Polito, *Savage Art,* 349.

to us from beyond the grave."[71] As *The Killer Inside Me* ends, "Smoke poured up through the floor. And the room exploded with shots and yells, and I seemed to explode with it" (244). From this place within the explosion, Ford concludes:

> And they all lived happily ever after, I guess, and I guess—that's—all. Yeah, I reckon that's all unless our kind gets another chance in the Next Place. Our kind. Us people. All of us that started the game with a crooked cue, that wanted so much and got so little, that meant so good and did so bad. All us folks. Me and Joyce Lakeland, and Johnnie Pappas and Bob Maples and big ol' Elmer Conway and little ol' Amy Stanton. All of us. All of us. (244)

This conclusion constitutes an assault on coherence, because of the exploded perspective, because of the "happily ever after" promised to the murder victims, and because "all of us" that "did so bad" lumps murder victims in with murderers.

Another assumption about the value of telling "everything" is that a candid narrator is tantamount to a good and reliable character. Ford's insistence that he will "tell you everything" activates American assumptions about frankness, simplicity, and reliability—assumptions nurtured over a century of humble, unpretentious, and courageous characters in the Western tradition. An open book is not necessarily a comprehensible one, by design: there exists a canniness of narration in the echoes of Schreber, the insistences on dementia praecox, the very inconsistencies that "challenge the Western conception of the person as bounded and unique." Furthermore, the narrator's point-by-point reversal of the classic hard-boiled character outline reveals this satire, and so implies a wiliness of narration. More important, whatever Ford thinks, believes, wants, and remembers—and there is much of this, for he is a man of many musings—the most important and durable measures of his character are his actions. Twentieth-century history of the hard-boiled as a developing genre is the history of these knowing metaperformances, of orchestrated disconnections among thought, word, and action. They show the plain-speaking self-deprecator to be an empty mask devoid of morality or moral authority whose emptiness is apparent when we accord pride of place to action.

In his first account of a violent act, Lou Ford attributes inconsistencies of narration to his aggression: When Joyce attacks him, he falls down, then stands up: "My vision was clearing and I found my voice again. . . . I took

71. Ibid., 9.

off my belt and raised it over my head. . . . I don't know how long it was before I stopped, before I came to my senses" (12). Ellipses obscure the movements, and the act of violence is made to seem born of bewilderment. This ruse is soon abandoned, however, and all subsequent instances of violence are narrated with clarity and exuberance. The moments when he burns a beggar with a cigarette (15), beats Joyce Lakeland almost to death (50), shoots Elmer Conway (52), murders Johnny Pappas (120) and Amy Stanton (186), and stabs Joyce Lakeland (244) are narrated with zealous directness. Decisions about narration are driven by decisions about action. When he pursues the beggar, the man he intends to frame for Amy Stanton's murder, he announces, "I grabbed up the knife and took off after the heartless son-of-a-bitch" (188). This recounting pretends to root the chase in delusion—Lou the dementia praecox patient on a murderous rampage—but it is actually an invention in the service of premeditated action. Cassuto calls this "pile-on of pitiful details" a "narrative strategy of misdirected sympathy and perverted sentimentality."[72] Ford is fond of repeating the commonplace "the child is father to the man," and for him the character is father to the narrator. That is, what he is as a character—a murderer who wants to elude responsibility—shapes his decisions as narrator. He calls the bum "heartless" because he has decided to frame him, not the other way around.[73] This order of things is visible to the reader, and the absence of conscience it represents forms the foundation of the novel's disillusion.

NARRATIVE VOICE

In having Ford narrate his murders simply and directly, Thompson mocks the American association of frankness and action with "good," as well as the equation of the hard-hitting straight shooter and a basic moral rectitude. Indeed, it almost encourages nostalgia for heroes who cared about embodiment of virtue, which is ironic since Ford understands his actions and their consequences as fully as did any nineteenth-century romantic narrator. This novel goes a long way toward undoing the American association of directness with reason, and of reason with right. The demolition operates effectively in the first person. Lou Ford's account of prepubescent sexual abuse echoes that of Ralph Cotter, the narrator of Horace McCoy's 1948 *Kiss*

---

72. Cassuto, *Hard-Boiled Sentimentality*, 133.

73. In Michael Winterbottom's 2010 movie version of *The Killer Inside Me*, Donizetti's "Una furtiva lagrima" accompanies Lou Ford as he prepares to burn down his house. Ford also plays the piano, giving him an artistic side that he does not have in the book.

Tomorrow Goodbye, who alludes early on to the memory of "little-boy fright (which, I also was to find out, was not annihilative as grown-man fright)."[74] Cotter reports toward the end of the novel that as a child, he had hidden under his grandmother's skirt and touched her legs: she threatened to have him castrated, and to avoid this fate he murdered her. "It was there, the cloaca, as it most certainly had to be, as it inevitably had to be, αναγκη."[75] The use of the Greek for "necessity" or "inevitability" accords to his traumatic past an incontrovertible and ancient inexorableness. Cotter (or the uncertain subject operating under that name; we learn later that Cotter is not his real name) is destined to murder, with tragic but logical certainty. This novel, like *The Killer Inside Me,* ends with the narrator's death, recounted as a return to the womb: "There was another flash of fire and my eyes went out and now I could see nothing. . . . I was safe and secure in the blackness of the womb from which I had never emerged."[76] The character exists as a generator of pure action, the search for whose motivations becomes lost in the jungle of a scarring childhood experience, a concealment of his real name, and an improbable narrative ending that puts him back in the womb, in essence negating the entire character. And yet, the very existence of the narrative, in McCoy and in Thompson, belies the erasure of the accountable subject, precisely because it is the subject who is narrating.

Much as this disingenuous erasure resonates as a first-person phenomenon, it also operates in third-person narratives. In Patricia Highsmith's *The Talented Mr. Ripley* (1955), the narrator initially invites sympathy in her report of Ripley's childhood troubles, then undercuts that sympathy when she recounts Ripley's readiness to blame them. For instance, when he prepares to murder Dickie Greenleaf, he remembers his Aunt Dottie, who had called him a "sissy" and belittled him as a child.[77] The moments that follow the murder are replete with fear, but the fact and vehemence of the act are unmediated. At the same time, loneliness and pliability are Ripley's most salient characteristics: whereas hard-boiled characters stand at the far end of a *Bildungsroman,* Ripley seems not to have started his. Lee Horsley writes, "Our dominant impression of Ripley is not of psychological imbalance but of rational self-interest, and in fact part of his insidious appeal lies in his

---

74. McCoy, *Kiss Tomorrow Goodbye,* 5.

75. Ibid., 364.

76. Ibid., 372.

77. Highsmith, *Talented Mr. Ripley,* 40, 42. Like Jim Thompson, Patricia Highsmith also found success on the French screen, with the 1960 film *Plein soleil* starring Alain Delon as Tom Ripley.

sheer pragmatism. . . . He does not resort to murder except when it presents itself as the only reasonable means of securing his goal or preserving his freedom."[78] These assessments are both correct, and the fact of a character at once murderous and malleable complicates the attribution of blame. Reacting to Dickie's refusal of his friendship, for instance, he evinces pure distress:

> They were not friends. They didn't know each other. It struck Tom like a horrible truth, true for all time, true for the people he had known in the past and for those he would know in the future: each had stood and would stand before him, and he would know time and time again that he would never know them, and the worst was that there would always be the illusion, for a time, that he did know them, and that he and they were completely in harmony and alike. For an instant the wordless shock of his realization seemed more than he could bear.[79]

This third-person narration, thanks to Highsmith's inimitable combination of coldness and comprehension, reveals the troubled history of the subject. Leonard Cassuto writes, "If the sentimental action hero was supposed to quell Cold War fears, Highsmith and Thompson wrote the anxious fifties, giving those fears full reign."[80] But Ripley's nervous apartness is individual before it is national, and so too are his crimes. In *Ripley Under Ground,* the narrator explains, "The reason he had to speak with Jeff and Ed was simply that he felt scared and alone."[81] National anxiety may be the setting for crises of individual subjectivity, may even be their catalyst and the condition of their publication as narratives. But as both Thompson and Highsmith demonstrate, no amount of anxiety, national or individual, is a sufficient condition for dismantling the accountable subject. The subject resists attempts to erase it, even when such attempts come from the subject itself. A traditional conception of the individual thus persists, even in moments of disclaimer and disavowal, and indeed especially at such moments. For if national crises emerge as most destructive and demoralizing when they suspend individual accountability, then that accountability, paradoxically, rebounds with surprising force the instant it names its dissolution.

---

78. Horsley, *Noir Thriller,* 119.
79. Highsmith, *Talented Mr. Ripley,* 265.
80. Cassuto, *Hard-Boiled Sentimentality,* 18.
81. Highsmith, *Ripley Under Ground,* 230.

FORD'S DESCENDANTS

Jim Thompson was not the first or the only author to create an amoral character, but he is the first to put such systematic dents in both autonomy and accountability. And when the accountable subject devolves in his fiction, so too does the character model of American heroism. The hard-boiled is a fictional genre, but the devolution of the heroic model—which is at its root a model of spiritual authority and exemplarity—has broader implications, and the flagrant consistency with which Ford abandons the heroic role anticipates other such abandonments.

As Stephen King noted in the introduction to the 1989 Blood and Guts Press version of *The Killer Inside Me*, Lou Ford began a notable American character trend:

> I have no idea if Mr. Kraepelin is real or another product of Thompson's imagination, but I do know that the description ("difficult to study because so seldom detected. The condition usually begins around the period of puberty, and is often precipitated by a severe shock. . . . He reasons soundly, even shrewdly. He is completely aware of what he does and why he does it") fits a lot more people than one mentally disturbed deputy sheriff in a crossroads Texas town. It describes a generation of killers, from Caryl Chessman to Lee Harvey Oswald to John Wayne Gacy to Ted Bundy. Looking back at the record, one would have to say that it also describes a generation of politicians: Joe McCarthy, Richard Nixon, Oliver North, Alexander Haig, and a slew of others. In Lou Ford, Jim Thompson drew for the first time a picture of the Great American Sociopath.[82]

In King's estimation, just as hard-boiled character types derived from the personalities who took the nation in hand both spiritually and politically in the nineteenth century, so twentieth-century political character types have derived from the hard-boiled and its cinematic incarnations. Race Williams coming to the aid of the unfortunate in 1920s New York; Philip Marlowe rescuing self-destructors in louche Los Angeles: the character model of the plain-speaking, uncomplicated, instinctive man of honor has dominated not just the hard-boiled novel but the American political scene as well.

Although it may be obvious to say that Thompson puts forth a problematic and poisonous individual who dismantles hard-boiled ideals, what is important is how that dismantling occurs, and how it hamstrings eventual

---

82. Thompson, *The Killer Inside Me*, foreword by Stephen King.

conversations about accountability in the political as well as the narrative realm. The evocations of a tyrannical father, an overbearing social structure, a psychiatric diagnosis, an aw-shucks foolishness—a compendium of forces historical, biological, psychological, and social conspire to render the individual ineffectual as a source of solution, dominant as he may be as a source of the problem, precisely because these negative forces tend to diminish the individual as an idea, as an ontological entity. The borders of the individual *qua* individual are continually breached not only by the individual's own evocations of those forces but by critical responses that underscore their importance. Indeed, Thompson is so important because he takes all twentieth-century indications of a weakened sense of self, these disculpating or mitigating psychic circumstances, these gestures at postmodern fragmentation, these collapses or surrenders in the face of the Kantian Ought, and makes of them disingenuous red herrings.

Ford's vacillation between pride and denial and his evocation of the social frame as a deadening force (evocation echoed in critical examinations of Thompson and of *noir* as a genre) conspire to leave the individual *qua* individual shadowy, uncertain, and hard to hold accountable. Stephen King's comment on political figures of the mid- to late twentieth century can be read as a sort of dramatic throwaway line, particularly its glib attributions of pathology, but it is true that the same shadowy uncertainty surrounds the political operators he mentions.[83] A full examination of those resonances is far outside the scope of this chapter, but as characters, as public personae, as narrators, each of these four men combined, as did Lou Ford, self-directed action with renunciations of accountability. Alexander Haig famously complained of a sense of powerlessness in his memoirs: "You heard the creak of the rigging and the groan of the timbers and sometimes even glimpsed the crew on deck. But which of the crew had the helm?"[84] But Frances FitzGerald later described Haig as living "on a psychological edge. . . . Eternally choleric, always on the verge of a tantrum, he raised tempers even when he was warning against overreaction."[85] In 1984 Christopher Hitchens wrote, "Now, nobody has a higher opinion of General Alexander Haig than I do. And I

---

83. King is not the first to diagnose an entire generation; see Lasch, *Culture of Narcissism*.
84. Haig, *Caveat*, 85.
85. FitzGerald, *Way Out There in the Blue*, 171. James Chace writes in a review of Haig's book, "As his memoir so unwittingly reveals, Mr. Haig's only real complaint over American foreign policy today is that he is not in charge of it." Chace, "Turbulent Tenure of Alexander Haig," n. pag.

think he is a homicidal buffoon."[86] Greg Forter would later use this exact phrase to describe the main character of Thompson's *Pop. 1280*.[87]

Oliver North's testimony in the Iran-Contra hearings echoes Lou Ford's "I'll tell you everything": "Those are the facts as I know them. I came here to tell you the truth. The good, the bad, and the ugly, I'm here to tell it all."[88] When explaining that he does not remember a question that was posed: "My memory has been shredded." His testimony that the government provided him with the shredder, and that he prepared "a version of the chronology" that was not true, amount to absurd circumlocutions that resemble Lou Ford's disconnection of narrative authority from moral authority, or even of narrative authority from autonomy. Rhetoric is used to moderate responsibility rather than to claim it, which constitutes a radical reversal of the usual hard-boiled formula. The cloud that *noir* has cast over the mid-twentieth century can in many ways be put down to this inverse relationship between narrative authority and individual accountability.

In an analysis of Horace McCoy's 1948 *Kiss Tomorrow Goodbye*, in which the protagonist Ralph Cotter declares that he "came into crime through choice and not through environment," Lee Horsley had written: "There is no doubt that focusing on the psychopathology of a character can become an indulgence of horrified fascination at the sheer nastiness of the aberrant personality, combined with a reassuring sense that normative values and conventional lives are free from these evils."[89] In this formulation, the individual problem can be solved with a retreat into "normative values." The problematic individual, in other words, has not so much poisoned a place of relative integrity or purity "free from those evils" as ceded it to or displaced it onto the outside world. Where the classic hard-boiled described an individual in a struggle against corruption, with victory indicating transcendence and heroism, here the individual is the problem and normative convention the cure. Of course, the idea of the outside world as solution is both false and underwhelming. The idea of a conventional space outside the reach of individual corruption is illusory, particularly when the corrupt individuals in question are in positions of legal or political authority.[90] Furthermore, "normative val-

---

86. Hitchens, "Minority Report," 662. Michael Barone writes of McCarthy, America's "most hated senator," "McCarthy was a pathological liar, an uninformed and obscure politician with certain demagogic gifts who latched onto the anti-Communist crusade without much believing in it himself." Barone, *Our Country*, 235.

87. "In Nick Corey, Thompson in fact refashions his father in startling ways, turning him into a morally tortured and yet homicidal buffoon." Forter, *Murdering Masculinities*, 133.

88. "Iran-Contra Hearings," *New York Times*, July 8, 1987.

89. Horsley, *Noir Thriller*, 104.

90. Stanley Milgram writes of the consequences of trickle-down amorality: "Although a

ues" and "conventional lives" are not particularly compelling instruments of narrative resolution. Indeed, these serve as positive terms only when the alternatives are sufficiently disastrous: antisocial behavior, egoism, sociopathic violence. Convention, representing social and judicial stasis, eventually succumbs to another pendulum swing that will return to celebrate the individual. Normative convention, in other words, with no actual presence or narrative of its own, morphs into the enemy as soon as a sufficiently appealing or creative individual arrives. Hard-boiled crime fiction finds heroism in departures from convention, not in embrace of it. Furthermore, that seems to hold true whether the convention in question is a source of pollution or simply a dulling force of constraint. The twenty-first-century hard-boiled thus faces the challenge of how to present an individual who is at once exemplary and unconventional, autonomous and accountable.

---

person acting under authority performs actions that seem to violate standards of conscience, it would not be true to say that he loses his moral sense. Instead, it acquires a radically different focus. He does not respond with a moral sentiment to the actions he performs. Rather, his moral concern now shifts to a consideration of how well he is living up to the expectations that the authority has of him." Milgram, *Obedience to Authority, 8*. Milgram's experiment suggests that it does not much matter whether the leader is deemed moral or not, competent or not—the mere presence of the person in a structural position of authority is enough to dilute others' sense of agency.

CHAPTER 4

JEAN-PATRICK MANCHETTE

The Art of Falling Apart

THE FRENCH DISMANTLING of hard-boiled character follows a process parallel to the American. Culturally resonant heroic character attributes are exaggerated to the point of pathology, even as the conceptual outlines of character and subjectivity are diminished. The result, here as in the American tradition, is a two-pronged weakening of individual moral authority. First, the individual is invested with characteristics that constitute grotesque augmentations of early nineteenth-century ideals. Second, those augmented characteristics are represented as unbidden intrusions that impede full subjectivity. As in the American model, distortions of canonical character models undermine the beloved hard-boiled ideal of the individual for whom spiritual principles become secular personality attributes. They change the entire landscape of ethical responsibility and of what can be imputed to the individual: perhaps the outside world is too contaminating and deadening a force, or perhaps, much more simply, human self-interest can be expected to trump communal responsibility. And yet, those distortions and subversions amount to deliberately disculpating narrative strategies. Indeed, the idea of individual malaise and abdication as inevitable correlatives to the late twentieth century is itself transparently the result of such strategies.

THE *NÉO-POLAR*

The 1960s and 1970s saw a radical change in French crime fiction. Around May 1968 the *roman noir* made way for a more aggressive and politically explicit subgenre, the *néo-polar*. The term *néo-polar* was coined by Jean-Patrick Manchette, who wrote in 1981: "I came up with the word 'néopolar,' based on the words néopain, néovin, or even néopresident, which is how radical criticism points out illustrious names given to the same old things" [J'ai formé alors le mot "néopolar," sur le modèle des mots de néopain, néovin ou même néoprésident, par quoi la critique radicale désigne les ersatz qui, sous un nom illustre, ont partout remplacé la même chose].[1] As David Platten writes, "the *néo-polar* took its inspiration from the American 'hard-boiled' tradition of the 20s and 30s, in which Manchette, its leading light, detected an uncompromising, if nihilistic anti-fascism." He points out, however, that in contrast to the American hard-boiled, whose stock-in-trade was the disinterested detective, the *néo-polar* became "a site of resistance to the perceived violence of the State."[2] As a movement, it was informed by Manchette's vision of modern crime fiction that "talks about a world out of balance, liable to fall down and disappear. The *polar* is crisis literature" [cause d'un monde déséquilibré, donc labile, appelé donc à tomber et à passer. Le polar est la littérature de la crise].[3]

The principal thematic elements of the *néo-polar* are violence, anti-idealism, and the alienation of individuals; its principal stylistic features are a graphic vernacular and a rapid narrative pace, all of which enacts a crisis at the level of form as well as content. Both in criticism and in the writings of *néo-polar* authors themselves, the passage from *roman policier* to *néo-polar* is most often examined from the point of view of social critique. Virtually every discussion of the *néo-polar* mentions its jaundiced political perspective and its nihilistic vision of society. Writes Jean-François Gérault of Manchette's *néo-polar*, "The individual becomes a moveable pawn in a world that excludes him, a violent and pitiless world" [L'individu devient un pion manipulé dans un monde dont il a perdu les clés, un monde violent et sans pitié].[4] In these critical formulations, the individual as narrative focus and actor is subordinated to the social. Individuals are cast as those around whom events happen, as children of, rather than actors upon, a particular social atmosphere. Margaret Atack notes, "May 68 forged a collective 'nous'

---

1. Manchette, *Chroniques*, 200.
2. Platten, *Pleasures of Crime*, 93–94.
3. Manchette, *Chroniques*, 53.
4. Gérault, *Jean-Patrick Manchette*, 11–12.

uniting all those excluded and marginalized by bourgeois society and the capitalist state, students, criminals, the young, the Third World, all actual or potential victims."[5] The notion that broad sections of the population are "actual or potential victims" underscores society's dominance as principal character. Several *néo-polars* were constructed around actual events of the 1960s and 1970s that were known most broadly as news stories, not as individual experiences. Manchette's 1971 novel *L'affaire N'Gustro,* his first sole-authored novel, is about the 1965 disappearance of the Moroccan opposition leader Mehdi Ben Barka. The narrator of his *Nada,* which recounts the kidnapping and assassination of an American ambassador by a group of *gauchistes* who demand that their manifesto be read in the media, points to May 1968 graffiti on the walls. The police in that novel are able to identify the kidnappers from photographs of the May protests. Didier Daeninckx's *Meurtres pour mémoire* resuscitates the 1961 massacre of Algerian protesters in Paris, as well as the deportation of Jews from Drancy during the Second World War.

As Pierre Verdaguer writes, "the *roman noir,* particularly since the so-called *néo-polar* of the 1970s, has been dominated by a sense of failure, disillusionment, and even despair and existential disgust or *nausée,* to use a Sartrean term."[6] That nausea is shared, and caused by a shared social atmosphere, but it is not any less individual for that, nor any less intentionally and artfully cultivated. Social readings of Manchette miss this artfulness, the fact that his work sustains traditional concepts of the individual and casts individual abdications of accountability as the foundation of social disorder. This might seem a reactionary reading for a corpus that conjures various intricate ideological and subjective models, from the culturally constructed to the Foucauldian poststructuralist subject. But as we will see, the decision to evoke an existentialist "nausea" functions, at times quite transparently, as a dramatic distraction from individual moral choice at precise moments of problematic conduct. David Platten writes that Manchette "back-track[s] to a variant on the Rousseau model of primitive man; they are 'mauvais sauvages' denuded even of pre-reflective pity, their brains programmed to ensure the greatest chance of their material survival."[7] And yet, the bad savage is as much a construct as the noble one, albeit a construct built on absences and reversals—as paranoid a notion as its predecessor is idealistic. For in the *néo-polar,* the principal characters do with the French character model what Lou Ford had done with the American: build upon it, distort it point by

---

5. Atack, *May 68,* 135.

6. Verdaguer, "Politics of Food," 198.

7. Platten, *Pleasures of Crime,* 108.

point, then represent the resulting disaster as an insurmountable psychosocial problem.

THE EARLY *ROMAN NOIR*

The character who twists nineteenth-century romanticism into discontent and violence is not a *néo-polar* invention. Gallimard's *Série noire* had been creating such marginal characters since 1948, but it was the *néo-polar* that turned them into elements of a broader social disorder. As a point of comparison, I want to look at Terry Stewart's 1948 *La mort et l'ange*, the first French-authored novel in Gallimard's *Série noire*.[8] In that novel, an FBI agent named Maat poses as a prison guard to interview Ben Sweed, a serial murderer from Indiana awaiting execution. The candid chronicle of numerous murders introduces micromoments of self-conscious subjectivity before ending in execution, but for the most part Sweed presents himself as the unwitting instrument of "a force that moves in me."[9] Sweed resembles a perverse romantic positing violence as natural correlate to melancholy solitude and pastoral existence. He anticipates Manchette's characters in this perversion, but, crucially, with no element of serious social criticism.

Early in his prison interviews, Sweed recalls when he started killing. "I started when I had just turned nineteen, there in the wheat fields. I never thought that my age had anything to do with it. I just think you have to be conditioned for it" [J'ai commencé alors que je venais d'avoir dix-neuf ans aux blés. Remarquez que je n'ai jamais cru que l'âge avait quelque chose à voir dans le truc. Je crois seulement qu'il faut être conditionné pour].[10] Sweed is impotent as the result of a childhood injury, schoolmates mocked him, and he found refuge in violence: his alienation constitutes his conditioning. He recounts his violence as a near-equivalent for melancholic poetic expression in nineteenth-century romanticism. The nineteen-year-old wandering the fields is a commonplace of French romantic literature: at that age, Lamartine was complaining of *ennui* on the banks of the Saône, Chateaubriand was departing for America (where he compared fields of wheat to a "choir of pas-

---

8. That collection had until 1948 published only Anglophone crime fiction in translation; in fact, *La mort et l'ange*, written under an American pseudonym, pretends—with the collusion of the series editor—to be "translated from the American."

9. As Sweed observes, "I have a force that moves in me, I think that's all" [J'ai une force qui bouge en moi, et je crois que c'est tout]. Stewart, *La mort et l'ange*, 84. This line already mocks the countless romantic writers and characters who represented "force" as a vital and welcome creative energy.

10. Ibid., 21.

toral angels to whose help we have appealed" [comme le chœur des anges champêtres dont on a imploré le secours]), Hugo was composing his *Odes,* and Musset was "first taken by the illness of the century" [je fus pris d'abord de la maladie du siècle].¹¹ Sweed's amoral recountings of his actions echo the solitude, alienation, and discourse of these authors' romantic heroes, but in such a way as to cast himself passively as the biblical weed in the wheat field.¹² At another moment, referencing romantic fondness for nature in bloom and echoing the language of Genesis, Sweed says, "Every step I took, I had the chance to destroy someone. It grew in me like seeds in the ground" [A chaque pas que je faisais, j'avais une occasion de mettre quelqu'un en l'air. Ca venait à moi comme la semence dans la terre].¹³ Conscience for Sweed is an ironic negative rather than a basis for conscious subjectivity. His evocations of wheat fields and seeds in the ground route his violence through the discourse of scriptural inevitability, dismissing the accountable self.

Toward the end of the novel, he complains, "I have too many thoughts, too many shadows. It's like the plague and it's destroying me" [J'ai trop de pensées, trop d'ombres. C'est comme la peste et ça me démolit].¹⁴ Evocation of the plague further contributes to the sense that thoughts and shadows are visited upon the subject (or carrier) from above or at least from the outside. If his conscience is obscured by shadows, then he would have no control or even sense of his role in an evolving narrative, his own or others'. On the other hand, to call one's own murderousness a "plague" at the end of 1948, one year after Camus's famously allegorical novel, is to underscore the disingenuousness of the comparison and to cast the renunciation of responsibility as an ostentatiously sinister narrative choice. At the end of *La peste,* Rieux understands his story as one of "all those who, unable to be saints and refusing to submit to pestilences, tried their best to be healers" [tous les hommes qui, ne pouvant être des saints et refusant d'admettre les fléaux, s'efforcent cependant d'être des médecins],¹⁵ while Sweed represents assaults on the autonomous self as coming from wheat fields, earth, and pestilential shadows. What I mean to point out is that the 1940s *roman noir* abandonment of accountability—connected as it is in Manchette to the distortion of nineteenth-century character models—functioned as the foundation of social disorder rather than its product. What in the *roman noir* was the deliberate action of the unrepentant

11. Lamartine, *Correspondance,* 235; Vinet, *Chateaubriand,* 46; Chateaubriand, *Génie,* 2:381; Musset, *La confession d'un enfant du siècle,* 24. See also Chateaubriand's fascination with George Washington, who at nineteen commanded a Virginia militia (327).

12. Matthew 13:24–30.

13. Stewart, *La mort et l'ange,* 159.

14. Ibid., 173.

15. Camus, *La peste,* 279.

criminal returns in the *néo-polar* as the normal state of the "moveable pawn in a world that excludes him."

Both the French and the American post–hard-boiled traditions create an apparently tautological existential catastrophe: the principal "social" problem is a consistent sublimation of individual characters to social forces, and those forces are so powerful and problematic that the individual is made increasingly unable to stand up in their midst. Lou Ford consigns to some historicopsychological trash bin the Race Williams heroic model of empathic connection, transcendence of a traumatic past, and an instinctual ethical sense. Furthermore, by trotting out a traumatically overbearing father-panopticon and the specter of mental illness, he also undermines the very possibility of accountability, setting the scene for individual deterioration as a product—rather than a cause or correlative—of social or atmospheric deterioration. In the novels of Jean-Patrick Manchette, the dismantling of the heroic model uses a similar approach. First comes a point-by-point undoing of heroic characteristics, namely, an ethical sense of the aesthetic and its limits, a respect for French cultural and literary history, and an empathic and readerly interest in other people; second comes a blaming of that undoing on other forces, or, as Dominique Manotti puts it, a casting of "existential disenchantment" as an accompaniment to political disillusions ("l'effondrement des espérances politiques s'accompagne nécessairement d'un désenchantement existentiel").[16] Just as Thompson turns Leatherstocking into Lou Ford, so Manchette turns the desultory and melancholic aesthete of nineteenth-century romanticism into a bored, self-absorbed *spectacliste*. A moveable pawn seems in some sense helpless. And yet, as we will see, the *néo-polar* ultimately illuminates the role of individual character and responsibility just as much as the American post–hard-boiled.

LE NOUVEAU ROMAN POLICIER

In a formal sense, the reduction of the individual as accountable social creature—reduction of communication, of psychology, of personality—participates in a broader literary movement, analogous to the blurring of character in the French *nouveau roman*. As Ann Jefferson, Jean Ricardou, and others have pointed out, the *nouveau roman* enacts the "death of fictional character" and the institution of the "grammatical person."[17] As Robbe-Grillet stated,

---

16. Frommer and Oberti, "Dominique Manotti," 46.
17. Jefferson, *Nouveau Roman*, 58; Ricardou, *Pour une théorie du nouveau roman*.

The novel of characters belongs entirely to the past, it describes a period: that which marked the apogee of the individual. Perhaps this is not an advance, but it is evident that the present period is rather one of administrative numbers. The world's destiny has ceased, for us, to be identified with the rise or fall of certain men, of certain families. . . . To have a name was doubtless very important in the days of Balzac's bourgeoisie. A character was important—all the more important for being the weapon in a hand-to-hand struggle, the hope of a success, the exercise of a domination. It was something to have a face in a universe where personality represented both the means and the end of all exploration.[18]

Le roman de personnages appartient bel et bien au passé, il caractérise une époque: celle qui marqua l'apogée de l'individu. Peut-être n'est-ce pas un progrès, mais il est certain que l'époque actuelle est plutôt celle du numéro matricule. Le destin du monde a cessé, pour nous, de s'identifier à l'ascension ou à la chute de quelques hommes, de quelques familles. Le monde lui-même n'est plus cette propriété privée, héréditaire et monnayable, cette sorte de proie, qu'il s'agissait moins de connaître que de conquérir. Avoir un nom, c'était très important sans doute au temps de la bourgeoisie balzacienne. C'était important, un caractère, d'autant plus important qu'il était davantage l'arme d'un corps-à-corps, l'espoir d'une réussite, l'exercice d'une domination. C'était quelque chose d'avoir un visage dans un univers où la personnalité représentait à la fois le moyen et la fin de toute recherche.[19]

In Robbe-Grillet's assessment, the end of the *novel* of characters is an organic result of the end of the *world* of characters. The formal elements of the *nouveau roman* map out a world view, as the "death of the fictional character" echoes the demise of a certain sort of universe, of the "falsely reassuring map of human experience."[20] Patrick Raynal, an editor of the *Série noire,* in fact complained that the *nouveau roman* was mired in conceptualism and claimed realism and relevance for the *roman policier*:

You had to write under the "empire of the sign." That's what literature is officially becoming: Duras, Sollers, Robbe-Grillet, Butor, etc. Everything else is considered a little . . . low-rent, not really presentable . . . and a little stupid. The *roman noir,* but also all the literature that was really fictional, and every-

---

18. Robbe-Grillet, *For a New Novel,* 28.
19. Robbe-Grillet, *Pour un nouveau roman,* 28.
20. Gratton, "Postmodern French Fiction," 243.

thing that was excluded as "para-literature," started arguing, "Listen, we're novelists, and we just want to tell stories."

On ne peut plus écrire que sous "l'empire du signe." La littérature officielle deviant ça: Duras, Sollers, Robbe-Grillet, Butor, etc. Tout le reste est considéré comme un peu . . . merdeux, pas vraiment présentable . . . un peu bête, aussi. Le combat qu'a mené alors le roman noir, mais aussi, avec lui, toute la littérature vraiment Romanesque, et tout ce que, par exclusion, on a appelé "paralittérature," c'était en fait de dire, "Attention, nous sommes des romanciers, nous voulons simplement raconter des histoires."[21]

Despite this protestation, however, the *néo-polar* matches the *nouveau roman* in demonstrating that personality is not "the means and the end of all endeavor." It situates that negation in the context of social criticism: there is no room for a central personality, heroic or otherwise, in a period of "administrative numbers." But whereas the *nouveau roman* does much to dismantle character as formal construction, the *néo-polar* undermines character as an "inner source of action." It muddies the traditional concept of the individual and by extension the concept of accountability. And yet in the *néo-polar* those concepts continue to assert themselves and the genre ends up resuscitating, albeit in twisted form, the "novel of characters." "Regularities" take the form of absences (of innovation, enthusiasm, and reflection), but these absences are so systematic and relentless that the *néo-polar* ends up as a photographic negative of the abandoned nineteenth-century novel of characters, and the crisis to which Manchette alluded becomes a crisis of responsibility. In this chapter as in the previous one, I will concentrate primarily on one author and one novel. The principal character of *N'Gustro* is neither a detective nor a policeman, but a former soldier who had been stationed in Algeria. I will also consider two of Manchette's other novels, one a narration by a private detective, the other a third-person account of a professional assassin.

L'AFFAIRE N'GUSTRO

L'affaire N'Gustro (1971) is Manchette's first sole-authored novel, and it alternates between first- and third-person narration. In the first chapter, the principal character, Henri Butron, prepares to listen to a recording he has just

---

21. Raynal, "Le roman noir," 91–92.

made of his own life story, a story he finds fascinating.[22] But before he can listen to it, two men burst into the office and shoot him. They take the tape and deliver it to their boss, the *maréchal* Oufiri, who listens to the recording and laughs. The second chapter starts with Henri Butron narrating his life, starting in 1960 at the Lycée Pierre Corneille, where he studies philosophy before being arrested and joining the army. In the rest of the book, Butron's narration is interspersed with descriptions of his murderers listening to the recording of that narration. The novel is nominally about the murder of Ben Barka (the title's N'Gustro), a Moroccan opposition leader and head of the National Union of Popular Forces who disappeared in Paris in 1965. Butron serves as N'Gustro's bodyguard but eventually, through carelessness and boredom, turns him over to the people who murder him. In its titular plotline and in other narrative elements—clashes between youth groups to right and left, a military stint in Algeria, membership in the OAS—the novel would seem to concentrate on political phenomena of the 1960s rather than on character. And yet, the indisputable nucleus of the narrative is its main character and sometime narrator, Henri Butron. Dieudonné N'Gustro does not appear until two-thirds of the way through the novel, and he is much more an *affaire* than a character. Butron, on the other hand, is palpable and present. A disgruntled thug in the vein of *A Clockwork Orange*'s Alex, he is ostentatiously devoid of feeling and attachment, violent, unpleasant, antisocial, and smug. The character's antisocial nature, his violent tendencies, and his disdain for social conventions and human beings in general make him a sort of "man of the crowd" for a contaminated society—the center of a narrative that Franck Frommer called "one of the strangest French polars of the last thirty years" [l'un des polars français les plus étranges de ces trente dernières années].[23]

On the one hand, it seems obvious that the principal character in a world deadened by commercialism and 1968-era malaise would be antiheroic and antisocial. Butron's most obvious literary ancestors are Albert Camus's Meursault in *L'étranger* and Anthony Burgess's Alex in *A Clockwork Orange*. Other precedents include Stendhal's Julien Sorel, Maupassant's Georges Duroy in *Bel-Ami*,[24] Sartre's Lucien Fleurier in *L'enfance d'un chef*, Nimier's Olivier Malentraide in *Les enfants tristes*, and Céline's Ferdinand Bardamu in *Voyage au bout de la nuit*. These novels are not *polars* and do not (with the excep-

---

22. Manchette, *Romans noirs*, 125. Subsequent references to this work will be given parenthetically.

23. Frommer, "Jean-Patrick Manchette," 90–91.

24. Butron, like Duroy, is invited to cowrite with his lover an article about his time as a soldier in Algeria. Butron's would be titled "Le Retour du petit soldat," whereas Duroy's was titled "Les Souvenirs d'un chasseur d'Afrique."

tion of Stendhal) address questions of heroism as such. The *néo-polar* does, however, demonstrating that the strongest foundation for a demoralizing atmosphere is a demoralizing central character. And the strongest recipe for a demoralizing central character is the point-by-point elimination or perversion of those character traits that the culture has embraced as heroic, combined with the intimation that such elimination marks the decline of subjecthood and the inexorable disappearance of individual conscience.

In Butron's case, point-by-point dismantling of the nineteenth-century character model operates through a series of perversions of romanticism and spiritual authority. For instance, Chateaubriand warns against disrespect for God, parents, and nation: "He who renounces the God of his country is almost always a man with no respect for the memory of his forefathers; tombs do not interest him, he takes no pleasure in remembering his mother's words, her wisdom, her tastes" [Celui qui renie le dieu de son pays est presque toujours un homme sans respect pour la mémoire de ses pères; les tombeaux sont sans intérêt pour lui; il n'a aucun plaisir à se rappeler les sentences, la sagesse, et les goûts de sa mère].[25] Contrastingly, Butron declares, "Everyone for himself, and God for nobody" [Chacun pour soi et Dieu pour personne], calls his father and mother "old idiots" [vieux con/vieille conne], passes gas during his mother's funeral, and recalls that whereas he used to trust in the idea of a nation, "I hadn't really looked at what a putrid ant farm the Earth is. There are borders, sure, but all they do is make money for the people in charge" [J'avais pas bien regardé cette petite fourmilière puante qu'est la Terre. Il y a des frontières, certes, mais elles ne servent qu'à faire gagner de l'argent aux dirigeants] (152–53).

Butron is also uninterested in the pastoral scenes so popular with romantics: "I have no particular feeling about Nature, I only like seeing landscapes in the movies, I can tolerate sitting on a lawn if there's something to drink, but anyway, it's better than the grime and the suburbs" [Je n'ai aucun sentiment particulier à l'égard de la Nature, je n'aime les paysages sauvages qu'à voir au cinéma, je tolère les pelouses s'il y a à boire, mais en tout cas ça vaut mieux que les crasses et les banlieues] (213). He uses the flowered discourse of the romantics with Ben Sweed's sense of ridicule. As he watches the Amiral N'Gustro advance toward him: "His walk recalls temples swaying in an earthquake, at the start of some ancient cataclysm" [Sa démarche évoque le vacillement des temples en proie aux premières trémulations séismiques, dans quelque début de cataclysme antique] (193). The mention of an "ancient cat-

---

25. Chateaubriand, *Génie du christianisme*, 2:156.

aclysm" recalls nineteenth-century writings on the "ancient cataclysm that destroyed a godless world" [cataclysme antique qui causa la destruction d'un monde impie],[26] but the great swaying temple that is N'Gustro will be eliminated with Butron's help.

For Chateaubriand's narrator, "in bread and wine, we see the consecration of human nourishment that comes from God" [dans le pain et le vin matériels, on voit la consécration de la nourriture de l'homme, qui vient de Dieu].[27] In keeping with a God-centered sense of proportion, he also writes, "reflecting on the pointlessness of time, I thought only of eternity" [réfléchissant sur la vanité du temps, je n'ai plus songé qu'à l'éternité].[28] Butron echoes this sentiment about time's pointlessness, but without its humble associations or spiritual undertone: "All we have is a pathetic scrap of time, relative to eternity; so let's not sacrifice, let's enjoy the good things. Food, Beaujolais" [Nous n'avons qu'une parcelle dérisoire du temps, au regard de l'éternité; aussi, ne nous sacrifions pour rien, aimons les bonnes choses. La nourriture, le Beaujolais] (130). In a sense, this is a mere turning of spiritual sustenance into *nourritures terrestres*. But the departure of God-centered morality accompanies a more general contraction of communication, thought, and social consciousness. A "paranoid" reading might call this social criticism or point to the historical abandonment of virtue as an idea. I would instead call it the production of a *noir* atmosphere through calculated dismantling of the subject.

"I BELIEVE I WAS AFRAID . . ."

Butron confides to women that he tortured prisoners in Algeria, hoping to seduce them with interesting stories and existential woes. As he recounts in one instance, "I believe I was a bit afraid. Not of being punished. But of the idea that such things were even permitted, not just to me, but to all mankind. Mankind abandoned in space, on this pitiful little globe we call Earth" [Je crois que j'avais un peu peur. Non pas peur d'être puni. Mais peur à l'idée que de telles choses étaient permises, non seulement à moi, mais à l'Homme. L'Homme abandonné dans l'espace, sur ce petit globe dérisoire qu'on appelle la Terre] (136). This pretended distress at existential abandonment is a rather comic version of Chateaubriand's rendition of Tasso's warrior, standing in the

---

26. Lenoir, *Étude sur le spiritisme*, 30.
27. Chateaubriand, *Génie du christianisme*, 1:39.
28. Chateaubriand, *Œuvres*, 1:208.

light of the moon ("this beautiful globe" [ce beau globe]), "his face turned to the sky, as to his only hope. . . . His other hand rested humbly and piously on his chest, as if to ask God's pardon" [son visage tourné vers le ciel, comme le lieu de son unique espérance. . . . Son autre main, d'une manière humble et pieuse, reposait sur sa poitrine, et semblait demander pardon à Dieu].[29]

In addition to these general mockeries of romantic antecedents, Butron also reverses Nestor Burma's hard-boiled cultural ambassadorship, with its respect for literature and literary history, awareness of the ethical parameters of the aesthetic, and readerly interest in others. Manchette's protagonist disdains historical monuments: "I wander around my neighborhood at night pissing on monuments, especially the one with the stone guy and his stupid placard: Art inscribes a symbol within a dogma, or some somber crap like that" [J'erre dans mon quartier la nuit, compissant les monuments, notamment celui où il y a le gustave de pierre avec sa petite pancarte de merde: L'Art, c'est inscrire un symbole dans un dogme, ou quelque sombre péterie du même genre] (196). This scene evokes Simone de Beauvoir's recollection of Sartre urinating on Chateaubriand's tomb ("Chateaubriand's tomb seemed so ridiculously pompous in its false simplicity that to show his contempt, Sartre pissed on it" [Le tombeau de Chateaubriand nous sembla si ridiculement pompeux dans sa fausse simplicité que, pour marquer son mépris, Sartre pissa dessus]).[30] Sartre had also said that his "first encounters with Beauty" came through popular writers like Arnould Galopin (creator of the Ténébras phantom bandit and the detective Allan Dickson), rather than through the well-constructed phrases of Chateaubriand.[31] His contempt for the tomb's pomposity, like Butron's contempt for the "stupid placard," falls in line with néo-polar political critiques and underscores the familial connections between the roman noir and existentialism. But Butron's theories of art and subjectivity are themselves pastiches of existentialism, and as narrator, he uses all such isms to undercut the thoughtful subject. Art for him is a dull consolation in the absence of violence.[32] Time means nothing to him (184), nor does individual existence (189).

---

29. Chateaubriand, Génie du christianisme, 2:303.
30. de Beauvoir, La force de l'âge, 114.
31. Sartre, Les mots, 57.
32. "We made a plan to meet at the CineClub and see Hiroshima mon amour. I remember hoping there would be sex and violence, with a title like that. I was disappointed on that score, but I must admit the movie is a work of art" [Nous prenons rendez-vous pour aller au ciné-club voir Hiroshima mon amour. Je me rappelle que j'espérais qu'il y aurait du cul et de la violence, avec un titre pareil. Ce soir je serai bien déçu, à ce point de vue, mais je dois reconnaître que le film est une œuvre d'art] (114).

Pleasure, unsurprisingly, is ostentatiously detached from ethical concerns. With this detachment, Butron undoes not just the romantic model but also the principal characteristics and ethical resonance of Nestor Burma. In a street brawl, he is disturbed by the unpleasant sounds his wounded opponent is making (140). When the police arrest him, he finds pleasure in pain: "I'm not gay or a masochist, but I admit it feels good to be roughed up by a bunch of strong brutes, especially your intellectual inferiors" [Je ne suis pas pédé ni maso, mais je dis franchement qu'il y a de la jouissance à être manipulé brutalement par un groupe de fortes brutes, surtout quand elles vous sont inférieures intellectuellement] (132). Instead of the comic understatement found in *120, rue de la Gare,* this "jouissance" is a perverse performance of dissociation. Butron finds even more gratification in perpetrating violence, stealing a man's car and beating him with its tire jack (131). When in another episode he sees an wounded policeman, he is pleased at the chance to do further violence: "The officer is crawling on the ground, barely conscious and covered in blood. I rush in all excited and kick him in his filthy, bleeding face. When I get home, there's a tooth between the upper and the sole of my shoe . . . . My spirits are high. I couldn't care less about politics, but life has got some pretty good moments" [L'officier rampe à terre, peu conscient, tout sanglant, je me rue joyeux, je botte la face immonde et qui dégoutte. Rentrant chez moi, entre empeigne et semelle de ma pompe bon marché, je trouve une dent, une canine, net cassée. . . . Mon âme est très légère. Je me fous de la politique, mais il y a de bons moments dans la vie] (185). What separates N'Gustro from the existential continuum, even as he has literary predecessors there, is his resolute jollity and the unapologetic directness of his violence. Butron as narrator mocks and imitates the "nauseous" existentialist, thereby demonstrating, ironically, what Chateaubriand had warned against: poetic verbosity devoid of "that moral tint without which nothing is perfect."

On the one hand, some of Butron's discourse ("I believe I was afraid . . .") is not much different from any other instance of disingenuous seduction. What is innovative about Butron is that while he uses romantic language without meaning it, he also contemplates—or pretends to contemplate—his own character, his own value, his existence. These contemplations focus on character as such—the "fictional character" that Robbe-Grillet outlined as well as Currie's "Character" as compendium of attributes—as a narrative center, even while intimating that that center is hollow. Pretenses at introspection reveal the absence of a "there" there, but this is Butron's narrative point. In the end, the novel reveals, it takes an accountable subject to dismantle itself, and that dismantling is Butron's masterpiece.

THE UNCONSCIOUS

Butron can be read as the aggressively self-conscious embodiment of a lost generation, a sort of modern cipher. His interest in speed, violence, sex, and movies and his constant undercurrent of ennui echo the dull roar of television, consumerism, and the *société de spectacle*. But when we approach Butron not as a cipher but rather as a narrator eager to look like a cipher, we can discern a deliberate dismantling of heroism and subjecthood. Butron's most exploratory statements about his own character and worth are at the same time the most obfuscatory for the notion of character as well as responsibility. Musing on his interviews with Jacquie Gouin, his occasional lover and mother of his girlfriend Anne, he says, "I can't honestly say that I've hatched a long-term plan for forging my personality, but I'm sure it's already there, guiding me unconsciously. I believe in the unconscious" [Je peux pas dire à présent en toute franchise qu'un plan à long terme pour forger mon propre personnage a d'ores et déjà éclos dans mon cerveau, mais je suis sûr que c'est déjà ça qui me guide inconsciemment. Je crois à l'inconscient] (153). The unconscious in this formula is the guiding motor, invisible but ever-present, that creates his character. But for Butron, the unconscious is less a fountain of ideas than a convenient straw man, a scapegoat for possible accusations. When he sets up N'Gustro to be intercepted and "disappeared," Butron cites the unconscious again: "I am ready to swear that part of me knew what was going to happen. An unconscious part of me. I very much believe in the unconscious, in Freudianism and things like that" [Je suis prêt à jurer qu'une partie de moi-même savait ce qui allait arriver. Une partie inconsciente de moi-même. Je crois beaucoup à l'inconscient, au freudisme et à ce genre de choses] (220).

Butron's shambolic ode to the unconscious, which devolves instantly into a mention of "Freudianism and things like that," recalls that Flaubertian character famous for wandering into abstractions and incarnating culture's dullest common denominator. (It is not surprising that Flaubert, incomparable when it came to putting blame everywhere and nowhere, finds such echoes in Butron.) Flaubert's pharmacist Homais, a noncharacter or postcharacter *avant la lettre*, defends his religion much as Butron defends his unconscious: "I believe in the supreme Being, in a Creator, whatever he is, it doesn't matter to me, who put us here to do our duty as citizens and fathers" [Je crois en l'Être suprême, à un Créateur, quel qu'il soit, peu m'importe, qui nous a placés ici-bas pour y remplir nos devoirs de citoyen et de père de famille].[33] The falling apart of sentence content, from the precise "supreme Being" to the

---

33. Flaubert, *Madame Bovary*, 116.

still proper-named but unspecified "a Creator," to the even vaguer "whatever he is, it doesn't matter," is mirrored in Butron's slide from "the unconscious" to "Freudianism" to the broad and indistinct "things like that." To "believe" in the unconscious and in "things like that" is as absurdist as it was for Homais to believe in "the supreme Being, in a Creator, whatever he is, it doesn't matter," made more ridiculous in the curious detail that Butron believes in the unconscious "very much." In the hands of this narrator, the unconscious seems as incoherent a source of belief as was God in the secularizing nineteenth century.[34]

To continue to use Flaubert as point of reference, as a window onto character-as-absent narrative center, we can consider what Flaubert wrote about God in a letter to Louise Colet: "The author in his work should be like God in the universe, everywhere present but visible nowhere. Because art is a second nature, the creator of that second nature must proceed like that of the first: in all its atoms, in all its aspects, one must sense a hidden and infinite impassivity" [L'auteur dans son œuvre doit être comme Dieu dans l'univers, présent partout et visible nulle part. L'art étant une seconde nature, le créateur de cette nature-là doit agir par des procédés analogues: que l'on sente dans tous les atomes, à tous les aspects, une impassibilité cachée et infinie].[35] Jonathan Culler, reading that invisibility as an element of Flaubert's deliberate "uncertainties," proposed: "It is not so much God's objectivity Flaubert desires as his absence: the world will be totalized in a negative fashion, its order shown to be that of an ironic joke, but the author of that joke will be as difficult to pin down as the God who for so many centuries managed to escape, with the aid of his theologians, his obvious responsibility for the world's evil."[36] In *L'affaire N'Gustro,* it is Butron, deconstructing his character, evoking the unconscious and orchestrating his own diffuse absence, who bears responsibility for trouble in the novel. "Everyone for himself and God for nobody," claims Butron: God is absent from this novel, but human agency is alive and well. What Gregory Currie called "regularities of behavior that are robust under variation of circumstance" dominate the story, even though the regularities in question are negative, the actions violent, and the words indifferent, but the individual as such, as actor and conscious subject, is nonetheless the definite center. Similar to Flaubert's "difficult to pin down"

---

34. Gérault writes of Manchette, "His goal, like Flaubert, like Dashiell Hammett, is to describe and stigmatize a bourgeois society that he finds hypocritical, corrupt, and stifling" [Son but est, comme Flaubert, comme Dashiell Hammett, de décrire et stigmatiser une société bourgeoise qu'il trouve à la fois hypocrite, corrompue et étouffante]. Gérault, *Jean-Patrick Manchette,* 32.

35. Flaubert, *Œuvres complètes,* 2:204.

36. Culler, *Flaubert,* 79.

or absent God, "difficult to pin down" or seemingly absent individual subjectivity is the nucleus of the *néo-polar*'s *noir* vision.

The unconscious in Manchette's novel is rather indistinct as a choreographer of personality. And yet, in invoking the unconscious, Butron has done what Ford did with discussions of his sickness and his panoptical father: placed an escape valve in the coherent outlines of his character, a reason to read him as a series of personality fragments and dismiss him, to abandon the hope of understanding him, and certainly of holding him to account. Whereas Lou Ford raised the diagnosis of dementia praecox, Butron evoked a deliberately confounding but culturally resonant discourse of psychoanalysis, existentialist philosophies, and situationist social criticisms to cloud the parameters of his own accountability. In fact, numerous similarities between Butron and Ford as characters, narrators, and erasers help make the case that Butron's literary and sometimes Sartrean musings are carefully designed to eviscerate accountability. Both men are emotionally volatile sons of doctors, both are resentful of their fathers' authority, both sit in their fathers' chairs, drinking coffee, smoking cigarettes, and looking at themselves in their fathers' mirrors.[37] Ford though remained a stronger master of the narration, compared to Butron. Lou Ford narrates until the end of *The Killer Inside Me,* rather than being murdered in the first chapter as Butron was, but more than this, he sounds as though he is in control even as he evokes the morbid psychiatric ailments that theoretically obviate control. For Ford, being in his father's home office "was like coming out of the darkness into sunlight, out of a storm into calm" (27). Butron, on the other hand, comes undone in his father's house: "I kick the copper umbrella stand against the front door. The umbrellas go all over. I laugh and go into the kitchen, where I make a Nescafé. I have this idea to shit all over the carpets. I get hold of myself" [D'un coup de pied j'envoie rouler contre la porte d'entrée le porte-parapluies décoré en cuivre. Les pébroques se répandent. Je ricane et passe dans la cuisine où je me fais un Nescafé. Je suis dévoré par l'idée de chier partout sur les tapis. Je me maîtrise] (147).

As narrators, both characters address the reader and defend their gradual narrative expositions. "I haven't said anything yet about the N'Gustro affair. Wait. I have to set the scene" [Je n'ai pas dit un mot encore de l'affaire N'Gustro. Patientez. Tout le décor doit être mis en place] (170). And then, "I prom-

---

37. After his father's death, recounts Butron, "I smoke while I shave, always looking in the mirrors" (147) [je fume en me rasant, je ne cesse de me regarder dans les miroirs]. Writes Lou Ford, "The phone rang. I wiped my hands against my pants, and answered it, looking at myself in the laboratory mirror—at the guy in the black bow tie and the pink-tan shirt, his trouser legs hooked over his boot tops" (108).

ise I'm getting to it now" [Promis je relate à présent] (197). Lou Ford, having announced that he killed Amy Stanton, also insists on sound narrative methodology: "I'll tell you everything. But I want to get everything in the right order. I want you to understand how it was" (180). Both narrators insist that they are honest and sincere. Butron says, "I don't have to lie now. I have a fully developed life, I can be sincere because I've attained great authority" [Je n'ai pas besoin de mentir à présent. Ma vie s'est développée et je puis être sincère parce que j'ai acquis une grande souveraineté] (160). This declared candor echoes Lou Ford's "I want to tell you, and I will, exactly how it happened" (179). Butron's grandiose sincerity, however, recalls nothing so much as the "pompous false simplicity" of Chateaubriand's tomb—an amoral fascination with his own discursivity.

Butron functions as the French counterpart to Ford in his evasion of accountability, but he accomplishes that evasion through a particularly French postexistentialist discourse, one based on the early nineteenth-century model of the bored, languishing romantic. It is in that persona that he addresses the political idea of the individual as a product of circumstances. At the same time, he pretends to refuse that idea, to claim "great authority." Where Ford claims dementia praecox but evinces cold and emotionless calculation, Butron claims control but evinces disorder: "I get hold of myself" declares a control that his narrative and his actions do not actually demonstrate. On the one hand, that lack of control has a political cast—Butron is a right-wing character in the hands of a left-wing author, who could use Butron to ridicule right-wing insistence on individual responsibility. But on the other hand, and more broadly, Butron reveals "everyone for himself and God for nobody" to be the foundation of, rather than the response to, dismantled individual accountability.

INDIVIDUAL VALUE

As Pierre Zima wrote, discussing Marcel Proust's combination of psychology and psychoanalysis, "The fundamental and indelible difference that separates the *Recherche* from traditional psychological novels must be understood in terms of the difference between psychoanalysis and the 'philosophical' psychology of the seventeenth or eighteenth century. In psychoanalysis, ambivalence is so strong that the individual's identity and the very notion of the Subject are put in question" [La différence fondamentale et ineffaçable qui sépare la 'Recherche' des romans psychologiques traditionnels devrait être comprise parallèlement à la différence entre la psychologie "philosophique" du XVII ou du XVIIIe siècle et la psychanalyse. Dans cette dernière, l'ambivalence est si forte que l'identité de l'individu et la notion du Sujet elle-même sont remises en question].[38] Once the unconscious is evoked, Butron's actions cease to be the character's principal problem, and instead his being, the parameters of self, the invisibility of his motivations, and the "very notion of the Subject" become themselves the problem. Butron's search for motivation and understanding, quite by design, goes nowhere and discovers nothing. When another character questions his reasons and his empathic capacities, he switches back to an old-school protection of character as pure formal entity resistant to examination. Jacquie accuses, "'It's not possible,' she continues, 'to be that alone and egotistical, it becomes a mental illness. Because you don't grasp other people's feelings, you don't even know that those feelings exist, because you don't have any. And sooner or later, to have no heart, it's like not having any intelligence'" ['C'est pas possible,' poursuit-elle, 'seul à ce point, tellement égoïste, ça devient de l'infirmité mentale. Parce que tu ne connais pas les sentiments d'autrui tu ne sais même pas qu'ils existent, parce que tu en manques toi, tu en manques tellement. Et un moment, le manque de cœur, ça devient comme le manque d'intelligence' (175)]. Butron merely warns her not to insult his intelligence.[39] The questioning of subjectivity comes to a dead end when the Subject as such refuses to be questioned, and instead asserts its pure solidity as agent of thought and action.

In his most philosophical monologue, Butron announces,

> I couldn't care less about the masses. Only Butron Henri interests me, the masses won't save him. What do I have in common with those office and factory guys? Exactly, says Anne, that proves that your problem is social. If she were to be believed, I was the product of circumstances. Listening to her, I was the product of circumstances, their toy. That's what they all say. To make excuses for me. I don't need any excuse. I'm happy with what I've done. I know my value. And we were people of value. We had abandoned things and ideas that got in the way of pleasure. And all ideas get in the way of pleasure, I say.

> Je me fous de la grande masse. Butron Henri seul m'intéresse, c'est pas la grande masse qui le sauvera. Qu'est-ce que vous voudriez que j'aie de commun avec les mecs des bureaux, des usines? Précisément, me racontait Anne, c'est ce qui prouve qu'il est social, ton problème. À l'en croire, j'étais

---

le produit des circonstances. Qu'est-ce que j'ai pu l'entendre dire, que j'étais le produit des circonstances, et leur jouet. Tous ils reprenaient la chanson. Pour m'excuser. J'ai jamais eu besoin d'être excusé. Ce que j'ai fait, je suis content. J'ai conscience de ma valeur. Car nous étions des gens de valeur. Nous avions rompu avec les choses, avec les idées qui empêchent de jouir. Toutes les idées empêchent de jouir, je dis. (181–82)

In this meandering articulation of value and entitlement, Butron bounces from one ontological framework to another, from one conception of character to another. It is worth a moment to untangle these, since this one paragraph contains numerous contradictory visions of character and a shrewd undoing of conscience. Butron starts out by asserting that he has nothing in common with factory and office workers; he does not mention what sets him apart, but Anne diagnoses a general "social problem," a misanthropic alienation. When Anne notes that Henri's problem is social, she means that he fails to connect with other people, to feel and act as a social being. Furthermore, since Anne's principal interest is in social commonality for political purposes—in a solidarity with "office and factory guys" that stands to improve the conditions of workers—Butron's social problem, his inability to form social connections, becomes a "social problem" in the sense of a problem affecting society and social justice causes. But because Anne's mention of Butron's "social problem" is followed immediately by "To listen to her, I was the product of circumstances," it is clear that Butron reads the directionality of the "social problem" differently than Anne does. He essentially hears "social problem" as "a problem that society has caused," a problem whose source resides outside him, and in any case, a problem he denies. From there, however, Butron (who introduces himself in the third person) wanders into a confounding compilation of positive assertions and emphatic denials.

On the one hand, his insistence that "I don't need any excuse. I'm happy with what I've done" denies the blaming of circumstances and hints instead at justification and even pride in his actions. In this sense, Butron departs from Lou Ford, claiming an individual agency that Thompson's character sometimes evaded. The next phrase, however, in which he claims to "know his value," abandons the topic of agency as such and celebrates the dominance of pure and formal individual worth. This statement echoes somewhat Sartre's "existence precedes essence," but having "value" or being conscious of one's value cannot constitute a coherent alternative to needing to be "excused." It might make sense as an alternative to needing to be praised, for instance, but to claim consciousness of value—rather than of actions, responsibility, or identity—as an alternative to "needing to be excused" is to slip from the realm of actions and characteristics, which might be held to ethical standards and thus necessitate excuse, to the realm of the individual as pure fact. To return to Lukács's description of the novelistic character as resident of a secular world, "The inner importance of the individual has reached its historical apogee: the individual is no longer significant as the carrier of transcendent worlds, as he was in abstract idealism, he now carries his value exclusively within himself."[40] So too does Butron carry his value exclusively within himself, but that value, cited as an antidote not to a meaning-giving God but to a need for excuse, has nothing to do with the "inner importance of the individual." It is more along the lines of "value" as situated within the frame of existentialist philosophies. As Sartre writes, "Value is affected with the double character, which moralists have very inadequately explained, of both being unconditionally and not being" [La valeur, en effet, est affectée de ce double caractère, que les moralistes ont fort incomplètement expliqué, d'être inconditionnellement et de n'être pas].[41] Butron's use of the word amplifies the ambiguities in this discourse, particularly with first-person plural that lacks antecedent. Indeed, this character's interest in "value" is limited throughout the novel to money. With these evocations of value generated in the view of others, value generated in one's own estimation, value generated by the pure fact of existence, and value generated by the consumer market, ideas of "value" cancel each other out, as each replaces—at least for the duration of its utterance—the others. When Butron then declares, "We had abandoned things and ideas that got in the way of pleasure," he has wandered away both from the claim of value and from the resistance to excuses, returning to value-free pleasure and to his person as pure locus of sensation.

Here, as in Thompson, the character is narrating himself into a deliberate abstraction, into value without substance, words without intention, actions without emotion, pronouns without antecedents. On the one hand, the introduction of the lexicon of psychoanalysis, nascent discourses on self-esteem, sociological forces, and consumerism can be read as a political statement—a presentation of the individual within a corrupt social frame. Manchette was a partisan of the Situationist International, a compendium of existentialism, Marxism, anarchy, and avant-garde art whose principal text, Guy Debord's *La société du spectacle,* articulated the alienating and inauthentic nature of contemporary life. Using as a point of departure the idea of spectacle, Debord

---

40. Lukács, *Theory of the Novel,* 117.

41. Sartre, *Being and Nothingness,* 68; *L'être et le néant,* 136. Writes Benoît Pruche, "Ma valeur est mise en cause et je me vois ramené à des questions fondamentales: quelle est ma place dans l'Univers? Qui pourrait me l'annoncer, sinon les autres?" Pruche, *Existant et acte d'être,* 29.

described society ("a carnivorous plant" [une plante carnivore], according to
May 1968 graffiti) as placing numerous obstacles between human beings and
reality. In a phrase reminiscent of Manchette's antiteleologies and of Butron's
anti-ambition, Debord writes: "Society based on modern industry . . . is fundamentally *spectacliste*. In the spectacle, image of the reigning economy, the
goal is nothing, development is everything" [La société qui repose sur l'in-
dustrie moderne . . . est fondamentalement spectacliste. Dans le spectacle,
image de l'économie regnante, le but n'est rien, le développement est tout].[42]
It is tempting to see Butron as the voice and face of *spectacliste* inauthenticity. Indeed, his interest in movie making and in money—and in making
money through movies—supports this reading. It is also tempting to concur
with Anne and read Butron's claims on his value as the confused ramblings
of a selfish character with a "social problem," one whose difficulties in relat-
ing to others are matched by his difficulties in communicating. But for all
the obfuscation that arises around this character, and indeed because of that
obfuscation, the traditional individual continues to arise and assert itself.
Butron embraces the unconscious but avoids self-examination, declines to
be excused but resists accepting responsibility, and claims to be a person
of value while pointing out that so is everyone else. And yet, at the same
time, his posturings, interventions, and eventual demise align with what
Robbe-Grillet called the "novel of characters." Like Stendhal's Julien Sorel,
who promises to "only count on the parts of my character that I've tested"
[je ne compterai que sur les parties de mon caractère que j'aurai éprouvées]
and to "only say things that he believed to be false" [des choses qui lui sem-
blaient fausses à lui-même],[43] Butron enters the French army determined to
"hold onto my convictions, my revolt. The main thing was that I would learn
to keep those inside as I launched myself into the social world" [J'y pourrais
garder mes convictions, ma révolte; l'essentiel était que j'apprendrais à les
conserver au-dedans de moi-même tandis que je me lancerais dans le jeu
social] (133). The end of Butron's life also resembles that of his 1830 predecessor. At the end of *N'Gustro*, Butron, who has brawled relentlessly through
the entire narrative, declines a friend's gun when he is actually in danger,
preferring to wait alone in the dark. "He wanted to leave me his gun. Maybe
I should have accepted, but I was sick of asking other people for help. It's
me they're trying to kill. So it's me who should face it. Sitting in the dark, I
am content" [Il voulait me laisser son flingue. J'aurais peut-être dû l'accep-

---

42. Debord, *Œuvres*, 769. A. D. G., a rare right-wing author of the *roman noir*, read such
contextualizations as so many attempts at excuse: "A. D. G. attacks the decadence of modern
urban life and decries the hypocrisy of those who would sooner blame the ills of society than
the individual who commits the crime." Johnston and Marshall, *France and the Americas*, 321.

43. Stendhal, *Le rouge et le noir*, 97, 216.

ter, mais j'en avais marre de faire appel aux autres. C'est moi, pas eux, qu'on essaie de détruire. C'est moi qui riposte, c'est justice. Assis dans le noir, je suis content] (228). Because Butron is murdered in the first chapter, the entire narrative draws him to his death, aligning him with other protagonists who meditate on the eve of execution. For instance, in the prison interlude in *Le rouge et le noir,* Julien Sorel, unwilling to appeal his death sentence, "felt strong and resolute, like a man who sees clearly into his soul" [se sentait fort et résolu comme l'homme qui voit clair dans son âme].[44] That same peace in solitude appears in the last paragraph of Camus's *L'étranger,* when Meursault (Julien Sorel's twentieth-century descendant, whom Butron also echoes in his apathetic funeral attendance) awaits execution: "Sounds of the country-side were drifting in. Smells of night, earth, and salt air were cooling my temples. The wondrous peace of that sleeping summer flowed through me like a tide. Then, in the dark hour before dawn, sirens blasted. They were announcing departures for a world that now and forever meant nothing to me" [Des bruits de campagne montaient jusqu'à moi. Des odeurs de nuit, de terre et de sel rafraîchissaient mes tempes. La merveilleuse paix de cet été endormi entrait en moi comme une marée. À ce moment, et à la limite de la nuit, des sirènes ont hurlé. Elles annonçaient des départs pour un monde qui maintenant m'était à jamais indifférent].[45]

Butron's reference to his value similarly recalls *L'étranger*'s prison medita-tions. As Meursault muses:

> But I was sure about me, about everything, sure of my life and sure of the death I had waiting for me. Yes, that was all I had. But at least I had as much of a hold on that truth as it had on me. I had been right, I was still right, I was always right. I had lived my life one way and I could just as well have lived it another. I had done this and I hadn't done that. I hadn't done one thing and I had done another. And so? It was as if I had waited all this time for this moment and for the first light of dawn to be vindicated.[46]

> Mais j'étais sûr de moi, sûr de tout, plus sûr que lui, sur ma vie et de cette mort qui allait venir. Oui, je n'avais que cela. Mais du moins, je tenais cette

---

44. Ibid., 653.

45. Camus, *The Stranger,* 122; *Œuvres completes,* 117. Writes Franck Frommer: "Manchette veut aller tellement loin dans la transgression et l'exercice de style, qu'il choisit un narrateur fascistoïde, petit mec sans envergure et indifférent (avec une référence explicite, dans une scène d'enterrement, au Meursault de *L'étranger*), mais dans la personnalité duquel se font jour toutes les contradictions politiques, économiques et sociales de cette fin des années gaulliennes," Frommer, "Jean-Patrick Manchette," 91.

46. Camus, *The Stranger,* trans. Matthew Ward, 120–21.

vérité autant qu'elle me tenait. J'avais eu raison, j'avais encore raison, j'avais toujours raison. J'avais vécu de telle façon et j'aurais pu vivre de telle autre. J'avais fait ceci et je n'avais pas fait cela. Je n'avais pas fait telle chose alors que j'avais fait cette autre. Et après? C'était comme si j'avais attendu pendant tout le temps cette minute et cette petite aube où je serais justifié.[47]

I have cited these echoes of prison meditation and insisted on this line of character ancestry because *Le rouge et le noir* and *L'étranger* are character-driven narratives, focused on a character who clashes with his culture (Julien) or whose insistent alienation sounds the end of the *Bildungsroman* (Meursault). Butron, on the other hand, would seem to live in a world whose thematic foundation is that the individual, truncated and disillusioned at every turn, is more or less beside the point. This does not just mean that he abandons the pursuit of good character, although he does. The point is that the idea of examining character itself as a narrative nucleus, as the locus of action and point of the story—this too recedes. And yet, as much as Butron obscures the *idea* of character, his actions, words, and attitudes are remarkably consistent. His emphatic and precise reversals of the romantic ideal, discussed earlier in this chapter, and his reversals of the classic hard-boiled model, his cruelty to men and women, friends and lovers, not to mention the death of N'Gustro that he all but orchestrates, reveal a narrative intentionality that paints the entire *noir* decline, the entire crisis that the *néo-polar* chronicles, as centered on personal agency.

THE INDIVIDUAL AND THE FRENCH STATE

Compared with Nestor Burma's embodiment of literary historical and cultural memory, Butron's lack of appreciation of French culture as such can be read in part as an indictment of that culture. Manchette's novels are consistently described as containing mordant social criticism, but this raises the question of what "social criticism" actually means. For one, there is not much "society" in the conventional sense going on in Manchette's novels. Populated towns, places of employment, and even family units are absent. Characters appear in bars, cars, streets, beaches, each other's apartments, evidence of a population in transition or at sea—in a sense, the individuals in Manchette's fiction seem more to be sharing a habitat than forming a society. Except when a dense crowd functions as a grotesque *corps de ballet* in brawls or explosion

---

47. Camus, *Œuvres complètes*, 117.

scenes—succumbing to or reeling in the face of catastrophe is one of the last and best remaining communal activities in Manchette's world—a critical mass of people participating in social conventions is markedly absent from Manchette's fiction. Indeed, even social solidarity is missing. "Social" in the *néo-polar* carries instead an elemental and anthropological cast, one that emerges, and whose failings are underscored, any time that individuals come into contact with one another. The basic mechanisms that allow people to live among others—communication, consciousness of others as others, listening, some minimal participation in communal structures—all come apart in the *néo-polar*. The individual character in the *néo-polar* ceases to be a social creature in most senses of the word: not just disillusioned, not just corrupted, but blurred, washed out, reduced, and disconnected. Manchette's society, then, means a group of individuals, and this simple definition undermines the complex ideological models that his characters continue to reference. A society in decline means the decline of the individual as sentient and social being.

While the American hard-boiled model devolves into unromantic individualism without the intervention of culture as such, the French *néo-polar* lays its troubles at the feet of a culture in decline. In a sense, the fact that the blurring of "character" corresponds to a social problem—and that both connect to a devolution of the French character model—has to do with a specifically French symbiosis between individual identity and cultural identity. While personality and character always depends to some extent on social interaction (otherwise personality and character become as trees in an unseen forest), French political culture conceives of the state as inextricably intertwined with individual identity. As Stewart Field notes, "the state has defended and inculcated particular ideas of the nation and *république* in which are expressed positive abstract notions of France and Frenchness."[48] These notions are not demanded just of civil servants, but also of regular citizens—individuals like Butron who might have no particular interest in representing or being represented by the state. In other words, an individual's failure to represent the state ("I couldn't care less about politics") does not just cause a decline to society, it *is* that decline. As Jacqueline Hodgson writes, "At the heart of the French republican tradition, as it might broadly be described, is the sovereignty of the French people and as the only body to enjoy the mandate of these citizens (through the election of politicians), this power is exercised in practice by the state, as the nation's representative. In this way, sovereignty of the people becomes sovereignty of the state."[49] The idea that

---

48. Field, "State, Citizen, and Character," 542.
49. Hodgson, *French Criminal Justice,* 16.

sovereignty of the people becomes sovereignty of the state refers at a basic level to practical consolidation of power. Sovereignty of the state, in other words, is supposed to render in unadulterated form a people's sovereignty that would, without that rendering, remain necessarily theoretical for lack of embodiment and consolidation. But underneath that notion of equivalence or embodiment is a more literal resonance of *becoming,* one that implies an instinctive or intuitive manner, an individual interiority that morphs into part of the state. When Henri Butron declares that he doesn't care about politics and opines that the apparently functioning state is a "putrid ant farm," the symbiosis between individual and state still stands. As Müller writes of the antiheroes of French crime fiction, "They are unhappy and their unhappiness belongs to society" [Ils sont malheureux et leur malheur est celui de la société].[50] This comment echoes Hodgson's remark that "the sovereignty of the people becomes the sovereignty of the state," simply in negative form, for it is nihilism, not sovereignty, that the *néo-polar* projects.

MORGUE PLEINE

Henri Butron uses ostentatiously vacuous philosophical posturing to undercut the notion of accountability. But his methodical undoing of classic romantic and hard-boiled characteristics—actions that could be put down to his simple antiheroism—are just as present in Manchette's other characters, professional assassins or private detectives. I will examine two more instances of that undoing so as further to illustrate the paradoxical power and centrality of the *néo-polar's* apparently "moveable pawn." Going in chronological order, I will look now at the novel that most closely resembles a classic detective novel in its formal construction. This is *Morgue pleine,* published in 1973, featuring Eugène Tarpon, former *gendarme* turned private detective. Tarpon also appears in *Que d'os!* (1976). In both novels, the character gives an impression of fadedness. Whereas Butron's blurriness was conceptual, a product of garbled pseudo-introspection, Tarpon's incompleteness is in the domain of affect. In action, word, thought, understanding, and communication, he seems washed out, though he is present in every scene. Bored lassitude is a common pose in the hard-boiled, and it recalls the studied indifference of Nestor Burma in his understatements of the camp experience. But whereas Burma pursues the criminals, understands the crime, and announces his collected research to the assembled group, Tarpon bumbles through all of

---

50. Müller and Ruoff, *Le polar français,* 76.

Morgue pleine. We learn that during his police days, he shot a demonstrator, but his remorse emerges as vague bewilderment. When he shoots another man in the course of the investigation, "So once again I'd killed someone and didn't know why. I thought I was going to be sick" [Comme ça, j'avais encore tué quelqu'un et je ne savais pas pourquoi, de nouveau. J'ai cru que j'allais être malade] (521). We learn that he is contemplating returning to the country to live with his mother, but he abandons this plan. When a client comes to his office looking for help, a drunken Tarpon declares that nothing can be done, punches him in the stomach, and sends him on his way. At the end of the novel, he wants to find the client: "I wanted to tell him not to give up hope, that I'd take his case, basically that there were ways to keep on swimming and paddling in this messed-up world" [Je voulais lui dire de ne pas désespérer, que je voulais bien m'occuper de son affaire, somme toute, qu'il y avait encore moyen de nager et de se dépatouiller, dans cette chierie d'univers] (578). He never does find him.

Tarpon's contributions to the novel's *noir* atmospheric bleakness are his lethargy, hesitation, and confusion. He is an agent of reaction rather than of action. When he hits someone, "I hit him because he scared me" [Je l'avais cogné parce qu'il m'avait fait peur], he admits, though he has not even won the fight and is immediately cornered by another gunman (491). When he meets with the murder victim's father, the man's tears "freaked me out" [Il me foutait les jetons] (495). His most consistent experience is one of disorientation. He is unsure what is happening, he feels incoherent (494), he doesn't know what to do (491), he decides he can't do anything (492), and he doesn't understand what people are saying (512). The woman who had sought his help when her roommate was murdered had this assessment: "You're in the dark, huh?" [Vous êtes dans le noir, hein?] (535). The "noir" that surrounds Tarpon is more incomprehension than menace, directionless as the fish for which he is named. As the novel opens, he is depressed (453). As he alienates and then punches the only client who has come to see him, he is ashamed, and when the client leaves, "I started really drinking" [Je me suis vraiment mis à boire] (464).

Physically, Tarpon is awkward and almost clownish. "He slid down the stairs like a luge, and I slid down on top of him, like in the 'Seven Wonders' show at Cinerama" [Il s'est mis à descendre l'escalier comme une luge, et moi, j'étais accroupi sur lui et je descendais avec, comme aux Merveilles du Cinérama] (490). He wrings his hands (497), he tries to disarm someone but cannot (513), he trips on the sidewalk and falls on his face (546–47), he falls down again and gets gravel in his palms (547), and his voice is "hysterical and quavering" [hystérique et chevrotante] (549). Mentally, he is usually worn out

(486), inebriated, disoriented, asleep (453), or passed out. He has not much mental acumen for the investigation: "Sure, her story didn't hold up, but what does, these days?" [Bien sûr qu'elle ne tenait pas debout, son histoire, mais qu'est-ce qui tient debout, de nos jours?] (518). "Who has the money for a decent investigation these days?" [Qui peut se payer une enquête bien faite, de nos jours?] (522). At the end of the novel, it is Tarpon's journalist friend who writes the article explaining the crime, noting that the criminal "hadn't counted on the dazzling intuition of Eugène Tarpon" [c'est sans compter sans l'intuition fulgurante d'Eugène Tarpon] (576). The mention of Tarpon's dazzling intuition is of course intended to be ironic.

The elements of character fundamental to the hard-boiled, namely, volition, consciousness, an innate sense of ethics, and courage, are more present in Tarpon than they were in Butron, in that Tarpon is not a perverse bad actor; but each element is reduced, barely hinted at, or dulled by distraction, alcohol, boredom, and fatigue. The absence or reduction of these elements in turn creates a flatness of affect and casts "regularities of behavior" not as bedrock but as lackluster baseline. Tarpon does seem to have a minimal sense of ethics, in that he declares remorse for harms done and for good deeds not done. When Charlotte Schultz aka Memphis Charles comes to him claiming her roommate has been murdered, he is willing to help her, but not until she has knocked him out with his own telephone. Even then, his first impulse is to go back to sleep (469). When a random *gauchiste* is wounded in a fight, he worries whether she has received medical attention. But when no real answer is forthcoming, "I closed my eyes. Maybe I was going to wake up in my little room with Mommy bringing me hot chocolate in bed because I was sick and delirious, seeing things that weren't there and all that" [J'ai fermé les yeux. Peut-être que j'allais me réveiller dans ma chambrette et maman m'apporterait mon chocolat au lit parce que j'avais été bien malade, j'avais déliré, vu des choses qui ne sont pas et tout ça] (510). He understands that the murderer had had a troubled childhood, but he has no sense of how he became a murderer and no energy to think about it. "As to how he came to do it, I don't know the details. I haven't had time to think about details. I'm on so much medication, I keep falling asleep" [Quant au passage à l'acte, je ne sais pas les détails. Je n'ai pas eu tellement le temps de réfléchir aux détails. Je suis bourré de médicaments. Je n'arrête pas de somnoler] (572). With Tarpon's general placid innocuousness, with his continued somnolence, it soon becomes clear that it is not understatement that he is practicing but a studied nullity, a dearth of intention that remains in force, as it were, until the end of the novel.

What matters in the present argument is that the very characteristics that make Tarpon so subdued a specimen—trepidation, weariness, bewilderment—are precisely those of early nineteenth-century romantic heroes, in exaggerated form. In *Mémoires d'outre-tombe*, the narrator laments, "Everything bores me. I carry my tedium around every day, weary of life" [Tout me lasse: je remorque avec peine mon ennui avec mes jours, et je vais partout bâillant ma vie].[51] Chateaubriand's René is a model of forlorn inaction: "This aversion to life that I had felt since childhood came back with renewed force. Soon my heart supplied no more nourishment for my thoughts, and all I felt of my existence was a profound sense of weariness" [Ce dégoût de la vie que j'avais ressenti dès mon enfance, revenait avec une force nouvelle. Bientôt mon cœur ne fournit plus d'aliment à ma pensée, et je ne m'apercevais de mon existence que par un profond sentiment d'ennui].[52] From Vigny's "I laid down my head, as if presenting it to the knife. I was delirious. What was I doing?" [Et j'allongeais ma tête, comme la présentant au couteau. J'étais dans le délire. Eh! que faisais-je?][53] to Tarpon's "I was delirious, seeing things that weren't there and all that," from Chateaubriand's "I was slipping into that fatigue well known to men who travel the world: no distinct memories remained; I felt myself living and vegetating with nature in a sort of pantheism. I leaned against a magnolia tree and fell asleep" [Je déclinais peu à peu vers cette somnolence connue des hommes qui courent les chemins du monde: nul souvenir distinct ne me restait; je me sentais vivre et végéter avec la nature dans une espèce de panthéisme. Je m'adossai contre le tronc d'un magnolia et je m'endormis][54] to Tarpon's "I haven't had time to think about details. I'm on so much medication, I keep falling asleep" are but short steps. The transposition of spiritual contemplation into the realm of sensation has apparently set it on uncertain ground, for Tarpon, without turning "bad," nonetheless lapses into sedation. He never sees the lead woman again, and the villain in the story "kills himself with a nail" [se suicide avec un clou] (578), reducing the story's end to a miniature point and an uncertain image. Surprised, abducted, insulted, attacked, disoriented, tired: in a sense, his most active and also incongruous act is the story's very narration, for it hardly seems that he would have the energy necessary for such sustained production of words. *Que d'os!* puts more emphasis on Tarpon's partnership with Charlotte Malrakis (not the same Charlotte as in *Morgue pleine*) but nonetheless has him

---

51. Chateaubriand, *Mémoires d'outre-tombe*, 299.
52. Chateaubriand, *Atala, René*, 134.
53. Vigny, *Stello*, 246.
54. Chateaubriand, *Mémoires d'outre-tombe*, 336.

"knocked out like a steer" [camé comme un bœuf] and, at the end, "mainly tired" [surtout fatigué] (699).[55] He produces, generates, discovers, and decides almost nothing. But he lives, breathes, and recounts, and this is enough to make him the narrator of the novel and its center—a center whose salient characteristic is the absence of intention and action.

A CHARACTER WHO DOESN'T EXIST SUFFICIENTLY

To underscore that individual absence is a constructed character attribute, I turn to Manchette's last published and most praised novel, *La position du tireur couché* (1981), which was made into an American movie, *The Gunman*, in 2015. Written in the third person, it tells the story of Martin Terrier, a hired assassin who wants to leave the hitman profession and return home to marry his high school sweetheart. Terrier is in essence an entire classic crime fiction plot contained in one character: he is the murderer, the one who wants to stop the killing, the one investigating the obstacles to stopping, and the would-be restorer and embodiment of bourgeois order. Already, however, this summary becomes misleading, since Terrier does not articulate a "want" but rather performs a series of actions. The name Terrier (and the narrator calls him this, rather than Martin) implies a burrowing prairie animal and a small dog—unthreatening, but not very indicative of complex humanity. Indeed, there is virtually no direct report of Terrier's internal world. As Platten writes, "Martin occupies a single plane of existence where there are no highs or lows, since the emotional life of this character is extinct."[56] As Manchette wrote *La position*, he recorded in a journal the progress of his novel: "In *La position du tireur couché* as it stands now, the problem is that by representing the emotional blockage of the main character by a near-total absence of reactions, I've made a character who doesn't exist sufficiently" [Dans *La position du tireur couché* tel qu'il se présente actuellement, le problème est qu'à vouloir représenter le blocage émotionnel du personnage central par une absence presque complète de réactions, j'ai obtenu un personnage qui n'existe pas suffisamment] (873).

Since existential crises framed by Sartre and Camus presented "insufficient existence" as a philosophical as well as literary conundrum, it is worth a moment to parse the measures of sufficient existence Manchette is using. It is unclear what the operating standard of existence is, or what purpose it

---

55. In *The Snarl of the Beast*, it is the monstrous villain, not the detective, who "hit[s] the pavement like a stockyard steer" (50).

56. Platten, *Pleasures of Crime*, 105–6.

serves—to generate compassion in the reader, to constitute intent under the law for purposes of prosecution, to drive a narrative arc, to interest other characters. Insufficient existence has legal consequences and can keep one out of prison, as we see in the book's conclusion. But it also raises the question of what constitutes a character and a "narrative actor" as well as a sentient, social, and moral being.

Itziar Giger and Jean-Paul Bronckart have studied verb tenses in the *polar* and noticed a preponderance of the *passé simple* in Manchette's 1977 novel *Fatale*. Their study divides the story's verbs into verbs of movement (there are 60), verbs of speech (17), and verbs of sentiment, perception, or psychology (6).[57] *La position* replicates this proportion and if anything tilts it even farther away from "sentiment, perception, or psychology." The first page of the novel is filled with *passé simple* action verbs, whose final "a" creates a somewhat ludicrous sound effect. There are very few verbs of emotional expression, and those there are seem ironic or unconnected to surrounding content. On learning that his former girlfriend has been raped, tortured, and murdered, "For a moment he seemed to reflect. He did not seem shocked. Perhaps he felt a little sorrow" [Un instant il parut réfléchir. Il ne semblait pas ressentir un choc. Peut-être éprouvait-il un peu de peine] (896). We do see recounting of past emotion, though, principally rage: "That night, blinded by rage and humiliation, Martin almost came to blows with his father" [Ce soir-là, aveuglé de rage et d'humiliation, Martin manque se battre avec son père] (898). This character also has a father whose story becomes definitive. Charles Terrier had been shot in the head during some postwar black market business ventures; the bullet remains in his head and when he drinks, he becomes clownish. Martin's mother runs off with a truck driver, leaving baby Martin to be raised by his father. At the end of the novel, Martin has also been shot. He lives with a bullet in his head, works as a waiter in a brasserie, and becomes clownish when he drinks. Bar patrons give him cocktails to make him act foolish, just as they had to his father. In the end, he lives in a "little lodging" [un petit logement], having retreated into the sort of subterranean "terrier" that his name implies (978).

Uri Margolin remarks on the various components of action (context, manner, content, and so on) that allow acts to "serve as signifiers with regard to the characteristics and personalities of narrative agents. . . . Some physical acts, once identified, can be characterized in isolation and serve immediately as a source of characterization of the doer as well. These involve primarily acts with general, codified, context-free symbolic significance: bowing deeply for

---

57. Giger and Bronckart, "Le temps du polar."

respect, tearing out one's hair for despair, smiling for friendliness, etc."[58] Terrier's acts, from machine-gunning strangers for money to frowning and smiling, seem as detached from their doer as they do from their context. When acts seem to be meaningless, one possible conclusion is that this is a world in which acts do not have meaning, in which, as Platten puts it, "human beings are diminished to the status of agents . . . where the professional assassin is the ultimate arbiter of market forces."[59] Here, however, that diminishing, absence, elision, or dissociation of the human actor emerges as the work of the narrator and not of society. The difference between a *noir* atmosphere and a non-*noir* atmosphere, I would propose, is quite simply the presence of a sustained and self-conscious character. In this sense, the *néo-polar* is a character-centered *mise en scène* of the vacuities introduced by existentialism and enacted through the *nouveau roman*. For even as it represents individual character diminished by deadening social forces, it also showcases the narrative decision to play up that diminishing, and to create the character that does not exist sufficiently.

YAPPING TERRIER

At the end of *La position,* a man called only "blue suit" [complet bleu] explains to Terrier that he, Terrier, will publish a "book of recollections" [livre de souvenirs]. Terrier will not actually write this book, however, as someone else will already have written it—he will lend his name as author and correct the "verifiable inexactitudes" [inexactitudes vérifiables] (975). In fact, Terrier will learn from this manuscript what has happened to him, who shot him, who murdered his girlfriend, who the principal actors have been; all this understanding will then help him with his eventual court testimony. The publishers, however, find the manuscript "ridiculous." Publication is canceled and legal prosecution abandoned. Blue suit explains the cancellation to Terrier:

> —There will be no testimony, said blue suit. Everything is canceled. It's over. You've been declared legally not responsible, so there's no case. We'll spread the word that you're at a psychiatric clinic in the States . . . . You can call yourself lucky.
> —Lucky? yapped Terrier.
> —You massacre three dozen people and they put you nicely back at square one! yelled blue suit. You don't call that lucky?

---

58. Margolin, "Doer and the Deed," 208.
59. Platten, *Pleasures of Crime,* 105.

—I don't know, murmured Terrier slowly.

—Il n'y aura pas de témoignage, dit complet bleu. Tout est annulé. L'opération est terminée. Vous êtes déclaré légalement irresponsable. Sur le plan judiciaire, vous avez un non-lieu. On fera savoir que vous êtes interne aux Etats-Unis dans une clinique psychiatrique. . . . Vous pouvez vous vanter d'avoir de la chance.
—De la chance? glapit Terrier.
—Vous massacrez trois douzaines de personnes et on vous remet gentiment sur la case départ! hurla l'autre. Vous n'appelez pas ça de la chance?
—Je ne sais pas, dit lentement Terrier à voix basse. (976)

In this scene, the declaration of legal irresponsibility and the dismissal of the case coincide with the loss of the chance of authorship. Unable to provide testimony, Terrier becomes a character without sufficient legal existence to stand trial, the silent gunman reduced to a yapping dog. In the French legal tradition more so than in the Anglo-Saxon, an audience in court amounts to a recognition of the character's humanity. Stewart Field notes that the French *cour d'assises* contains a *comparution de curriculum vitae* and quotes a French judge as stating, "you will be judged on the facts but through the personality." He writes, "In American 'contractual society,' an offence is a deliberate breach of that contract, whereas in the French 'political community,' it is the straying of a sheep."[60] And yet, in Terrier's case, even had he been heard, even had his book been published and his testimony recorded, that testimony would still be based on a manuscript he did not write and did not actually experience as such. The "I don't know" when Terrier contemplates these options, when he envisions a prison term as compared to life as a waiter in a backwater brasserie, one sort of "terrier" existence against another, is probably his most human moment of expression.

Another *néo-polar* writer, Jean-Bernard Pouy, stated in an interview, "Manchette brought in something very important, he brought a specificity to the French novel. For once there were French *noir* novels that were not copies at large of the Anglo-Saxon, American models, but in which there was a true French voice."[61] The "true French voice" in question undoubtedly comes from Manchette and other *néo-polar* authors, but not from Manchette's best-known character. Indeed, there are numerous instances in Manch-

---

60. Field, "State, Citizen, and Character," 524, 538.
61. Elfriede Müller, Interview of Jean-Bernard Pouy, January 29, 2004, trans. Steve Novak, http://www.europolar.eu/europolarv1/2_dossiers_entretien_Pouy_angl.htm (accessed February 17, 2016).

ette when at moments of strongest human pathos, the narrative turns to pure aesthetic spectacle and abandons character voice and thought. Once reunited with Anne, for instance, Terrier leaves for a walk and returns to find her in bed with one of the guards. Terrier loses the power of speech and is reduced to (or perhaps it is more correct to say expanded into) an interesting visual object. The narrator states also that Verdi's *Trovatore* is on the turntable, the duet "Miserere" announcing the death of Manrico and Leonora's devotion, and that a setter is barking outside (941). Terrier becomes unable to speak when he sees the couple, but he had not said much before that. With his speechlessness, his strange appearance and sounds, the opera with the man destined for death, and the dog (a double for Terrier) barking in the distance, the perceiving subject turns into a spectacle, a visual and musical scene. On the one hand, this turning renders a deadening modern environment in which loud noises and fast motion distract from human feeling; Manchette's most vibrant writing is undoubtedly in such scenes, in which the narrator turns artist, television director, and anarchist musician.[62] But it is worth considering that these vibrant cacophonies—echoes, it could even be argued, of Manchette's own agoraphobic crises—emerge at emotional turning points for the characters. At those precise times when the character's sentiment is of principal interest, narrative focus shifts to noise outside. This shift echoes on the one hand the multimedia nature of the *néo-polar,* the elements of punk rock, absurdist theater, and distracting spectacle that infuse the genre, but it has an important moral resonance. In a third-person narration, the narrator's decision to concentrate on the distant barking dog, the operatic chords, the sexual position of the couple, and Terrier's labored breathing turns a moment of emotional upset into a circus, but it does not indicate anything about Terrier as a person and a character. In first-person narratives, however, those concentrations on aesthetic diversion do contain an ethical resonance for the character and ultimately anticipate one of the most important modern obstacles to individual moral authority: a systematic and deliberate diversion of attention.

As Müller writes, citing Dominique Manotti's statement that "the crumbling of political hopes always brings existential disenchantment," "Anchoring that subjectivity within the social, that is the art of the *polar*" [Ancrer cette subjectivité au sein du social, voilà l'art du polar].[63] There is no doubt that Manchette paints the decline of the subject as a social phenomenon. But it is equally incontestable that the social, reciprocally, has no other anchor

---

62. The Monoprix chase and explosion scene in *Folle à tuer* is an ideal example.
63. Müller and Ruoff, *Le polar français,* 112.

and expression than the individual. Again, this is not to suggest that any given individual can reverse broad social phenomena. Rather, it is to wonder why the individual is elided and accentuated in novels that focus on social criticism. It is also to propose that reading the individual and the social as mutually exclusive sites of responsibility may be a misreading. Manotti writes, "We have to reinvent the *noir*. Write the *roman noir* of globalization, of capitalism taking over with no one to stop it. Write the novel of these bad men who make our world, as Ellroy might put it" [Il faut reinventer le noir. Écrire le roman noir de la mondialisation, du capitalisme triomphant sans adversaire structuré, sans limites. Écrire le roman de ces hommes mauvais qui font notre monde, dirait peut-être Ellroy].[64] Even in this formulation, however, which accords pride of place to globalization and capitalism, she points to "these bad men who make our world," as though a group of individuals had been mentioned. In the American tradition, the principal character resists individual responsibility by pointing to concrete opposition or restrictions on his own movement, or by hinting at a traumatic experience that impedes complete subjecthood (Lou Ford). In the French tradition, that resistance appears in the form of ennui and malaise, or from outside cacophonies that distract from or drown out the individual. Lou Ford perceived or claimed to perceive, which for purposes of accountability amounts to the same, that he was a victim. In Martin Terrier's case, the narrator accords to him as little perception as possible, as little evidence as possible of actual existence. And yet there is much action that is readable. Harming others and being kind to others function as "general, codified, context-free acts" that, as Margolin puts it, "serve immediately as a source of characterization of the doer."

To some extent, in the individual-social duality that characterized the traditional hard-boiled or *roman noir*, the individual as such has slipped out the back door and left the "social" to function as the scene of the narrative, its principal villain, and the source of possible reparation. Here again, however, there is considerable slippage in the meaning of "social," since the alienated *néo-polar* character is isolated not just from other people but also from basic mechanisms of thought and communication. The ostensible result of this isolation is a vacuum in which there can be no complete individual, for the simple reason that individual moral choices, individual conduct full stop, becomes manifest only when people come into contact with or think about one another, and Manchette and other *néo-polar* authors have shrunk this contact significantly. As Simon Blackburn writes in 2014, "Our sense of self is reciprocal with our sense of other people, and their sense of us. We discover

---

64. Manotti, "Le roman noir," 109.

ourselves only in the social world. Moral notions enter into the most important dimensions of self-consciousness, and our sense of self is largely made
up by them. They compose our identity."[65] What Blackburn describes is a conscious interaction between individuals—and between the individual and society—that starts to demystify the social. The twenty-first-century corrective to
the Butron phenomenon, to the character at once detrimental and indistinct
and to the social at once invisible and incontrovertible, will follow a culturally
specific pattern. The French solution to the self-absorbed but unaccountable
protagonist is a character who thinks less about himself, more about others, and more about the ideas he wishes to live. The contemporary French
hard-boiled, or restorative hard-boiled, presents an abiding distrust of facile
verbiage as well as of certainty. In place of oratorical flourishes, we see an aesthetic of hesitation and conscientiousness. We also see a much greater emphasis on partnership, not to distract from individual accountability and sense of
self, but to render these possible once more, and to restore the "social" in all
senses of the word.

---

65. Blackburn, *Mirror, Mirror,* 28.

CHAPTER 5

CONTEMPORARY HARD-BOILED

Rebuilding a Culture Hero

IN BOTH American and French post–hard-boiled narratives, individual character takes on a deliberately fragmented quality. Character, such as it is, crumbles under the residue of heavy-handed upbringing, hypocritical bourgeois society, mental illness, commercialism, social pressure, fatigue, boredom, and confusion. The dismantlings of both heroic character models and accountability described in the third and fourth chapters are extreme examples of that crumbling but nonetheless represent a broad mid-century trend. To take up once more Currie's notions of "character" and "Character," an introspective character dissects his Character and lays the pieces at the feet of forces outside his control. Meanwhile, the character with a small C, the narrative agent and actor, remains strikingly intelligible and reliable. He drives the narrative. As a result, the laconic, pessimistic Frenchman and the reckless, resentful American are cultural commonplaces in the 1960s, 1970s, and 1980s.

On both sides of the Atlantic, the individual's focus on intractable demons made him an unreliable repository or generator of public order. This was not because those demons were insurmountable but because narrative focus on them, the character's immersion within them, had made the trustworthy maverick almost an anachronism. The idea of a privately generated set of ethics and the absence of declared conventional morality, sources of liberation in the classic hard-boiled, now signified the mood swings of a dangerous loose cannon. Jim Thompson's Ford describes his lawyer Billy Boy in terms almost identical to those employed by Race Williams: "His ideas of right and wrong didn't jibe too close with the books" (234). Billy Boy himself then announces, "A weed is a plant out of place. I find a hollyhock in my cornfield, and it's a weed. I find it in my garden, and it's a flower. You're in my yard, Mr. Ford" (236–37), which echoes the dismissal of absolute values and the affirmation of the subjective. But when the flower in question is criminally insane and ready to burn down his own house, or even just disengaged, bored, tired, and unwilling to be held to account, then "not jibing too close with the books" becomes worrisome rather than liberating.

I want to return for a moment to Mikhael Bakhtin's earlier-cited comment on Dostoevsky's fiction, "Living an idea is somehow synonymous with unselfishness."[1] Bakhtin's "ideinost," or profound investment or immersion in an idea, was rather peculiar to nineteenth-century Russian ideas of social justice—Tolstoy's interest in the liberation of the peasants, for instance. After the Second World War and after decades of unhinged or deluded characters of all stripe, "living an idea" showed itself to be as much problem as solution, encompassing at once idealism and dedication, obsession and delusion. On the one hand, living an idea (the abstract notion of justice, a particular social ideal, the importance of an institution, or even the investigation at hand) seemed preferable to, and sufficient to stop characters from, thinking always about themselves. At the same time, the twentieth century gave ample examples of individuals living even potentially reasonable ideas to the point of madness, and the mid-century hard-boiled showcased characters living some rather very questionable ideas. In Jim Thompson's *Pop. 1280,* for instance, Nick Corey lives the idea of doing the Lord's work. "I said I meant I was just doing my job, followin' the holy precepts laid down in the Bible. It's what I'm supposed to do, you know, to punish the heck out of people for bein' people. To coax 'em into revealin' theirselves, an' them kick the crap out of 'em" (206). In his case, living an idea is code for messianic delusion. That parodic excess of individual grandeur is more extravagant than most, but lesser contaminations of the "idea" abound.

As Lee Horsley implies, those contaminations are the fault not of ideas themselves but of the people living them.

> The psychologising of the criminal and the concomitant movement away from treating crime as the product of socio-economic deprivation is sometimes judged to weaken the capacity of the gangster narrative to act as a critique of the capitalist system. There is no doubt that focusing on the psychopathology of a character can become an indulgence of horrified fasci-

---

1. Bakhtin, *Problems of Dostoevsky's Poetics,* 71.

nation at the sheer nastiness of the aberrant personality, combined with a reassuring sense that normative values and conventional lives are free from these evils.[2]

With the turn to "normative values," however, the pendulum prepares to swing again; for compared to "libidinal investment" in the classic hard-boiled character,[3] "normative values" are an underwhelming corrective to criminality. When the "lived idea" at hand is the importance of "normative values and conventional lives," living that idea can easily mean submission to statis, corruption, or uselessness. After all, it was disaffection with normative values and conventional lives that encouraged the classic hard-boiled celebration of the individual a century ago.

RESTORING MORAL AUTHORITY

In the late twentieth and early twenty-first centuries, crime fiction in the hard-boiled mode engages deliberately with "living an idea" of individual moral authority and accountability. It also engages with the various material conditions and communal norms that encumber that authority. This chapter examines the contemporary resuscitation of the individual as viable autonomous entity and of shared values as other than deadening, impersonal, fraudulent, or corrupt. Indeed, I propose that that resuscitation is a principal concern in popular culture writ large. From the best sellers cited in this book's introduction, to political discourse on individual and collective responsibility, to public discussion of political corruption both American and French, to television dramas that depict social systems deteriorating, to debates about juvenile justice and the age limits of accountability, to research on "bandwidth" poverty,[4] popular culture on both sides of the Atlantic has addressed individual moral authority almost as a microcosmic measure of national identity. This is one reason I broaden the category of hard-boiled crime fiction in this final chapter to include television, for in that most widely resonant medium, analyses of accountability find the strongest both popular and intellectual representation.

Insistence on individual moral choice, again, is neither reactionary nor utopian. It simply means that naming the social as source of disorder has often been an unproductive and truncated endeavor. Rather, naming *either*

---

2. Horsley, *Noir Thriller*, 104.
3. Breu, *Hard-Boiled Masculinities*.
4. See Mullainathan and Shafir, *Scarcity*.

the social *or* the individual as source of disorder has been problematic, particularly because in much social discourse, the individuals most called to account are curiously those who have the least social capital and power. A more relevant and provocative undertaking would be to focus on those who have the most, and this is where the hard-boiled comes in. The relationship between social problems and individual moral agents is alive and ongoing. While moral agency must certainly be considered in view of collectively produced ethics, the hard-boiled has always insisted on individual authors as well as on individual resonances. To be an individual and to be part of a system are not mutually exclusive, either for heroes or for public enemies. In the twenty-first century, when individual moral choice often seems subsumed under collective productions or impositions, the hard-boiled continues to insist upon it as a source of reparation.

Broadly stated, contemporary crime narratives remedy crises of accountability and character dissolution in two ways. One way is to reintroduce early nineteenth-century character outlines and laconic dedication to action, thus reinstating the maverick individual as throwback. Another way is to ramp up emphasis on institutional or collective models of social protection and to cast individuals in service to these models, acknowledging the precariousness of the individual *qua* individual and moving away from the hard-boiled model. And yet, these models, in some ways diametrically opposed, fuse into a contemporary balance. These modes of correction—and it is indeed correction, for the contemporary hard-boiled is consistently and explicitly dedicated to damage control, though the source of that damage varies—each cast the resurrection of individual moral authority as a common goal. Much of the work of restoration has to do with reversing the character tendencies described in the third and fourth chapters. Characters return to the discursive and behavioral outlines of the nineteenth century, before psychoanalysis, before the modern age of the self. Bakhtin's standard was living an idea, not declaiming or advertising an idea, and yet living an idea, like unselfishness, entails some thought of it, and in novels, much talking about or around it. It also entails considerable thought about the potential perils of living an idea, since by the time the contemporary hard-boiled endeavors to resurrect the individual, some of the road earlier traveled has been burned. But that is the precise and particular value of the contemporary hard-boiled: it plays out the relationship of the individual to the idea, and of idea-living individuals to the good of society. Throughout the American and French narratives examined in this chapter, we see contemporary resurrection of empathic presence, responsiveness to others, and a diminished focus on one's own interest. Furthermore, the idea of national identity functions as a powerful corrective repository of "normative values," even as it looms as a villainous or boringly conventional foil. Finally, partnerships and collaborations become crucial, not just in the sense of shoring up individuals, but of expanding their boundaries and developing the individual as social being.

Ultimately, the contemporary hard-boiled examines how "living" the idea of morality, justice, patriotism, humanity, ennobles and animates the individual, even as it encounters the duplicitous faces of convention. The content of the lived ideas varies subtly from culture to culture, as do the manners of living and sharing them, but common to both twenty-first-century models are a surprisingly explicit return to nineteenth-century character outlines and an active engagement with questions of accountability and social function. Contemporary hard-boiled characters stand in the public view, both as representatives of national justice within their narratives, and as popular fictional characters in the world. In this sense, they are similar to political personalities, at once visible representatives of national justice and embodiments of what "living an idea" could look like, for better or worse, in each respective national setting.

THE CONTEMPORARY FRENCH CORPUS

French crime fiction in the post *néo-polar* years includes a rich variety of characters. These include Gabriel Lecouvreur, or Le Poulpe, who was dreamed up by Jean-Bernard Pouy, Serge Quadruppani, and Patrick Raynal and developed through the contributions of numerous authors from 1995 to the present; Franck Thilliez's Lucie Hennebelle and Franck Sharko; Brigitte Aubert's Elise Andrioli; Antoine Chainas's Paul Nazutti; Daniel Pennac's Benjamin Malaussène; and Jean-Claude Izzo's Fabio Montale. I focus on a character who resuscitates the nineteenth-century romantic model while fusing maverick eccentricity to national intactness, and whose claim to hard-boiled status combines Nestor Burma's cultural ambassadorship with Chandler's "honor without thought of it." This is Fred Vargas's *commissaire* Jean-Baptiste Adamsberg, a romantic-inspired hero in some ways more Maigret than Burma. And yet, to take up Lukács's terms once more, his living of ideals as "subjective facts" casts him as both generator and interpreter of moral authority. Furthermore, his evolution over the past two decades demonstrates individualism nourished in connection with others and thus increasingly "social" in nature.

Fred Vargas is the author of numerous crime novels, most of which center on Parisian police *commissaire* Adamsberg (several others concentrate on the so-called three Evangelists, or scholars of various historical periods who solve mysteries as amateur detectives). Vargas is credited with nothing less than the rejuvenation of French detective fiction, not just in France where her novels are best sellers, but across the world. Readers first encounter *commissaire* Adamsberg in *L'homme aux cercles bleus* (1991), and for the second time in *L'homme à l'envers* (1999). Since then, Adamsberg has appeared in seven more novels. I will start with *L'homme à l'envers* and then consider briefly the sixth Adamsberg novel, *Sous les vents de Neptune* (2004), in which Adamsberg himself is suspected of murder. The plot of *L'homme à l'envers* is as follows: in the southeast of France, sheep are being killed in large numbers by what seems to be an enormous beast. A visiting Canadian biologist, Lawrence Johnstone, studies wolves and tracks their movements; he becomes curious about the fallen sheep. When a local woman is also killed, however, Lawrence and the villagers begin to talk of a werewolf; suspicion falls on a recently disappeared loner, Massart. Three characters band together to pursue Massart: Soliman, the adopted son of the murdered woman; Le Veilleux, a local shepherd; and Camille, plumber and musician, current girlfriend of the biologist, and former love of the Parisian police *commissaire*. As the killings continue and the murderer eludes the group, the aforementioned *commissaire*, the highly intuitive and meditative Jean-Baptiste Adamsberg, is himself brought in to help investigate. In the end, Adamsberg solves the crimes, which turn out to be the work not of a village werewolf but of Lawrence himself, through a pathological and generations-old search for vengeance. *L'homme à l'envers* is published in English as *Seeking Whom He May Devour*, though the literal translation is *Man Inside Out*, which is how one of the characters describes the phenomenon of the werewolf.

During the first half of the book, Camille, Soliman, and Le Veilleux form a motley investigative team, but they soon decide that some support from actual law enforcement would be helpful. Faced with the challenge of locating a policeman who will not look askance at their werewolf–murderer–sheep-eater theories, Camille proposes to contact Adamsberg. Soliman asks Camille: "How is he then, as a cop? No scruples?" [Comment il est alors, comme flic? Pas de scrupules?] to which Camille answers, "Plenty of scruples and not many principles" [Beaucoup de scrupules et pas beaucoup de principes].[5] Adamsberg's scruple-principle distinction fashions Chandler's "honor without thought of it" to the French twenty-first century. The distinction paints Adamsberg as entirely instinctive both in his conduct with others and in his performance as police *commissaire*. As a result, he becomes

---

5. Vargas, *L'homme à l'envers*, 185. Subsequent references to this work will be given parenthetically.

a sort of fantasy French civil servant, his mindfulness reflecting positively on French culture as a whole. From his introduction in *L'homme aux cercles bleus,* Adamsberg comes at policing for reasons interior, private, almost sensorial: "I wondered why I was a cop. Maybe because in this job there are things to look for and a chance of actually finding them. That makes up for the rest" [Je me demandais pourquoi j'étais flic. Peut-être parce que dans ce métier on a des choses à chercher avec des chances de les trouver. Ça console du reste].[6] When Camille insists that Adamsberg has scruples but not principles, her companions at first assume she means that he is corrupt. And yet the distinction between scruple and principle takes for granted that Adamsberg is a reliable protector of the people—again recalling the Burma model—and concentrates on why. The *Oxford English Dictionary* defines *principle* as "a general law or rule adopted or professed as a guide to action; a settled ground or basis of conduct or practice; a fundamental motive or reason of action, esp. one consciously recognized and followed" and as "an inward or personal law of right action; personal devotion to right; rectitude, uprightness, honourable character." The dictionary's cited examples of this definition's usage include: "If I were to choose any servant . . . I would choose a godly man that hath principles" (Cromwell, July 4, 1653). And from *Moll Flanders:* "Thus my pride, not my principle, kept me honest." *Scruple,* on the other hand, though it may well have the same net behavioral result as principle, takes the form of feeling rather than of "inward or personal law." The *OED* defines it as "a thought or circumstance that troubles the mind or conscience; a doubt, uncertainty or hesitation in regard to right and wrong, duty, propriety, etc.; esp. one which is regarded as over-refined or over-nice, or which causes a person to hesitate where others would be bolder to act." Given examples include, from Bishop Jeremy Taylor: "A scruple is a great trouble of mind proceeding from a little motive" (1660), and from Father Frederick Faber's *Growth in Holiness:* "A scruple is a vain fear of sin where there is no reasonable ground for suspecting sin" (1854). Indeed, *scruple* is most often used in connection with religious nervousness.[7] *Merriam-Webster* defines scruple in terms of principle ("an ethical consideration or principle that inhibits action"), but includes the element of "mental reservation." The *OED* tells us Cicero first used "scrupulus" (rough or hard pebble) figuratively to designate a cause of uneasiness or anxiety. According to that usage,

6. Vargas, *L'homme aux cercles bleus,* 44.

7. Further, *scruple* is often used as a synonym for a pathological oversensitivity. See Jenks, *Blind Obedience;* Casey, *Nature and Treatment of Scruples;* Van Ornum, *A Thousand Frightening Fantasies.* In *The Doubting Disease,* Ciarrocchi describes *scruple* as arising from an "overly sensitive moral conscience" (5).

Adamsberg is to "scruples" as the princess is to the pea—he carries within him the mandate to remain ethical without thought of it. In some ways, the dominance of scruple in Adamsberg aligns with the dominance of sentimentalism as Leonard Cassuto outlines it in *Hard-Boiled Sentimentalism.* For Cassuto, "the hard-boiled detective relies on reason only in concert with intuition—that is, feeling. Sentimentalism strikes a similar balance between reason and feeling."[8] The scruple-principle distinction, however, breaks down the reason-feeling opposition even further, for it starts to question what thought is and who is responsible for it.

NARRATIVE MODESTY

Chandler's formula of the character who is heroic "without thought of it, and certainly without saying it" referred to first-person narrators, and the Adamsberg novels' third-person narration does much to transmit subtlety. It is relatively easy for Adamsberg to avoid "saying it" when a narrator is saying it all for him. But even as a character, Adamsberg functions as a third-person narrator, which is to say that his focus is on others. When he thinks about himself, it is as a vehicle for the investigation, and he is principally concerned—this is the main focus of his scrupulousness—with clear thinking. When a person is found dead in a sheep pen and the story of the mad sheep-killing wolf takes a more sinister turn, "Only at moments like this, when reality fell in line with his darkest imaginings, did Adamsberg lose his poise and become almost scared of himself. He had never had complete confidence in his inner depths. He was as wary of those depths as of the charred bottom of a wizard's cauldron" [Dans ces seuls instants, quand la réalité venait absurdement rejoindre ses plus obscures expectatives, Adamsberg chancelait et se faisait presque peur. Le fond de lui même ne lui avait jamais inspiré tout à fait confiance. Il s'en défiait, comme du fond calciné de la marmite d'un sorcier] (87). In this formulation, Adamsberg emerges as a sort of Saint Francis of criminal investigation, or channel for the truth of events and ideas. Various reviewers describe Adamsberg as "zen-like" because of his temperament and stillness, but the term also speaks to his focus on pure receptivity. For instance, the narrator tells us that "Adamsberg never reflected, he found it sufficient to dream, then to sort out his catch" [Adamsberg ne réfléchissait jamais, il se contentait de rêver, puis de trier la récolte] (85). Rolls has written that Adamsberg's detective practice is "fetishistic in its deployment of

---

8. Cassuto, *Hard-Boiled Sentimentality*, 13.

a Baudelairean prose poetics through which the hyperclarity of his vision alights on both the manifestly important evidence and the small, everyday occurrences that pass otherwise unnoticed."[9] What interests me here is that contemplation for Adamsberg is less an action than an experience; encountering his own thoughts becomes akin to watching images on the television (and indeed, it is through television that he encounters the sheep killings to begin with). All his policing movements emerge from a sensorial impulse in which professionalism seems beside the point. There are few instances of the verb "to think" [penser], but the noun "thought" abounds. For instance: "Adamsberg's thoughts contained a fair amount of pebbles and seaweed, and he often got tangled up in them. He had to throw a lot out, eliminate a lot of it. He was aware that his mind tended to serve up a muddled conglomerate of thoughts, and that for other people it didn't necessarily work that way" [Il y avait pas mal de cailloux et d'algues dans les pensées d'Adamsberg et il n'était pas rare qu'il s'y emmêlât. Il devait beaucoup jeter, beaucoup éliminer. Il avait conscience que son esprit lui servait un conglomérat confus de pensées inégales et que cela ne fonctionnait pas forcément de même pour tous les autres hommes] (85).

Returning to the terms that Lukács introduced in his comments on subjective fact, his notion of "aims given to [the individual] with immediate obviousness, [involving] hindrances and difficulties but never any serious threat to his interior life," I would propose that Adamsberg's openness to thought resonates as almost premodern. When one character asks him, "You know these things, or you think them?" [Tu sais ces choses ou bien tu les penses?] Adamsberg responds, "I don't know anything. . . . I just want to see" [Je ne sais rien. . . . Je veux voir] (242). In this sense, Adamsberg is not just a zen meditator but also an anachronism, going back beyond nineteenth-century romanticism to a frame of mind in which the value of his own subjectivity is never equal to the import, the weight, of what is "given" to him. This receptivity, like the distinction between "his mind served up thoughts" and "think," like the distinction between scruple and principle, makes Adamsberg a Lukácsian "unproblematic individual."[10] And yet, his "thoughts" in

---

9. Rolls, *Paris and the Fetish*, 107.

10. Véronique Denain cites her interview with Fred Vargas, in which the latter noted that "while in the public's mind the male character is neutral, any female character is inevitably going to be categorized according to a handful of stereotypes." Dénain then elaborates: "No particular expectations or qualities are ascribed to a male hero whereas a woman is immediately assimilated to one of thirty or more possible roles which are virtually impossible for a writer to counteract: from 'the whinger' to 'the mother,' from 'the victim' to 'the bitch,' the female character's actions will be interpreted to fit one of those stereotypes." Desnain, "Women in French Crime Writing," 93.

themselves are understood to be more problematic than the "immediate aims" given to Lukács's epic heroes. Intervening centuries of modernity have blocked the channel of such giving and muddled the translucency of ideas. As Adamsberg acknowledges: "He was aware that his mind served up" [Il avait conscience que son esprit lui servait] maintains the integrity of "conscience," separate from "thoughts" and responsible for their evaluation. As such, this description stands in diametric contrast to Butron's "I believe in the unconscious." The French "conscience" corresponds to both conscience and consciousness and connects one to the other. Scruple, as "a great trouble of mind proceeding from a little motive" or as "a vain fear of sin where there is no reasonable ground for suspecting sin," implies an automatic delicacy that conscience does not, but both speak to a mindfulness of one's responsibility as generator and animator of ideas. In attributing to Adamsberg both scruple and conscience, the novel has the *commissaire* oscillate between an instinctual "honor without thought of it" and an awareness of his own responsibility.

The notion that thoughts are independent and unreliable functions as a corrective to snarls of thought into which various self-obsessed characters fell—at times deliberately—in the *néo-polar*. Too much thought, however, does away with the instinctive quality that underlay the hard-boiled character as conservator of sentimental virtues (Cassuto), as deserving of libidinal investment (Breu), and as embodiment of secular morality. Adamsberg's continuous alternation between the two poles places him in an ideal twenty-first-century dimension: a fusion between the unselfishness of "living an idea" and the conscious responsibility to ensure the soundness of ideas as he lives them.

CLOSING THE CASE

For most of the novel, Adamsberg's temperament and the novel's criminal plot run parallel to one another, with the truth of the crime emerging as though from a dream. The problem is that both the individual and the institution have practical as well as symbolic limits: while a solitary individual can conduct a criminal investigation, only a civil servant can actually close it. Contemplation can drive or even substitute for deduction, but it cannot substitute for arrest and the judicial process. Someone actually has to put on the handcuffs, and the very idea of judicial resolution is inseparable from official function. Official function is potentially redolent of all the "Oughts" that scruple and reverie would seem to circumvent, but this novel cushions its characters from the leaden weight of government even in the moment of arrest.

At the end of the novel, Adamsberg sets out for a midnight walk and is attacked by Lawrence. Rolls writes, "This departure from the road marks a move away from the central thrust of the narrative. The shift is apparently from an evidentiary-based investigation to an instinctive one. . . . The movement here is away from the whiteness of rationality toward the darkness of myth and primal forces."[11] I would go further than this and propose that the entire novel moves to replace or at least conflate an evidentiary-based investigation with an instinctive one. Adamsberg reaches for his gun, finds it unloaded, and is on the point of being killed when Soliman, who does have a gun, comes upon him and holds up the murderer. Adamsberg, then, worried that Soliman will be too scared to shoot, disables the suspect by throwing a rock at his head. They then tie up Lawrence with Adamsberg's holster and shirt. Policemen come and lead out the criminal, and "a third policeman gave [Adamsberg] back his shirt and his holster" [un troisième gendarme lui rendit sa chemise et son holster] (303). In this entire episode, the narrator takes pains to remove Adamsberg from formulaic police procedures. First, the *commissaire* is unarmed. Second, he is saved by Soliman, a civilian, not because the latter is a deliberate crime fighter, but because his mother was the murderer's first victim, and he has become fond of Adamsberg. Third, Adamsberg disables the murderer with a rock, an emphatically natural geological counterpoint to police-issue weapons. The rock echoes the story of David and Goliath, but whereas David promised to give the dead bodies of the Philistines "to the wild beasts of the earth," Adamsberg passes Lawrence to the policemen who process him into the French system. The rock also echoes Adamsberg's "scrupulus" (rough pebble) as well as the thought "pebbles" in his mind. Fourth, other police, not him, perform the act of arrest. Fifth, those other policemen hand Adamsberg his shirt and holster as they are leading the criminal away; it is therefore not until the criminal is gone that we see Adamsberg in police-issue clothing. Sixth, the entire process takes place in the country under the night sky, recalling the bucolic setting of the romantic poets. And last but not least, Adamsberg's announcement to Camille that Lawrence was the killer is more therapeutic than judicial in nature: "He was split in two, the quiet man and the tormented child. . . . They never gave him a chance at a normal life. It's the truth. Think of it that way" [Il était en deux bouts, l'homme tranquil et l'enfant déchiré. . . . Ils ne lui ont pas laissé une seule chance de vivre. C'est la

---

11. Rolls, *Paris and the Fetish*, 94–95. He observes elsewhere that "Adamsberg becomes the very model of a flâneur-detective." Rolls, *Mostly French*, 22.

vérité. Penses-y comme ça] (307). Adamsberg will not judge Lawrence, and yet it will happen, the courts will do it, and far off-screen.

The entire process of arrest seems as uncodified and as rooted in the personal as possible. It animates Rousseau's idea of the noble savage, as powerful as an animal: "Pit a bear or a wolf against a brave, agile, and vigorous savage, as they all are, armed with stones and a good stick, and you will see that the peril will at the very least be mutual, and that after several such experiences, wild beasts who do not like to attack each other will be equally disinclined to attack man, whom they will have found every bit as ferocious as themselves" [Mettez un ours ou un loup aux prises avec un sauvage robuste, agile, courageux comme ils sont tous, armé de pierres, et d'un bon bâton, et vous verrez que le péril sera tout au moins réciproque, et qu'après plusieurs expériences pareilles, les bêtes féroces qui n'aiment point à s'attaquer l'une à l'autre, s'attaqueront peu volontiers à l'homme, qu'elles auront trouvé tout aussi féroce qu'elles].[12] At the same time, the sort of empathic understanding that Adamsberg demonstrates at the moment of arrest distinguishes humans: "Man is not a dog or a wolf. It is necessary only to establish basic social relations, to give his feelings a morality that beasts cannot know. Animals have heart and passions, but the holy image of what is honest and beautiful lives only in the heart of man" [L'homme n'est point un chien ni un loup. Il ne faut qu'établir dans son espèce les premiers rapports de la société pour donner à ses sentiments une moralité toujours inconnue aux bêtes. Les animaux ont un cœur et des passions; mais la sainte image de l'honnête et du beau n'entra jamais que dans le cœur de l'homme].[13] When we read Adamsberg as restoring the waning individual of the *néo-polar* without compromising the genre's resistance to deadening political structures, the detective's tendency to act in concert with—but also detached from—police procedural structures makes cultural sense.

Vargas's novel envelops any deadening intrusion of "conventional lives and normative values" in a redemptive individualism. Crucially, it also separates the individual as social being from the individual as cog in the social machine. As Adamsberg novels accumulate, his storied reliability intensifies, as do the quirkiness of the people who surround him and the importance of human connection to the investigation. In *Sous les vents de Neptune*, for instance, he is saved from erroneous imprisonment in Canada by clinging, literally, to the back of his lieutenant, Violette Retancourt. In *Dans les bois éternels*, his team saves Violette's life when the murderer attacks her. In *Un*

---

12. Rousseau, *Discours*, 136.
13. Rousseau, *Lettre à Mr. d'Alembert*, 116.

lieu incertain, Adamsberg is almost murdered by his own (recently emerged) son Zerk, then saved by an alexandrine-spouting recruit, Veyrenc. In the 2011 *L'armée furieuse,* Adamsberg (reconciled and teamed with Zerk) encounters a man who speaks backwards, that man's six-fingered brother, and another brother who believes his bones are falling into powder. These eccentricities undermine the linguistic, philosophical, and even physiological conventions that normally mark communities,[14] and in Adamsberg's France, communities build themselves on other grounds. In *L'homme à l'envers,* the usual anthropological commonalities of religion, national identity, creed, origin, and ethnicity are so notably absent from the novel's human groupings that entire communities as well as individuals appear to run on scruple rather than principle. The coming together of eccentrics and loners largely puts to rest the leaden force of the Kantian Oughts, the idea being that characters who don't bother to use last names, who mistrust the police, and who call priests "jackass" to their faces are unlikely to be silently bending under the weight of top-down bourgeois "shoulds." Their scruples are unlikely to be made up of internalized principle, since the characters are eccentric enough to be isolated from the usual channels of principle and convention, which saves these communities from being "imagined," to use Benedict Anderson's term. Civilization in Fred Vargas is a collectivity of the proverbial noble savages.

STATE SOVEREIGNTY, OR SYNCHRONICITY WITH THE STATE

The communities in this novel are emphatically human rather than national. Indeed, distrust of nationalism and its institutions is endemic to its characters. And yet, that distrust functions in such a way as to support, rather than undercut, a rather idealized vision of the French state. Jacqueline Hodgson's earlier-cited statement that "the sovereignty of the people becomes the sovereignty of the state" applies again here, for if scruple, rather than principle, makes for an exemplary civil servant, then the sovereignty of the individual (and his scruples) can become the sovereignty of the state without ceasing in the process to be the sovereignty of the individual. Sovereignty in this formulation is not so much transferred as shared. Whereas Müller had written of the *néo-polar*'s antiheroes that "they are unhappy and their unhappiness belongs to society," in Vargas's fiction, Adamsberg's scruple belongs to soci-

---

14. Platten writes that Veyrenc's "pseudo-Racinian language within the text—Vargas has invented numerous examples—signposts both the diegetic and non-diegetic importance of figurative language in the novel." Platten, *Pleasures of Crime,* 239–40.

ety.[15] His scruples are *representative* and can thus transcend, albeit in all modesty, the boundaries of the individual.

Despite Camille's assertion that Adamsberg has not many principles, he never comes across as unprincipled, any more than Race Williams comes across as unethical. The distinction could thus remain purely academic; it is important, however, because it attributes Adamsberg's internal compass, his decisions, his conduct, his investigations, everything, to intuition rather than conscious decision. The distinction would not have the same resonance were Adamsberg an independent detective, or even a lower-ranking policeman; the stakes of his scruples would be too low, their personal nature beside the point. As a scrupulous *commissaire*, Adamsberg constitutes a French counterpoint to the ethical maverick Race Williams. When the decidedly unaffiliated Williams uses the strongly affiliated term "ethics," that term, combined with Williams's ethical actions, removes the sharp edges from his maverick independence. When, on the other hand, the classically affiliated Adamsberg is attached to the independent term *scruples,* the intuitive nature of the term removes the deadening or coercive nature of "normative values and conventional lives." When a good policeman's scruples step in for principle, or come to the result one expects of principle, the result is a sort of ideal society: a police department, a crime-fighting force, a judicial system, a nation, in short, based on a natural and coincidental congruence of private temperament and public interest.

As political historian Sudhir Hazareesingh describes, the notion of natural "becoming" that Hodgson outlines is fundamental to France's self-image. He writes, "The presence of the State is maintained through its self-image as the guardian of the long-term interests of the nation. This self-image is constantly projected to the population, reminding French citizens of the benevolent and paternalistic vocation of their State." The notion of "constant projection" implies a state that needs perhaps protest too much. Indeed, Hazareesingh writes that "the French State is almost unique in the extent to which its public discourse reflects its inflated view of itself." The state attempts to embody desirable personal characteristics (benevolence and paternalism suggesting, respectively, personal will and familial standing). The appeal of Adamsberg as *commissaire* lies in his being benevolent and paternalistic in fact but not in words—that is, not on principle. He himself does not remind or project, and in a sense seems to have no metaconsciousness of himself as state representative or even person in society, which makes any principle-directed "rule

---

15. Sara Poole describes Adamsberg's "moral mission" as "a mission to follow up an intuited source of cruelty." Poole, "Rompols Not of the Bailey," 97.

or code of conduct" beside the point. Camille's friends are surprised to hear that this "special cop" is a *commissaire* rather than a mere inspector. As Hazareesingh writes, "French higher civil servants (*hauts fonctionnaires*) regarded themselves as embodying a particular institutional vocation: the defence of the public interest. Only a highly trained, disciplined, and efficient body of public servants could act as the guardians of the long-term interests of society, because only they had as their prime motivation an abiding attachment to the common good." The higher the ranking of the civil servant, the more that servant's scruple becomes a happy accident, both for the individual and for the state.[16]

Scruple, conscience, improvised societies, nicknames, mistrust of the government, and endless personal peculiarities ensure that personal sovereignty runs parallel to rather than underneath state sovereignty. And yet, the state and its legal institutions become a sort of honorary person, bearing the canonical characteristics of the French character exemplar. When a British reviewer calls Vargas's work "a baked Camembert among the smorgasbord of chilly Scandinavian realism that dominates the foreign crime fiction market," the gastronomic allusion catches Vargas's peculiarly French conflation of culture and state.[17] In terms of character outlines, Adamsberg echoes the nineteenth-century romantic model more precisely than any other French detective, even Maigret. That echoing draws on private contemplativeness as element of the French *patrimoine*. Claire Gorrara, noting that one in five books sold in France is a *polar*, writes that "from being classified as a *genre mineur*, crime fiction has come to be recognized as an important part of France's *patrimoine culturel*."[18] The early nineteenth-century French male romantic hero, postrevolutionary, solitary, nostalgic, melancholic, sometimes pro-Royalist, sometimes protorepublican model, emerged in French literature at the moment when the people's sovereignty and state sovereignty were becoming linked, and when spiritual virtues morphed into character attributes. It was also in the early nineteenth century (1829) that *sergents de ville*, patrolling police forces, were introduced in Paris. As Christine Horton recounts, early directives to the *sergents de ville* "state that 'our action with regard to the public . . . will never assume the character of repression or violence,'" and that they should "cause themselves to be remarked by good

---

16. Hazareesingh, *Political Traditions in Modern France*, 151, 152, 153.

17. Jack Kerridge, "Fred Vargas: 'I Write My Novels in Three Weeks Flat,'" *The Telegraph*, March 6, 2013, http://www.telegraph.co.uk/culture/books/bookreviews/9900139/Fred-Vargas-I-write-my-novels-in-three-weeks-flat.html (accessed February 17, 2016).

18. Gorrara, "French Crime Fiction," 210.

bearing, regular conduct and honest and moderate words and deeds."[19] The romantics were not fond of the term "scrupules," using the word to designate unreasonable hesitation or cowardliness.[20] Adamsberg's principal characteristics, however, are precisely those of the inwardly directed and sentimental romantics: dreaminess and self-containment, fondness for nocturnal promenades, artistic disposition, and apparent nonchalance. Sara Poole writes, "Part Mr. Spock . . . he is also part Cassandra."[21] The description of Adamsberg's childhood at the beginning of *L'homme à l'envers* establishes most of his qualities: "His whole childhood in the Pyrenees had been shrouded in the voices of the elders who told of the last wolves to live in France. And when he walked the mountain paths at night, at the age of nine, . . . he could feel their yellow eyes following him all the way" [Toute son enfance pyrénéenne avait été enveloppée des voix des vieux qui racontaient l'épopée des derniers loups de France. Et quand il parcourait la montagne à la nuit, à neuf ans . . . il croyait voir leurs yeux jaunes le suivre tout au long des sentiers] (12). Poole points out that "elemental and/or natural imagery (the boundary blurs) is in these works not only a stylistic feature which defines characters, but an indulgence of those characters."[22] Adamsberg is part René, pausing to ruminate against a tree on a dark and windy night, and part Leatherstocking, with fields of corn and clouds drifting toward the west.[23] His characteristics hark

---

19. Horton, *Policing Policy in France,* 12, quoting Stead, "New Police."

20. In Lamartine's *Raphael*: "Je ne leur ressemble ni par la patrie, ni par le cœur, ni par l'éducation. Élevée par un mari philosophe, au sein d'une société d'esprits libres, dégagés des croyances et des pratiques de la religion qu'ils ont sapée, je n'ai aucune des superstitions, des faiblesses d'esprit, des scrupules qui courbent le front des femmes ordinaires devant un autre juge que leur conscience" (180). In Hugo's *Lettres à la fiancée*: "Pardonne-moi et ne t'en prends qu'à toi, car c'est toi qui par tes scrupules et tes craintes, me conduis à ces tristes et insipides dissertations" (90). In both of these examples, scruple is coded as feminine, and in particular as a feminine weakness.

21. Poole, "Rompols Not of the Bailey," 96. Séverine Gaspari quotes from Vargas's *Les Jeux de l'amour et de la mort* to describe Adamsberg's "dure douceur ou douce dureté." Gaspari, "Fred Vargas," 43.

22. Poole, "Rompols Not of the Bailey," 104.

23. The habits of solitary ambulation, especially at night, and of resting by trees in a landscape of clouds and wind is well established both among melancholic romantic heroes and French detectives. In Lamartine's *Raphael*: "Je marchais, pour dépenser le temps, d'un bout à l'autre d'un pont qui franchit la Seine presque en face de la maison que Julie habitait. Combien de milliers de fois n'ai-je pas compté les planches de ce pont qui résonnaient sous mes pas!" (265) In Lamartine's *Jocelyn*: "Je connaissais trop cette fatale route; mes genoux fléchissants m'entraînaient vers la voûte; j'y marchais pas à pas sur des monceaux mouvants de feuillages d'automne entassés par les vents" (2:380). In Hugo's *Le Rhin: lettres à un ami*: "Pendant que je marchais, je voyais les étoiles paraître et disparaître aux crevasses du sombre édifice, comme s'il était plein de gens effarés, montant, descendant, courant partout avec des lumières. Comme je revenais à l'auberge, minuit sonnait" (40). One hundred years later, in *Les vacances de Maigret*: "Il marchait le long du remblai, en s'arrêtant de temps en temps. Il

back to a time when virtues were emerging in narrative as character attributes, and when character attributes—even behaviors—carried a shade of virtue. The heavily romantic resonances of the character thus connect scruple to French nation-building to state sovereignty.

Moreover, despite the nonchalance with which Adamsberg practices (though the word seems too assiduous) his profession, he is explicitly identified with France and with Frenchness. Adamsberg demonstrates some unconscious linguistic chauvinism: we learn that when talking about Lawrence, "Adamsberg pronounced 'Laurence,' he had never been able to reproduce English sounds" [Adamsberg prononçait "Laurence," il n'avait jamais pu reproduire un son anglais] (206), and because Lawrence is American, the narrative does become explicitly about the opposition of the insider to the outsider, which in turn underscores the association of policeman with state. When Lawrence speaks, he tends to eliminate the human subject from his sentence. "Disappeared." "Didn't say to leave." "Won't die wondering" (76, 132, 299). In contrast to Adamsberg, who lives within the broad channel of his "je," the absence of the pronoun speaks here to a disconcertingly blank interiority. Once it is revealed that Lawrence was made a puppet of his murderous father, his suppressions of the first-person pronoun resonate as part and parcel of his posttraumatic pathologies. Like the post–hard-boiled characters unable to transcend a traumatic childhood, Lawrence is without accountability or scruple. And yet, in the scruple-principle opposition, Lawrence aligns with principle: "He'd swept up the ageless and odorless droppings on the floor. . . . It had to be done, on principle" [Il avait débarrassé le sol d'un fumier hors d'âge et à vrai dire inodore. C'était pour le principe] (15). When the Canadian who acts on principle turns out to be, as Adamsberg puts it, "a tormented child," then principle becomes an unreliable base. And the comparatively untethered notion of "scruple," paradoxically, becomes a surer road to understanding moral authority.

This is not to suggest that Vargas is running a public relations campaign for the French government; the Frenchness/nationalism in question has nothing to do with the blood purity or idealization of the political extreme right. Rather, Adamsberg exemplifies the way in which the idea of individual subjectivity enters into master narratives of French identity. It is not individualism that underlies the notion of the sovereignty of the people, or rather not American-style individualism, but the fortuitous convergence and continual regeneration of individually held qualities. And yet, part of France's

---

regardait la mer, les silhouettes multicolores qui devenaient de plus en plus nombreuses dans les vagues du bord" (17). In L'amie de Madame Maigret, the divisionnaire walks for the pleasure of walking.

self-image is the very *idea* that the private sphere can at once prosper and enter into moral and aesthetic harmony with state interests. In all hard-boiled literature, there stands a fundamental ambivalence between narrative momentum that relies on freedom from affiliation and narrative resolution that compresses it. This compression is literal as well as figurative, for the resolution of the crime generally marks the end of the narrative. In addition, a state that absorbs the sovereignty of the people inevitably domesticates that sovereignty precisely by embracing it, by naming the *idea* that individuals happen to live. Critics and historians have long noticed France's fondness for its abstract nouns ("liberté, égalité, fraternité"). A state that keeps Adamsberg as *commissaire* and validates him in the name of state interest thereby claims him, his individualism, and even the "holy images" of honesty and beauty at which he has arrived through scruple alone. By placing scruples at the root of Adamsberg's exemplary policing, Camille places the man, his scruples, and his entire temperament—his reverie, languor, nonchalance, indolence—onto the conveyer belt of "becoming." And as Rolls points out, "it is quite possible to read Camille, the love object of the detective and the killer, via the lens of republican iconography. In such an allegorical role, Camille stands as Marianne, and her plight is to be torn between two lovers, one American and the other French."[24] Adamsberg's moral superiority to Lawrence is in many ways code for a superior sense of accountability.[25] Those adults who accept responsibility, who live ideas and give them shape, are the ones who can represent civilization in the broadest sense—both the state named as such, and a community of adults dedicated to scruple and conscience.

SOUS LES VENTS DE NEPTUNE

What makes Adamsberg a character deserving of the hard-boiled name is his fusion of a culturally specific heroic character model with a consistent empathic presence, a "scrupulous" ethics of his own, and a sense of personal-turned-national responsibility. His expectations of others remain low, but his standards for his own conduct are high. I will take a moment to examine *Sous les vents de Neptune* (2004), for this novel explicitly considers those standards.

---

24. Rolls, *Paris and the Fetish*, 105.

25. It also points to a more classically French masculinity; Adamsberg's mispronunciation of "Lawrence" as "Laurence" in essence gives him a female name. Rousseau contrasted human to animal, and the novel thematizes these intersections, but the relevant divergence is also that between adult and child. In a subplot, Adamsberg convinces a young hooligan, Sabrina, not to shoot him by showing her a picture of her son.

Furthermore, it connects ethical responsibility to emotional presence in personal relationships—a particularly twenty-first-century issue that brings the classic hard-boiled model up against contemporary discourses of intimacy. In *Sous les vents de Neptune,* Adamsberg is drugged and framed for a murder by the same trident-wielding, psychopathic judge who had framed Adamsberg's own brother for murder decades before. Adamsberg's framing (this is the scenario that necessitates his ingenious rescue from Canadian justice on the back of his lieutenant) is foregrounded so that the reader never doubts his innocence. Adamsberg himself, however, is deeply troubled by the hours he cannot remember: "Was it the idea of losing a chunk out of his life that was so irritating, as if it had been confiscated without permission? Or was it that the alcohol was not enough of an explanation? Or, more seriously, was he worried about what he might have said or done in the missing hours?" [Était-ce que l'idée d'avoir perdu une parcelle de sa vie le contrariait, comme si on l'eût tronqué sans lui demander son avis? Ou que la simple explication de l'alcool ne lui convenait pas? Ou, plus grave, qu'il s'inquiétât de ce qu'il avait pu dire ou faire durant ces heures effacées?].[26] He never seems actually to believe that he could have committed the murder, though the Canadian police think he has, but he wants to remember where he has been. Furthermore, in his musings, this failure to remember is coupled with the failure to bring Judge Fulgence to justice and thus to avenge the framing of his brother. And these shortcomings, in turn, link to a more general failure in his personal relationships:

> Was it perhaps true that the absolute protection he felt he ought to have given Raphaël had kept him in orbit, far from earth, far from other people in any case, in a kind of weightless existence? And the same went for his relations with women too, of course. To allow himself to get carried away would have been to abandon Raphaël to die alone in his cave. And that was impossible. So it might explain why he had always fled from love, and even destroyed it? Had he really gone that far? (322)

> Et il était possible, pourquoi pas, que l'absolue protection due à Raphaël l'ait retenu en orbite assez loin du monde, à bonne distance des autres en tout cas, dans une apesanteur. Et bien sûr à distance des femmes. S'en aller dans cette voie, c'eût été lâcher Raphaël et le laisser crever seul dans son antre. Un acte impossible qui l'obligerait peut-être à s'absenter devant l'amour. Voire à le détruire? Et jusqu'à quel point? (369)

---

26. Vargas, *Wash This Blood Clean,* 175; *Sous les vents de Neptune,* 204. Subsequent references to these works will be given parenthetically.

In this economy of conscience, the capacities to bring the criminal to justice, form a loving partnership with another person, and declare with certainty that one had not committed a felony the previous evening are all of a piece. To be accountable for one's actions is to be counted, and thus to enter most fully into the social world. The fleeing from love arises from the failure to enact justice in society and in his original family, but it also proves his desire to redress that failure, to pursue justice rather than to "allow himself to get carried away." In this sense, Adamsberg is a contemporary version of the solitary 1930s American detective, casting his sometimes immature conduct with Camille as a side effect of the search for justice. Indeed, as if to compensate for his absence from Camille and to demonstrate that it is a matter of understandable emotional blockage rather than active sexism or caddishness, this novel puts the action and the case's resolution into the hands of women. Violette Retancourt saves Adamsberg from the Canadian police, Clémentine hides him in France, and the senior citizen superhacker Josette provides information that convicts the judge in absentia.

THESE ARE THEIR STORIES

In the United States, numerous contemporary novelists have taken up the hard-boiled mantle, many with considerable commercial and critical success. Among these are Robert Parker, James Ellroy, Walter Mosley, Sara Paretsky, Lawrence Block, Marcia Muller, James Sallis, George Pelecanos, Sue Grafton, and Barbara Fister. Rather than select one or more of these (or another, because this list is not exhaustive), I will examine some alternative but nonetheless central specimens of the contemporary American hard-boiled: ones taken from the small screen. In going from books to television, I am conscious of opening some avenues of analysis that will get too short a shrift here. And yet, television has generated some of the widest cultural conversations about moral authority and the individual as social being, and its immensely popular hard-boiled narratives deserve to be examined as such.

A glance over the past forty years of American crime television reveals that, very schematically stated, an abundance of eponymous crime fighters gave way in the 1990s to a reinforcement of the institutional or collective model. Where once there were *Mike Hammer* (1956–1959, 1984–1989), *Mannix* (1967–1975), *The Rockford Files* (1974–1980), *Baretta* (1975–1978), *Quincy* (1976–1983), *Magnum, P.I.* (1980–1988), *Cagney and Lacey* (1981–1988), *Knight Rider* (1982–1986), *T. J. Hooker* (1982–1986), *Remington Steele* (1982–1987), and *Spenser: For Hire* (1985–1988), television has turned in the last two decades to, among others, *Law and Order* (1990–2010), *Law and Order: Special Victims Unit* (1999–present), *Law and Order: Criminal Intent* (2001–2011), *NYPD Blue* (1993–2005), *CSI* (2000–present), *Criminal Minds* (2005–present), *Homicide* (1993–1999), *JAG* (1995–2005), *Third Watch* (1999–2005), and *NCIS* (2003–present). *Hill Street Blues* (1981–1987) was an early example. The twenty-first century has produced dramas that focus neither on the lone hero nor on the institutional corrective, but rather on the individual as social being. These series include *The Wire* (2002–2008), *The Killing* (2011–2014), *The Blacklist* (2013–present), and *True Detective* (2014–present). On the French side, the eponymous trend continues with *Julie Lescaut* (1992–2013) and *Léa Parker* (2004–2006), but these are accompanied by such company narratives as *RIS, Police Scientifique* (2005–present), *Braquo* (2009–present), *PJ* (1997–2009), and the ensemble series *Engrenages* (2005–present).

While the preponderance of chest hair and leisure suits has tarnished the philosophical gravitas of many 1970s and 1980s title characters, some of them are nonetheless the indirect narrative descendants of Leatherstocking's and Sam Spade's contained self-sufficiency. Writes Dana Cloud about *Spenser: For Hire* (based on Robert Parker's novels): "He can shoot bad guys, find counseling for a rape victim or reconcile an estranged father and son, quote Romantic poetry and wax philosophical on the state of society, make a soufflé, and go a round with his buddy Hawk in the boxing ring—all without any sense of personal fragmentation or contradiction."[27] Writes Gregory Waller on *Mickey Spillane's Mike Hammer*: "He is utterly unique in his world, a bona fide star. Always wearing a hat and a plain, unfashionable suit and tie, the experienced, self-confident Hammer looks like he stepped out of a hard-boiled detective movie of the 1940s."[28] The absence of "personal fragmentation" recalls the solidity of the trauma-resistant Race Williams—an unproblematic individual who stands as veritable instrument of drama and justice. And indeed, the two aforementioned television detectives were born as novel characters. The 1990s and the 2000s, however, saw a transformation in crime detective programs. *The Practice* edged out the individual detective, and an ethic of "We the People" replaced *I the Jury*. The title character detective drama has all but disappeared from the screen. Indeed, programs named for their main characters are for the most part comedies focusing on human foibles.[29]

---

27. Cloud, "Limits of Interpretation," 313.

28. Waller, "Mike Hammer," 119.

29. A notable exception, the medical show *House*, combined the heroic model with a throwback to the tormented, sometimes drug-addled detective characters of the mid-twentieth century.

Given the repeated insistence in contemporary procedural series that the "system" must be maintained even when it proves inadequate, I would propose that the transition to an institutional focus represents fundamental suspicion of unconstrained individual force. However, the individualist excesses to which such contemporary programs respond are not rooted in television. Rather, I would propose, the excesses implied in contemporary crime drama come from the real world of crime and politics, which continued the sort of personality trends embodied in Jim Thompson's fiction even as crime fiction retreated into more domesticated models. As Stephen King remarked in his introduction to *The Killer Inside Me,* the brute force and delusional certitude of Lou Ford was shared by politicians, making Thompson's a national as well as literary portrait of the "Great American Sociopath." King's observation points to the lived perils of autonomy detached from accountability. In what seems to be a direct response to abuses of power and declines in political answerability, American hard-boiled crime television since the late 1990s has been principally concerned with correcting grandiosity and self-delusion while resurrecting the empathic bond. To a surprising extent, these institution-driven dramas are dedicated to directing the characters' focus outwards, to "living the idea" of the importance of the rule of law and the downsides of careless and unbridled authority. The vaunting of the institution and abstract nouns such as justice, law, and country allows the characters to domesticate classic hard-boiled profiles. They walk a line between autonomy as breath of fresh air and autonomy as menace to social order, portraying maverick individualism as seductive, attainable, but needing to be formed to the common good.

LAW AND ORDER

I will start with a short discussion of *Law and Order,* which ran from 1990 to 2010 and marks a transition from unrestrained individualism to what I am calling a restorative hard-boiled model. *Law and Order* is not a hard-boiled drama, nor does it embody an "ethics of my own," but it does exemplify what passed for a corrective to rampant individualism in the 1990s. Every episode of *Law and Order* starts with a low male voice-over intoning, "In the criminal justice system, the people are represented by two separate but equally important groups: the police who investigate crime and the district attorneys who prosecute the offenders. These are their stories." The police and prosecutors are the people in our culture who, when a crime is committed, "respond" to the scene. In *Law and Order,* the strongest characteristic of the police and the prosecutors is steadiness. In the first episode (1990), the detectives shout at each other in the office, the lieutenant discloses that he is recovering from a drinking problem, and the district attorney remembers aloud his alcoholic father. In later episodes, even in episodes later that same season, there is no shouting. At almost no time in the original series do we see homes, cars, friends, families, pets, or paychecks; personal lives take place off-screen. The true spectacle in this series, the principal story told, is not the characters' dramatic response to crime, nor the plot's resolution thereof, but the absence of unbalanced conduct by the main characters, the absence of psychic commotion or unrest.

A television series differs from a novel in countless ways, including often, and especially in the case of *Law and Order,* the absence of a broad narrative arc. Tensions rise and fall over the course of individual episodes, but each episode is a contained unit. Dick Wolf, producer of the series, likened it to Campbell's soup and explained that "people feel comfortable going to something they know about. It attracts you because you know what you're getting."[30] The detectives and the prosecutors are able to respond with steady impassivity each episode, immune to both evolution and devolution. In their stasis, I propose, they respond to a powerful cultural dream of individual relationship to principle. *Law and Order* addresses the dismantling of "Character" as a whole by showing unrevealing movement rather than thriving interiority. The series replaces Martin Terrier's "extinct emotional life" with a sustained—but just as immobile and impassive—intimation of emotional presence. The absence of personal lives is more than just a matter of screen-time economy; it allows the characters to live the ideas of justice and procedure to the exclusion of everything else, thus suppressing problematic individualism.

To some extent, the impassiveness of the *Law and Order* cast speaks to a public fantasy about response to widespread violence. Throughout the program, not just the police and prosecutors, but every character, from the random couple who finds the body, to the witnesses, to the medical examiner, to the initial suspects and their families, to the courtroom spectators, to the incidental characters and bureaucracies that furnish information, to the juries, to the foreperson with the verdict, looks on with detachment. People standing around watching as suspects are hauled into the police car sometime in the initial half hour invariably look as though they were watching a television episode being filmed on their street rather than an actual friend or acquaintance being arrested. Witnesses questioned by the police can scarcely

---

30. Interview by author with Neal Baer, executive producer of *Law and Order SVU,* 2002.

be bothered to spare the time ("Are we finished here? I need to get back to work"), as if the appalling murder at hand were a minor distraction. Assistant District Attorney Jack McCoy (Sam Waterston) shakes his head at murders in his world the way the public shakes its head at murders in the actual world—on the one hand because *Law and Order* does take its stories from the news ("ripped from the headlines"), so the public and the characters are in a sense witnessing the same murders, and furthermore because they are witnessing them in the same way: as detached spectators.[31] *Law and Order's* steadiness of focus is a dramatic occurrence because television representation of violence does not just bring to us what we would otherwise not see, and does not just bring it to us contained, but implies that what it contains would, without that containment, be devastating for us.[32] At the same time, a corresponding dramatic vein centers on the characters themselves—on emotional response and on the individual's very self as a protected domain. Not only do the police and prosecutors protect the spectator from what Mark Seltzer calls "the pathological public sphere," they demonstrate that public servants carry within themselves a fundamentally impermeable and protected emotional world: that where scruple stood in the French model, static imperviousness stands in the American. Even the improbable impatience of the questioned witnesses conveys the main idea that all the show's characters are living, namely, the idea of work and responsibility. Duty trumps personality, in what I would propose is a particularly American response to individualist excesses, even if it eventually proves to be an unsatisfying one.

Philip Lane writes of *Homicide*: "The detectives of *Homicide* are very cool at the scene of a crime. They talk philosophy, engage in nonsensical repartee, discuss personal relationships and problems while standing over a corpse. They appear to be objective observers of a crime scene; but, in fact, their

---

31. Television spectators are of course not universally removed from daily violence. For one, in cities, suburbs, farms, and everywhere, domestic violence, as much a menace to society as street violence, is more common than television would have us think, and many times more common than dramatic gun battles. Second, there are numerous places in this country where street violence is an everyday occurrence, where interaction with the criminal justice system is a norm rather than an aberration, and where public discourse about violence is therefore more resigned than horrified. New York City, where *Law and Order* is set, contains some of these places. The point is that most residents of this country, and most spectators of *Law and Order*, do not have regular contact with police and prosecutors. And even those who do see shootings and robberies on their streets generally still see their first murder on television, not on their block. On the basis of sheer numbers, *Law and Order* addresses us, as most crime television addresses us, as spectators who know about violence from watching it on television or reading about it in the news. See Lee, "These Are Our Stories."

32. As Avital Ronell wonders in "Trauma TV," "What is television covering?" (309). And: "What video teaches, something that television knows but cannot as such articulate, is that every medium is related in some crucial way to specters" (313).

daily dosage of death eventually gets to them."[33] But in *Law and Order,* that dosage (and *Law and Order* ran longer than *Homicide*) does not "get to" the detectives. There is no accumulation of trauma, no boredom, no hardness, no increase or decrease in the capacity for empathy. Again and again, the camera remains focused on one face long enough to see an unwavering steadiness of regard, serious but not cold. The pain of violence, of contact with victims and sociopaths, never contaminates the characters' attendance record at the job or pushes them into a morass of depression or makes them uninterested in or hardened to human concerns. This vision in which social consciousness, ethical responsibility, and a fountain of calm flow forth from a seemingly inexhaustible source represents a vision of psychic security. But more than this, it represents a durable contentedness with living an idea that is always external. In addition to psychic intactness and empathic presence in the face of violence, the *Law and Order* characters represent characters content to live an idea—the idea of the rule of law—without acting upon or distorting that idea. Their dedication to the law, combined with their psychic intactness, constitutes their contribution to society, their acts of protection and service. They are the guardians and handlers of important abstract nouns, charged with ensuring their unimpeded circulation.

McCOY: The New York County District Attorney's office can't—no, won't knowingly convict a man of the wrong crime. What are you thinking?

CARMICHAEL: Well, I'm just taking a page from the Jack McCoy playbook. Nobody gets to bend the rules but you?

McCOY: I've bent the rules to convict the right person of the right crime. This isn't bending, this is turning the law against itself.

CARMICHAEL: You once hid a witness to get the result that you wanted.

McCOY: And I was wrong then. You're wrong now. Don't wait till you're facing a disciplinary committee to realize it.[34]

In their continued insistence on following the rules and answering to institutional authority, *Law and Order* characters depart from the menace created by the mid-century hard-boiled and the political characters who echoed it, characters who bore the specter of threat within them. The character who is as much problem as solution has become part of the landscape, part of the infrastructure, part of the preexisting symbolic environment, and the detec-

---

33. Lane, "Existential Condition," 146. *Homicide: Life on the Street* (1993–1999) ran parallel to *Law and Order;* at times, a two-part episode would start on one series and end on the other.

34. "Agony," *Law and Order: The Ninth Year.* Written by Dick Wolf and Kathy McCormick. Directed by Constantine Makris. Aired November 4, 1998. Universal, 2011, DVD.

tives' capacity to stand at a respectful distance from principal comforts the spectator against the prospect of such encroaching or unrestrained personality. It is remarkable that this program, the longest-running and most popular crime drama on American television, and one that constantly showcases the de facto insufficiency of the law, also represents the continuing suppression or domestication of interiority. This suppression, combined with the law's insufficiency, places the series in the eye of the individual-institutional hardboiled storm. The characters cannot convict every murderer, and even when a conviction is made, it is invariably presented as a drop in the ocean. These continual shortcomings allow the series to continue, but they also establish—again and again—that the value of the idea of the rule of law is not in its actual functioning, but in its essence, its very existence, its form, as echoed in the unbending narrative contours of each episode's editing.

Given that television is a medium that addresses spectators explicitly as consumers, the notion of a character as hero is more realizable than ever. And yet, while *Law and Order* gives a comforting vision of first responders as forming a sort of cultural security blanket, none of its characters would count as a culture hero. The act of listening suspends them between action and inaction. The characters are present but unobtrusive, lending an individual ear but not acting in any way that could code as troublesome. Indeed, there is a near evacuation of the self, since these are stories ("These are their stories") about living an idea without ruining it:

McCOY: I don't know what I find scarier, Abbie, clowns like these [suspects] having a free pass to break the law, or one of our own A.D.A.s taking their side.

CARMICHAEL: [The victim] is the bad guy here.

McCOY: He's alive. His sister and the babysitter are dead.

CARMICHAEL: It's overkill. But [the victim] is a coldblooded murderer. Like it or not, [the suspects] did us a service by catching him.

McCOY: A service? They're outlaws. I'm going to check on their weapons permits. I don't care if they forgot the period after their middle initial, I'm having their permits yanked.[35]

Law and Order plays as an antidote to the individualist excesses of the 1970s and 1980s. Its focus on abstract nouns and their institutions, its neutral costumes, its minimal facial movements—that such characters lasted for so long

---

35. "Hunters," *Law and Order: The Ninth Year*. Written by Dick Wolf and Gerry Conway. Directed by Richard Dobbs. Aired February 10, 1999. Universal, 2011, DVD.

demonstrates the powerful contemporary attraction of living an idea while maintaining a respectful distance from it. And yet the series, reliable and formulaic, does not propose a real reconciliation of personality with principle. Not for these characters the *ideinost* of the Russian nineteenth century, since the repeated allusions to constitutional parameters, combined with the minimal exposition of personal lives, hints at an individuality that varies inversely with dedication to principle. *Law and Order* provided an exit ramp from the hard-boiled dramas of individualism and its discontents, but in so doing merely deferred crime fiction's ultimate drive to examine, again and again, what the individual could do on his or her own steam. To return to this drive, I examine two HBO drama series, *True Detective* and *The Wire*.

TRUE DETECTIVE

The first season of *True Detective* (2014) tells the story of two police detectives in southern Louisiana who investigate what seems to be a ritual murder. The series partners the swaggering, adulterous, southern traditionalist Marty Hart (Woody Harrelson) with the brooding and taciturn Rustin Cohle (Matthew McConaughey). It alternates between Hart and Cohle's 1995 investigation of the murder and the 2012 police questioning of Cohle, who by then has scraggly hair, bad skin, a mustache, a taste for bottom-shelf beer, and no badge. There is some suspicion that Cohle had himself had a hand in the crime. Cohle walks through the job with a combination of absentmindedness and grim determination. Indeed, without the muscles, the movie star looks, and the steady gaze, the 1995 Cohle could be a Eugène Tarpon, prone to showing up drunk at dinners and responding to personal questions in incoherent sentence fragments. But this drama clearly endeavors to act out questions of moral authority, as well as to engage the decades of hard-boiled backstory that make those questions so fraught. The result is a radically stripped-down portrait of character that resurrects nineteenth-century American traits much as Adamsberg resurrects the French. The series has numerous shortcomings, outlined in review articles and online forums; Cohle, however, is the very embodiment of the post–*Law and Order,* postnihilistic hero, the embodiment of burdened individualism for the twenty-first century.

Instead of the dedication of the *Law and Order* cast, which showcased the acting out of procedural norms without the muddling intervention of personalities, *True Detective* is all interiority. Cohle is a bereaved father without friends, without intimate connections, without Gods or masters, without furniture—low on personality but rich in subjectivity. In the first episode, he explains his worldview: "I think human consciousness is a tragic misstep in evolution. We became too self-aware. Nature created an aspect of nature separate from itself. We are creatures that should not exist by natural law. We are things that labor under the illusion of having a self. A secretion of sensory experience and feeling programmed with total assurance that we are each somebody, when in fact everybody's nobody." When Hart then asks him why he gets out of bed in the morning, Cohle answers, "I tell myself I bear witness. The real answer is that it's obviously my programming, and I lack the constitution for suicide." These lines are presented as an excessively bleak foil to Hart's jovial conventionality—"My luck, I picked today to get to know you"—but the vocabulary of programming and self-awareness shows that this is a hard-boiled program for an era that has thought a great deal about the self as problem and solution. Emily Nussbaum, remarking on the overseriousness of the series and its principal characters, describes Rust as "a macho fantasy straight out of Carlos Castaneda. A sinewy weirdo with a tragic past, Rust delivers arias of philosophy, a mash-up of Nietzsche, Lovecraft, and the nihilist horror writer Thomas Ligotti." She then gets at the cultural appeal of the man and his gravitas: "Rust is a heretic with a heart of gold. He's *our* fetish object—the cop who keeps digging when everyone ignores the truth, the action hero who rescues children in the midst of violent chaos, the outsider with painful secrets and harsh truths and nice arms. McConaughey gives an exciting performance, but his rap is premium baloney."[36]

If Cohle's rap is baloney, it is because he moves with nonchalance across miles of post-Kantian philosophies of consciousness, and in so doing he contradicts himself several times. And yet, he carries on hitting the precise conceptual points that hard-boiled fiction has been covering for almost a century, and addressing them so as to show how embattled the ideas of autonomy and even moral authority have become in both the hard-boiled and political domains. It is hardly coincidence that the guilty parties in the show's various murders are connected to the ruling political and evangelical families in the state, and that the suspect is a "metapsychotic." If the suspect is a "metapsychotic," then Cohle is a metadetective, and indeed, nearly every one of Cohle's scenes is about individual reclamation of authority through either declaration or metaphoric reappropriations. In an early scene, for instance, we see the large wooden cross decorating the wall above the mattress in Cohle's apartment. Since the cross is the apartment's only decoration, Hart asks about it,

36. Nussbaum, "Cool Story, Bro." n. pag. http://www.newyorker.com/magazine/2014/03/03/cool-story-bro, accessed February 26, 2015. "The Long Bright Dark," *True Detective*. Written by Nic Pizzolatto. Directed by Cary Joji Fukunaga. HBO, 2014. Television.

and Cohle explains: "It's a form of meditation. I contemplate the moment in the garden, the idea of allowing your own crucifixion." The entire hard-boiled enterprise is about locating a self, or a portion of the self, or a series of impulses within what we are accustomed to calling the self, that can act and decide in a meaningful way, and that can balance freedom of action with genuine benefit to society. Cohle's appropriation of the cross is a philosophical version of Williams's "My ethics are my own," for an entire symbolic register is Cohle's own. We are constantly reminded that he is the generator of his own ideas—when Cohle describes the murder suspect as being "religious in some kind of way," his partner points out: "Every person within a thousand miles of here is religious in some kind of way. Except you." And yet, while the series takes pains to show Cohle doing a lot of thinking, he nonetheless mistrusts and deprecates thought, insisting on distanciation from subjectivity ("we became too self-aware," "we labor under the illusion of having a self").

To the Chandler formula of the man of honor "without thought of it, and certainly without saying it," Cohle seems to add "without wanting it and almost without tolerating it."[37] Again, if this rap is unbelievable, it is because the character both deploys and denigrates such a remarkable assortment of subjective mechanisms, and necessarily narrates himself into a philosophical corner while critiquing illusion, programming, constitution, and the entire "secretion of sensory experience" that is humankind. Robert Pippin, writing on Manfred Frank and the "priority and irreducibility of the subject" as counterpoint to "objectivism, the position that holds that the knowing, perceiving, and acting subject must be understood as just another, however unique, object in the world, in the best way objects in the world are understood, by modern science," points out that "awareness of the world must be something well beyond a receptor's capacity to receive and process and respond to sensory data" (this would be the programming that Cohle mentions as he describes humans as secretions of sensory experience), "it must be an awareness . . . being 'owned' individually." Cohle argues neither—again to cite Pippin on Frank—for "individual minds as primary bearers and sustainers of linguistic and general meaning" nor for "the issue of the normativ-

---

37. Nic Pizzolatto says, "If we're talking about hard-boiled detectives, what could be more hard-boiled than the worldview of Ligotti or Cioran? They make the grittiest of crime writers seem like dilettantes. Next to 'The Conspiracy Against the Human Race,' Mickey Spillane seems about as hard-boiled as bubble gum." Michael Calia, "Writer Nic Pizzolatto on Thomas Ligotti and the Weird Secrets of 'True Detective,'" *Wall Street Journal*, February 2, 2014, http://blogs.wsj.com/speakeasy/2014/02/02/writer-nic-pizzolatto-on-thomas-ligotti-and-the-weird-secrets-of-true-detective/ (accessed February 17, 2016).

ity and socially sustained normativity of meaning."[38] Rather, he stands as far from subjectivity as possible—not just from philosophies of consciousness, but from consciousness as a whole. Writer Nic Pizzolatto describes Cohle's philosophy as a "kind of anti-natalist nihilism." The "sinewy" descriptor is as relevant to his minimalist concept of self as it is to his extreme economy of movement and muscle tone. It modulates the pathological excesses of the American model. In a nod to the Europe of his philosophies of consciousness, even his aestheticism and literary sensibility are without thought of it. Painterly impressions of nature come to him unbidden through acid flashbacks, and he riffs on horror writer Thomas Ligotti to such an extent that Pizzolatto was accused of plagiarism.

If the *Law and Order* cast lived the idea of individuals subject to and otherwise responsible for getting out of the way of the rule of law, Cohle lives the idea of getting out of the way as an end in itself. As a result, he alternates between embracing isolation and wanting to be part of a greater whole. Asked what it means to be a pessimist, he explains, "It means I'm bad at parties," to which Marty responds that he is "not great outside of parties, either." In one of his 2012 questioning scenes, he states, "I know who I am. After all this time, there's a victory in that." Even the police work he does is presented as a matter of personal taste. When he leaves the station to track down prostitutes who might have known the murder victim, he presents it as a way to pass the time: "Mind if I escape? I got some names from vice. Just something to do." This character is a far cry from the clear-eyed, institutionally entrenched idealists of the *Law and Order* cast, and much closer to the ruminating *commissaire* Adamsberg. And yet, when asked why he chose to work in homicide, he quotes Corinthians: "The body is not one member but many. Now are they many, but of one body. I was just trying to stay a part of the body." This contradiction, this resistance to and simultaneous participation in the social body, reveals the conscious exertion that being "without thought of it" demands. In using the vocabulary of the body, he turns his participation in society into an exercise in individual wholeness, which honors his self-containment even while giving it a broader resonance. And yet, that exercise—and it is an exercise—is as laborious as it is necessary. Furthermore, as Emily Nussbaum points out in her discussion of the series's "shallow deep talk," the contemplations of subjectivity clash with a triviality in personal relations and in representations of women. The show concentrates on women as murder victims and vague romantic interests, not as characters. This is a

---

38. Pippin, *Persistence of Subjectivity*, 169, 170.

remarkable flaw of the first season, but not of Cohle as a character. His inability to form relationships is presented as one existential flaw among many.

A DREAM IN A LOCKED ROOM

The rise of hard-boiled individualism, its contamination, and contemporary gestures toward its resurrection raise fundamental questions about how even to talk about individual autonomy without simply going back and forth between the idea of independence and its negation. The broad historical arcs of detective fiction on both sides of the Atlantic indicate that the most valued culture heroes are those who both resist convention and come on their own steam to empathic treatment of others—it is not the substance of convention that characters resist, rather the very fact of convention—but again and again this is a false binary. Just as that opposition breaks down when Race Williams declares an ethics of his own that closely resembles an ethics of reciprocity, so it does when Cohle as drunken agnostic pessimist quotes the Bible. And the question thus becomes: how does one talk about—and then in fact make—individual decisions that are neither rote, flattened by Kantian Oughts, nor detrimental to the common good? Can autonomy be made to matter, and to have an enlivening rather than destructively entropic result? The hard-boiled genre traces the myriad obstacles and perils to such revitalization of autonomy but also, surprisingly, shows the way to its realization.

Cohle's speech illuminates the difficulty of living an idea in a way that gives living free rein and the idea transcendent importance. The hard-boiled genre is all about maintaining the balancing act of coincidence, where the character who could not care less about convention manages to do its office, and to do it better and more humanely than any institution could. Some of this has to do with avoiding "preexisting symbolic environments" where actions, ideas, places, and characters are already marked. It is telling that Nussbaum describes Cohle as delivering "arias of philosophy, a mash-up of Nietzsche, Lovecraft, and the nihilist horror writer Thomas Ligotti," since the entire conversation around autonomy has morphed into a sort of eternal sampling, to the point where originality has become a sort of anachronism, and innovation means citation of obscure references. Pizzolatto points out the similarities between *True Detective* and Camus's "existential stoicism,"[39] and

---

39. Dave Walker, "'True Detective' Writer Nic Pizzolatto Discusses Crime Fiction, Noir and Existential Questions," *New Orleans Times-Picayune,* July 8, 2013, http://www.nola.com/tv/index.ssf/2013/07/true_detective_writer_nic_pizz.html (accessed February 17, 2016).

were it not for his dedication to justice, this character could too come very close to the "pompous false simplicity" of Butron and Chateaubriand's tomb.

The history of the hard-boiled is the history of maverick action as an escape from leaden Kantian Oughts, but also of that action's associations with excess, madness, and eventual futility. If there is a lesson to be learned from the hard-boiled, it is that there are limitations not in autonomy's manifestations but in what it can do for the individual and for society. *True Detective* showed a detective struggling against those limitations as well as the boundaries of narrative and character. But that struggle, as painful as Cohle makes it seem, is the entire point. The sheer abundance of discourse around the character—his philosophies, actions, tone, and "sinewy weirdness"—indicates that when it comes to talking about autonomy, it is not a disembodied idea that one wants but a character living that idea and living it with others. Andy Greenwald writes of Cohle: "In the '90s he's all pinched stillness, a rubber band wrapped tight around a razor blade. That version of Rust Cohle keeps everything inside because he believes he's in control. The 2012 Rust has let everything go because he knows for certain he's not."[40] But the seventeen-year jump forward—to a man more tattered and tired, less handsome—also tracks a broader, culture-wide weariness with the exaltation and disappointments of individual autonomy—the same exaltations and disappointments that the hard-boiled genre has been tracking for almost a century. During interrogation, Cohle meditates on the limitations of subjectivity: "All your life, all your love, all your hate, all your memory, all your pain, it was all the same thing," he soliloquizes. "It was all the same dream—a dream that you had inside a locked room. A dream about being a person." These ruminations might indeed be self-protective, for as Shane Ryan writes, "Cohle, for his stoic demeanor and the absolute confidence of his delivery, is a man in a constant state of turmoil. He talks the talk of someone who has given up on life, but it's a defensive act, a last grasp for protection, when the staggering and heartbreaking truth is that he wants, deeply, those things that an unlucky fate has denied him."[41] But for the purposes of charting a hard-boiled history, and what is more a history of the hard-boiled's trust in the individual as repository of moral authority, the 2012 version of Cohle's character, his edge dulled by alcohol, stands as an incarnation of arguments about autonomy

---

40. Andy Greenwald, "True Detective: Six Questions for the Second Half of the Season," https://grantland.com/hollywood-prospectus/true-detective-six-questions-for-the-second-half-of-the-season (accessed May 5, 2014).

41. Shane Ryan, "*True Detective* Review: 'The Locked Room' (Episode 1:03)," http://www.pastemagazine.com/articles/2014/01/true-detective-review-the-locked-room-episode-103.html (accessed May 5, 2014).

and consciousness themselves. Cohle is devoted to standing apart from self, constitution, programming, illusion, and even self-awareness, but the energies he tries to dismiss in the name of those phenomena inevitably return. So too does the paradigm of the individual as generator of moral power.

MOMENTS WORTH IMITATING

What makes Cohle and other hard-boiled characters "fetish objects" is that they seem to take their ideals either from themselves or from some pristine platonic sphere; one very rarely sees hard-boiled characters imitating some-one else. Cohle's numerous discourses are notable for not referring to actual people. He has been clear that there is no one for him to emulate, not the sur-vivalist father or the absent mother. And yet, that is how people tend to learn, to choose their conduct—in imitation not of disembodied principles but of people or characters, even if the characters are there only to animate the prin-ciple. No one envisions "honor" in a vacuum, but rather as an embodied attri-bute. The hard-boiled plays on that paradox of imitation: it fastens morality to a set of characteristics, to a character outline that seems itself, somehow, improbably, to be born in a vacuum. Much research shows that people learn moral behavior by imitating, but the buck stops with hard-boiled characters who have no other apparent source than themselves.[42] What the hard-boiled offers, then, is a compendium of admirable moments—moments of living an idea that is at once one's own, and greater than oneself. *Law and Order*'s aggressively strict editing—no families, no homes, no tracking shots—sug-gests that impassivity and empathy are not eternally sustainable. So too with the laconic hard-boiled characters—Philip Marlowe and his epigrams, Race Williams and his bursts of energetic narration, Rust Cohle and his soliloquies in the car. In a sense, this is the hard-boiled's strongest fictional triumph: its editing of character portraits to make moments of force and compassion seem enduring, and its philosophical discourses constitutive. Even Chandler's iconic "down these mean streets a man must go who is not himself mean" gives an illusory picture of character solidity. It does not take much time to walk down a street, but we do get the sense that this "man of honor" is honor-able all the time. Indeed, Cohle's character only makes sense—and his solil-oquies can only be delivered—in the context of his partnership with Hart. What the contemporary hard-boiled showcases is less a character model than

---

42. Rushton, "Generosity in Children"; Eisenberg, *The Caring Child*.

a goal, a portrait of the endeavor to live an idea, and an outline of the community needed to do so.

THE WIRE

The real complexities of community are fundamental for the contemporary hard-boiled's treatment of individual moral agency. For while the outside world contains empathic listeners, it also contains material conditions and structural rigidities that impact subjectivity. In order to examine the meaning of individualism within collective structures—as well as the role of individuals in their creation—I turn to the television drama *The Wire*, which ran on HBO from 2002 to 2008. *The Wire* preceded *True Detective* in chronology, but its epic scale, its critical success, and its emphasis on the vital symbiosis of individualism and community make it an ideal concluding illustration of the restorative American hard-boiled.[43] *The Wire* showed characters constantly negotiating the sometimes considerable distance between ideas and realities, or between ideals and possibilities. It takes place in the East Coast American city of Baltimore, and each of its five seasons underscores the ambitions, failures, and corruptions of particular social groups and institutions. These include the police department, government, courts, public education, and media, as well as less legally codified systems such as the Barksdale drug organization, families, and a sprawling population of drug dealers, consumers, henchmen, bystanders, and casualties. Much of what makes *The Wire* valuable as a specimen of the restorative hard-boiled is its close proximity to the systemic hopelessness of the *néo-polar* and its characters' strong potential to follow in that suit. Indeed, the chess metaphor that the series's drug dealers use to discuss their own chain of command is reminiscent of Gérault on the *néo-polar*: "The individual becomes a moveable pawn in a world that excludes him, a violent and pitiless world."[44] I propose, however, that *The Wire*, even as it insists on the futilities of idealism and the crushing force of institutions,

---

43. To discuss this series in a book about hard-boiled crime fiction is to trust David Simon's early statement that it is a "novel for television" (http://www.borderline-productions.com/TheWireHBO/exclusive-4.html, accessed April 2, 2016) and endorse the editor of *Film Quarterly* in his comments on *The Wire* as a "major work of recent American fiction in any medium." White, "Make-Believe, Memory Failure," 4.

44. Gérault, *Jean-Patrick Manchette*, 11–12. Paul Allen Anderson remarks, in his excellent analysis of the series's often-used game metaphor, that understanding social control does not invalidate it: "The pathos of the pawn's situation is that increased self-awareness and knowledge about the game and its terms only increase recognition of one's limited agency and constraint." Anderson, "'The Game Is the Game,'" 380.

nonetheless opens up a provocative and complex space for individual morality. As such, it has suggestive implications for the attribution of accountability and the relevance of moral criticism in modern corporate capitalism.

In one sense, it is true, *The Wire* resists the very concept of individual autonomy. As numerous critics have noted, the series is an ensemble piece in the most fundamental sense, meaning that no one can transcend the ensemble. *The Wire* plays out the failure of one social system after another, one ambition after another. Anmol Chaddha and William Julius Wilson write: "Through a scrupulous exploration of the inner workings of drug-dealing gangs, the police, politicians, unions, and public schools, *The Wire* shows that individuals' decisions and behavior are often shaped by—and indeed limited by—social, political, and economic forces beyond their control."[45] David Simon also stated: "*The Wire* is making an argument about what institutions—bureaucracies, criminal enterprises, the cultures of addiction, raw capitalism even—do to individuals."[46] Much has been written about systemic oppression and this series insists upon it. And yet the series does represent a core group of characters who consistently maintain accountability and subjectivity within this badly failed social system. Because of that maintenance and because this is an ensemble series, it approaches a modern, somewhat more gender-inclusive, and intersubjective vision of heroism. Furthermore, through those examples, this series raises the glaring question: where are the authors of institutional failures? Where is the accountable subjectivity of those who win when institutions decay? Chaddha and Wilson note that the series's "focus on institutional practices effectively challenges alternative explanations that overemphasize the role of individual actors."[47] This is true, but most discussions of "individual actors" within oppressive systems focus, like the series itself does, on those actors on the receiving end of such systems. Those who contribute to and gain from institutional corruption are almost absent from the picture. There are a number of reasons for this absence, but through its very elisions, *The Wire* does encourage the viewer to consider who gains from iniquitous systems and what "honor" would demand of them.

WHY BOTHER?

Though there is no one dominant character in *The Wire,* its best contenders for the classic role of hard-boiled principal are Detective Jimmy McNulty

---

45. Chaddha and Wilson, "'Way Down in the Hole,'" 186.
46. Quoted in Penfold-Mounce et al., "*The Wire* as Social Science-Fiction?" 154.
47. Chaddha and Wilson, "'Way Down in the Hole,'" 183.

(Dominic West) and the stickup man Omar Little (Michael K. Williams), both of whom embody Race Williams's "my ethics are my own."[48] Detective McNulty, a Baltimore police officer, disregards protocol in order to investigate the murder cases that his more press-phobic superiors are ready to abandon.[49] As Roshan Singh and others comment, publicity for the series foregrounds McNulty as principal character.[50] He is described as "natural police," which puts him in the same camp as Adamsberg. But whereas being "natural police" in some sense intimates "honor without thought of it," no character in this series acts without thought for long. Series writer Rafael Alvarez, calling the show's Baltimore "a universe where hoped-for escapes to places that value individual desires do not exist," nonetheless insists that it "is making a case for the individual trying to get by in a society of harsh, indifferent institutions: bureaucracies on both sides of the law, the cultures of addiction—to power as well as dope—and raw capitalism."[51] This reference to the individual who "tries" goes to the heart of the series's representation of accountability. I said earlier that the hard-boiled character resides in the negativity of the outside world as in a permanent home, even as he counteracts that negativity through his own conscience. That conscience simply *is*. It is neither utopian nor anachronistic, it represents no solution, and it leads to no narrative conclusion. *The Wire* presents relatively little in the way of positive outside forces that can motivate a character; indeed, most outside forces produce frustration or disillusion.[52] All that this series has in the way of imperatives are internal, but it has those, and thus resists paranoid readings as well as utopian ones.

Alasdair McMillan comments that McNulty's pursuits of justice come from stubbornness rather than dedication to ethics: "What propels McNulty is ultimately revealed as little more than the raw will-to-power channeled,

48. As Fredric Jameson writes, "A work of this kind challenges and problematizes the distinction between protagonists and 'secondary characters.'" Jameson, "Realism and Utopia in *The Wire*," 359.

49. Jason Grinnell examines the relationship between ethics and professionalism in "Came to Do Good, Stayed to Do Well."

50. Singh, "*The Wire*," 111.

51. Alvarez, *The Wire*, 61.

52. Kristin Jacobson writes of McNulty's ultimate settling down: "McNulty's infidelities are not so much a rejection of or a revolt against domesticity but a character flaw that he, like the female protagonists in much sentimental fiction, must overcome." Jacobson, "HBO's *The Wire*," 161. It could be said that McNulty "must" overcome his character flaws in order to remain with his girlfriend, but this imperative on its own is not entirely convincing. She then argues convincingly that the female detective Greggs also has this character flaw to overcome, and that in its concentration on personal evolution, the series "develops feminine, not masculine, narrative structures" (Jacobson, "HBO's *The Wire*," 161).

organized, and individuated by discipline. He is driven not by an internal wellspring of the Good, but by a will 'to grow, spread, seize.'"[53] In other words, what seem to be good works are but side effects of his pushiness. McNulty does evince a certain grandiosity, but the point is that he continues to put his obstinacy into service to the greater good. This is not a picture of utopian individualism, but neither is it the chronicle of a loose cannon. Rather, McNulty demonstrates the resilience of individual conscience and the possibility of its continual maintenance. His plan to pursue a murder investigation into Marlo Stanfield (a drug dealer responsible for numerous murders) demands considerable narrative creativity as well as a meta-understanding of the police department. Knowing that his bosses are uninterested in pursuing Marlo, he invents a sensationalist serial killer who will be seen as deserving those resources—resources that McNulty will then divert into his pursuit of Marlo. It is true that McNulty's "ethics of his own" uses the corrupt police system to do what it would do in any case, which is pursue those who murder whites rather than those who murder blacks.[54] He does not change the system and does not believe he can. The point is that McNulty wants something, does something, and is able to put enough distance between himself and the system to manipulate it. The first result of this distance is condemnation of the system—one roots for McNulty and other team members, and when their scheme is frustrated and crushed by the higher-ups in the police department, that frustration translates into moral condemnation of the entire corrupt system. Furthermore, though his scheme fails in the end, the fact that it ever existed is evidence of individualism, of conscience, outside the system.

In this series the modern enemies of accountability and even subjectivity circle incessantly: these include corruption, scarce resources, crumbling infrastructure, inadequate technology, fear, trauma, crime, addiction, boredom, pessimism, despair, broken families, drug-dealing parents, and the list continues. And yet, both principal and secondary characters continually assert themselves as characters, as accountable and even ethical beings. These include dedicated police officer Kima Greggs, drug dealer–turned–boxing mentor Dennis "Cutty" Wise, policeman-turned-schoolteacher Roland "Prez"

---

53. McMillan, "Heroism," 57.

54. Leigh Claire La Berge writes, "The representation of black economic violence produces one form of seriality—that is, the series' realism. Conversely, white fictitious killing, the form of seriality that emerges in season 5, offers a critique of the series' previous realism and its reception. Black serial killing is read transparently as economic: it is treated as real within the narrative frame, and it is read as realist by the viewer; white serial killing is treated as psychological within the narrative frame and therefore read as not realist by the viewer." La Berge, "Capitalist Realism and Serial Form," 549.

Pryzbylewski, the Sherlock Holmesian Lestor Freamon, Port Authority officer Beatrice "Beadie" Russell, the loveable and doomed Wallace, and of course the righteous stickup man Omar Devone Little. As a witness for the prosecution in a murder case, Omar Little rebuts the defense lawyer's accusation that he is amoral, pointing out that he robs only drug dealers: "I ain't never put my gun on no citizen."[55] He then points out that his position is analogous to the lawyer's, as both are "parasites" of the drug trade. Despite the oppressive weight of the system, *The Wire* shows a sense of accountability—that "fragile achievement"—as an intrinsic and inescapable element of the living mind.

SOCIAL RESPONSIBILITY

In the aforementioned court scene, Omar Little points out the similarities between a criminal on the margins (himself) and the defense lawyer Maurice Levy. "I got the shotgun. You got the briefcase. It's all in the game, though. Right?"[56] The lawyer squirms at the comparison, the jury members chuckle, the judge looks startled, and the scene ends. I would propose that this moment, so popular with fans of *The Wire,* is so because it shows the rare spectacle of a mainstream individual being held to account. Levy is portrayed as unequivocally sleazy from the start, but the scene is striking because it shows a lower-power person holding a more powerful one to account at the very moment that power is being exerted. The satisfaction of this moment comes from its rarity. On the one hand, if there is a moral lesson to be learned from *The Wire,* it is that there is no "honor without thought of it," only continued endeavor with thought of it. But a corresponding and equally provocative lesson—visible in Levy's embarrassment—is that there is no dishonor "without thought of it." *The Wire's* attention to those whose choices are restrained shows social systems to be inescapable, but it also pushes us to consider the individual role in maintaining what seem to be collectively (which is to say anonymously or automatically) produced structures. For instance, it pushes us to wonder what would happen if those who contribute to and gain from social iniquities were held to as much meticulous account as those who struggle under them. In his reading of *The Wire's* "standstill of inequality and injustice," Younghoon Kim comments on the character of Tommy Carcetti, mayoral candidate: "Through Tommy Carcetti's political career, the show clarifies the point that policy changes or civil activism would not change the

---

55. "All Prologue," *The Wire*. Written by David Simon, Ed Burns, Joy Lusco Kecken, and Rafael Alvarez. Directed by Steve Shill. Aired July 6, 2003. HBO, 2006. DVD.
56. Ibid.

socioeconomic structures that have plummeted Baltimore into poverty and crime."[57] The fact of this broad conclusion illuminates (perhaps unwittingly) the absence of more powerful lawmakers from the central series cast. This is not a criticism of *The Wire*: the series is dedicated to showing *that* systems go wrong rather than examining why, and its dramatic focus is on local effects rather than abstract causes. The invisibility of those who have the most power is already part of the system and therefore part of the series' realism. And yet, that invisibility is itself a convention worth questioning. As Paul Allen Anderson writes, citing Adorno: "In order to reduce exposure 'by eliminating all linguistic traces of the will of the superior,' a high-power figure might say *business is business* to displace responsibility for an unpopular decision onto the abstract and nonmoral rules of the relevant institution or practice."[58] The high-power figure in Anderson's reading is Avon Barksdale, "king" in the dealing economy fond of repeating "The game is the game," but the series intimates that more could be learned by holding to account the orchestrators of broader economic structures. The elision of the individual that Lou Ford practiced has been reified and systematized in twenty-first-century finance and corporate capitalism, but it is as much a narrative construct here as it was there.

There are of course a number of obstacles, both practical and philosophical, to such accountings. One of these obstacles is the fact that dedication to money and power, or narrow self-interest, is in a sense antithetical to character nuance. Fredric Jameson's article on *The Wire* derides contemporary society's "loss of individualism and of bizarre eccentrics and obsessives—in short, its increasing one-dimensionality," and then points to the role of financial motivation in that one-dimensionality: "Meanwhile, the psychic realm has also been drastically reduced, perhaps in part as a result of the omnipresence of money as an all-purpose motivation, perhaps also as a result of the familiarities of universal information and communication and the flattening of the individualisms."[59] Financial motivation reduces rather than expands the individual as such, both in realism and in discussions of institutions, thus creating the tautological sense that one cannot discuss the individuals responsible for a system because such individuals are subsumed by the system.[60] To counteract that reduction and that tautology would constitute an important—and distinctly "reparative"—social analysis.

---

57. Kim, "Rogue Cops' Politics," 200.
58. Anderson, "'The Game Is the Game,'" 387.
59. Jameson, "Realism and Utopia in *The Wire*," 366, 367.
60. See Hobsbawm, *Age of Extremes*; Kotz, *Rise and Fall of Neoliberal Capitalism*; Phillips-Fein, *Invisible Hands*.

I do not claim that *The Wire* offers much hope for social change, but neither would I concur with Peter Dreier and John Atlas that the series "was the opposite of radical; it was hopeless and nihilistic."[61] What it does do is draw a contrast between the nuanced individual and the relentlessly corrupt system that is so stark as to call for sustained attention. It prompts the question of how a group of individuals becomes a system and why the individuals who are the least able to alter the system are the most present *as* individuals. Again, it has become almost a contemporary commonplace that those at the head of systems look out for themselves and that those on the margins look out for others, but *The Wire* encourages us to wonder why individual exemplarity must be relegated to dark alleys. This wondering perhaps constitutes the contemporary hard-boiled's most provocative contribution to modern moral criticism. If questioning the inexorability of systems allows even a small reversal of the "reduction of the psychic realm," then it is worth the trouble to frame narratives of social systems in a different way so as to start to reverse the "flattening of the individualisms" that Jameson found. A reparative reading can examine the system and its inexorability as products, ones with a material and narrative history, ones that actual individuals have generated, perpetuated, and tolerated.

---

61. Dreier and Atlas, "Dystopian Fable," 194. Jason Vest also points out that the series even "verges on civic nihilism." Vest, *The Wire*, 171.

CONCLUSION

THE PHILOSOPHICAL TERRAIN that the hard-boiled covers is in many ways identical to the terrain examined by numerous other disciplines, including philosophy, sociology, and psychology. In many disciplines, questions of autonomy and accountability are examined along political lines. But the hard-boiled, no matter what the political bent of its authors, has insisted on holding individuals to account, even when the bleakness at hand seems to be emanating from the very air. Like the epic, the hard-boiled underscores that an idea can be lived only through an individual and that regardless of social currents, the actions and decisions of the individual are crucial. Unlike the epic, however, the hard-boiled represents individual actions and decisions as born in a moral vacuum, or at least without moral support. The outside world is understood to be a problematic foil, rather than a source of meaning and encouragement, and as a result, individual moral choice must be continually regenerated. At the same time, the hard-boiled demonstrates again and again that such regeneration exists, and this demonstration counteracts dominant narratives of inexorable modern decline.

On the one hand, what makes the moral authority of the hard-boiled character appealing is its apparent effortlessness and continuity. Raymond Chandler's ideal hard-boiled character was a sort of cinematic still, placed against an evocative but nonetheless static backdrop. The idea of an individual who reaches within himself or herself to find a reliable, fully stocked well of "subjective facts" is a cornerstone of Western culture but is no less fictitious for that. Indeed, for every real study that shows the individual able to rise on his or her own steam, there is another pointing out the vital preconditions—health, education, family support, a caring adult—that make that success possible. And yet, in the mid-century post–hard-boiled, even those novels that seem to skewer society end up reinforcing the importance of individual responsibility. The more outside forces seem to be at fault, the more the individual points out those faults, the more that pointing out—as valid and as awful as the faults at hand may be—resonates as an evasion of responsibility. Even those attributions of blame that seem incontrovertible, such as mental illness, a disconnected parent, political disenchantment, the omnipresence of corruption, adolescent boredom, or a dead-end town, resonate as disingenuous when they are cited as reasons for misconduct, or reasons to not hold oneself to account. This disingenuousness is most palpable in first-person narration, since a character who pleads his own case in a carefully spun narrative has already made the dilution of subjective agency seem insincere. But it even operates in the third person, in Manchette's account of Martin Terrier's troubles and his decisions, in Highsmith's matter-of-fact description of Tom Ripley's cold guardian aunt. The hard-boiled responds, it seems, to a broad Western impulse to see individuals able to bear responsibility without evasiveness or self-pity. What Chandler called honor turns out to be accountability and competence.

Where these concepts could alter the landscape of moral criticism would be in their application to ostensibly unalterable systems. I gestured at that application in the last chapter, but it deserves further examination. The idea of the hard-boiled character as maverick—like moral criticism itself—poses no real threat to broad political and economic structures. Precisely because the outside world and "the age of absolute sinfulness" are lived without judgment, the hard-boiled character is not poised to overthrow those structures. At the same time, the consistently marginal position of such characters raises the question of why dominant economic and political narratives cast conscience as the domain of the marginal. The hard-boiled has for one hundred years foregrounded social consciousness and accountability as indomitable character attributes, and their absence from economic and political systems is conspicuous. It is a hard-boiled commonplace that exemplary characters on "mean streets" does not render those streets less mean. And yet, once we start to read that atmospheric stasis as itself a narrative construct, we can approach the ahistoricity and inalterability of social inequalities in the same way.

The visible outline of accountability and competence—of an exemplary character, in other words—varies from culture to culture. The American model is heavier on anti-intellectualism, plainspokenness, and declarations of personal independence, while the French model focuses on historical and cultural consciousness, aesthetic discernment, and verbal lyricism. Interestingly, it is these cultural variables—these characteristics that render the hard-boiled hero as heroic silhouette rather than as compendium of actions and choices—that have become the objects of cultural admiration. As Proust's narrator comments on the shallow Odette de Crécy, who prefers smooth-talking suitors to men of substance:

> People who enjoyed "picking-up" things, who admired poetry, despised sordid calculations of profit and loss, and nourished ideals of honour and love, she placed in a class by themselves, superior to the rest of humanity. There was no need actually to have those tastes, provided one talked enough about them; when a man had told her at dinner that he loved to wander about and get his hands all covered with dust in the old furniture shops, that he would never be really appreciated in this commercial age, since he was not concerned about the things that interested it, and that he belonged to another generation altogether, she would come home saying: "Why, he's an adorable creature; so sensitive! I had no idea," and she would conceive for him a strong and sudden friendship. But, on the other hand, men who, like Swann, had these tastes but did not speak of them, left her cold. She was obliged, of course, to admit that Swann was most generous with his money, but she would add, pouting: "It's not the same thing, you see, with him," and, as a matter of fact, what appealed to her imagination was not the practice of disinterestedness, but its vocabulary.[1]

> De ceux qui aimaient à bibeloter, qui aimaient les vers, méprisaient les bas calculs, rêvaient d'honneur et d'amour, elle faisait une élite supérieure au reste de l'humanité. Il n'y avait pas besoin qu'on eût réellement ces goûts pourvu qu'on les proclamât; d'un homme qui lui avait avoué à dîner qu'il aimait à flâner, à se salir les doigts dans les vieilles boutiques, qu'il ne serait jamais apprécié par ce siècle commercial, car il ne se souciait pas de ses intérêts et qu'il était pour cela d'un autre temps, elle revenait en disant: "Mais c'est une âme adorable, un sensible, je ne m'en étais jamais doutée!" et elle se sentait pour lui une immense et soudaine amitié. Mais, en revanche ceux, qui comme Swann, avaient ces goûts, mais n'en parlaient pas, la laissaient froide. Sans doute elle était obligée d'avouer que Swann ne tenait pas

---

1. Proust, *Swann's Way*, 227.

à l'argent, mais elle ajoutait d'un air boudeur: "Mais lui, ça n'est pas la même chose"; et en effet, ce qui parlait à son imagination, ce n'était pas la pratique du désintéressement, c'en était le vocabulaire.[2]

Classic hard-boiled crime fiction provides the practice and the vocabulary fused together. The mid-century post–hard-boiled separates one from the other. Contemporary crime fiction reconnects them, sometimes pretending that the disconnection never happened and that practice is borne of vocabulary, but more often underscoring the exertion needed to sustain the practice.

Even in contemporary crime fiction that has witnessed the evacuation of the silhouette, however, appearances nonetheless continue to dominate. Emily Nussbaum calls Rust Cohle "our fetish object," "the outsider with painful secrets and harsh truths and nice arms," and the nice arms are crucial.[3] The trench coat and the cigarette, the American laconic offhandedness, the French understatement and aesthetic discernment, are all much more culturally resonant than the idea that one should be responsible for one's own ethics (whether one is "religious in some kind of way" or not), or that a consistent empathic consciousness of others' troubles is advisable. The hard-boiled acts as a reminder, then, both of the importance of conscious effort and of the potential emptiness of the "vocabulary." The notion of a character who has already completed his *Bildungsroman,* or who has, better yet, sprung fully formed into conscious exemplarity is a strong Western illusion, a seductive image. Indeed, constructing and maintaining that image is part of the hard-boiled's charm. But as I have tried to show in the foregoing chapters, the hard-boiled has also done the crucial work of revealing the practice and the struggle underneath the vocabulary. What is more, it has done some of the work of revealing "honor" to be a common responsibility rather than a rare commodity. The idea of the industry magnate subsumed under the apparently insurmountable social systems he helped create is as much a fictitious diversion as Lou Ford's traumatic panopticon or Henri Boutron's ennui. Every historical period has such accountability-diluting diversions, the depersonalization of finance and corporate capitalism being one of the most formidable, but the hard-boiled consistently counteracts these diversions with its focus on individual choice and action.

The fact that the hard-boiled is a literary form is crucial because accountability, in all these texts, is inextricably interwoven with the ability to account, or recount, in narrative form. Those who are conscious of themselves as actors and narrators, who claim responsibility for their own subjectivity,

---

2. Proust, *Un amour de Swann,* 81.

3. Nussbaum, "Cool Story, Bro," n. pag. http://www.newyorker.com/magazine/2014/03/03/cool-story-bro, accessed February 26, 2015.

their own actions, and the effect of those actions on others, who concentrate not on their own troubles but on those of others, are not just "men or women of honor," which is a rather abstract term, but also strong narrative agents. This reading of the importance of individual competence of course itself poses an ethical problem. That is, there are ways in which the individual can use narrative voice and ethical decisions to create autonomy, but to actually place the responsibility for that creation on everyone, including those disenfranchised, discriminated against, or deprived, is to enter ethically as well as politically problematic territory. The enemies of free and complete subjectivity tend to go all the way down: persistent economic inequality, the challenge of behaving in an ethical manner when others do not, and the paucity of social and economic incentives have been well documented. Even the incitement to read, to see what narrative agency can do for someone's competence and confidence, is dependent on the availability of books, on literacy, not to mention the willingness to discern the practice underneath the vocabulary. There is certainly potential to read this book's argument as idealist or reactionary, since public discourse about accountability so frequently amounts to blaming the disenfranchised, but the more provocative use of the hard-boiled's insistence on individualism is to impute responsibility up the socioeconomic ladder as well as down. If honor without thought of it is an improbable phenomenon, so is dishonor without thought of it. It seems to matter little whether character as an idea maintains coherence or not. What the hard-boiled does is hold all individuals responsible for seeing themselves as narrative agents in their own lives and as actors in the lives of others.

BIBLIOGRAPHY

Abbott, Megan E. *The Street Was Mine: White Masculinity in Hardboiled Fiction and Film Noir.* New York: Palgrave Macmillan, 2002.

Abernethy, Thomas Perkins. *From Frontier to Plantation in Tennessee.* Chapel Hill: University of North Carolina Press, 1932.

Adams, Jon. *Male Armor.* Charlottesville: University of Virginia Press, 2008.

Allen, Frances, Michael B. First, and Harold Alan Pincus. *DSM-IV Guidebook.* New York: American Psychiatric Association, 1995.

Alvarez, Rafael. *The Wire: Truth Be Told.* New York: Simon & Schuster, 2004.

Anderson, Paul Allen. "'The Game Is the Game': Tautology and Allegory in *The Wire*." *Criticism* 52, no. 3 (2010): 373–98.

Anshen, David. "Clichés and Commodity Fetishism: The Violence of the Real in Jim Thompson's *The Killer Inside Me*." *Journal of Narrative Theory* 37, no. 3 (2007): 400–406.

Atack, Margaret. *May 68 in French Fiction and Film: Rethinking Society, Rethinking Representation.* Oxford: Oxford University Press, 1999.

Athanasourelis, John Paul. *Raymond Chandler's Philip Marlowe: The Hard-Boiled Detective Transformed.* New York: McFarland, 2011.

Auden, W. H. "The Guilty Vicarage." In *Detective Fiction: Crime and Compromise,* edited by Dick Allen and David Chacko. San Diego: Harcourt College Publishing, 1974.

Babington, Anthony. *Shell Shock: A History of Changing Attitudes to War Neurosis.* London: Leo Cooper, 1997.

Bakhtin, Mikhail Mikhailovich. *Problems of Dostoevsky's Poetics.* Minneapolis: University of Minnesota Press, 1984.

Barone, Michael. *Our Country: The Shaping of America from Roosevelt to Reagan.* New York: Free Press, 1990.

Bartschinger, Hans. "The Question of the Causation of Schizophrenia by Head Injuries, and Some Opinions on Them." *Dementia Praecox Studies: A Journal of Psychiatry of Adolescence* 3–4 (1920): 223–29.

Beecher, Lyman, *Sermons Delivered on Various Occasions*. Bedford, MA: Applewood, 2009.

———. *Six Sermons on the Nature, Occasions, Signs, Evils, and Remedy of Intemperance*. New York: American Tract Society, 1827.

Beekman, E. M. "Raymond Chandler and an American Genre." *Massachusetts Review* 14 (1973): 149–73.

Bennett, Jane. *The Enchantment of Modern Life: Attachments, Crossings, and Ethics*. Princeton, NJ: Princeton University Press, 2001.

Bird, Robert Montgomery. *Nick of the Woods: or, The Jibbenainosay; a Tale of Kentucky*. New York: Redfield, 1853.

Black, Joel. "Murder: The State of the Art." *American Literary History* 12, no. 4 (2000): 780–93.

Blackburn, Simon. *Mirror, Mirror: The Uses and Abuses of Self-Love*. Princeton, NJ: Princeton University Press, 2014.

Bourdelas, Laurent. *Le Paris de Nestor Burma: l'occupation et les "Trente Glorieuses" de Léo Malet*. Paris: L'Harmattan, 2007.

Breton, André. *L'anthologie de l'humour noir*. Paris: Pauvert, 1977.

Breu, Christopher. *Hard-Boiled Masculinities*. Minneapolis: University of Minnesota Press, 2005.

Bronfen, Elisabeth. *Over Her Dead Body: Death, Femininity and the Aesthetic*. Manchester: Manchester University Press, 1992.

Brooks, Peter. *Reading for the Plot*. Cambridge, MA: Harvard University Press, 1984.

Butler, Judith. *Subjects of Desire: Hegelian Reflections in Twentieth-Century France*. New York: Columbia University Press, 2012.

Caillois, Roger. *Le mythe et l'homme*. Paris: Gallimard, 1972.

———. *The Edge of Surrealism: A Roger Caillois Reader*. Durham, NC: Duke University Press, 2003.

Camus, Albert. *La peste*. Paris: Éditions Gallimard, 1947.

———. *Œuvres complètes*. Paris: Club de l'honnête homme, 1983.

———. *The Stranger*. Translated by Matthew Ward. New York: Random House, 1988.

Caruth, Cathy. *Unclaimed Experience: Trauma, Narrative and History*. Baltimore: Johns Hopkins University Press, 1996.

Casey, Dermot. *The Nature and Treatment of Scruples: A Guide for Directors of Souls*. Westminster, MD: The Newman Press, 1948.

Cassuto, Leonard. *Hard-Boiled Sentimentality: The Secret History of American Crime Stories*. New York: Columbia University Press, 2009.

Cawelti, John G. "Myths of Violence in American Popular Culture." *Critical Inquiry* 1, no. 3 (1975): 521–41.

———. *Adventure, Mystery, and Romance: Formula Stories as Art and Popular Culture*. Chicago: University of Chicago Press, 1976.

Chace, James. "The Turbulent Tenure of Alexander Haig." *New York Times*, 1984.

Chaddha, Anmol, and William Julius Wilson. ""Way Down in the Hole": Systemic Urban Inequality and *The Wire*." *Critical Inquiry* 38, no. 1 (2011): 164–88.

Chandler, Raymond. "The Simple Art of Murder." *Atlantic Monthly,* December 1944.

——. *The Big Sleep, Farewell, My Lovely, The High Window.* New York: Everyman's Library, 2002.

Chateaubriand, Francois-René, vicomte de. Atala, René, Les Abencérages, suivis du Voyage en Amerique. Paris: Didot, 1853.

——. *Génie du christianisme.* 2 vols. Paris: Calmann-Lévy, 1844.

——. *Mémoires d'outre-tombe.* Paris: Penaud frères, 1849.

——. *Œuvres.* 16 vols. Paris: Dufour, Mulat, et Boulanger, 1861.

Ciarrocchi, Joseph. *The Doubting Disease: Help for Scrupulosity and Religious Compulsions.* Mahwah, NJ: The Paulist Press, 1995.

Clark, Dorothy G. "Being's Wound: (Un)Explaining Evil in Jim Thompson's *The Killer Inside Me*." *Journal of Popular Culture* 42, no. 1 (2009): 49–66.

Cloud, Dana L. "The Limits of Interpretation: Ambivalence and the Stereotype in *Spenser: For Hire*." *Critical Studies in Media Communication* 9, no. 4 (1992): 311–24.

Cobb, Richard. *French and Germans, Germans and French: A Personal Interpretation of France under Two Occupations, 1914–1918/1940–1944.* Lebanon, NH: University Press of New England, 1983.

Cohan, Steven. "Figures beyond the Text: A Theory of Readable Character in the Novel." *Novel: A Forum on Fiction* 17, no. 1 (1983): 5–27.

Connelly, Michael. *Black Box.* New York: Little, Brown, 2012.

Cooper, James Fenimore. *The Leatherstocking Tales.* 2 vols. New York: Library of America, 1985.

Coquerel, Athanase-Laurent-Charles. *Sermons: 1e et 2e recueils, et sermons détachés.* Paris: Librairie de Marc-Aurel Frères, 1842.

Cotkin, George. *Existential America.* Baltimore: Johns Hopkins University Press, 2005.

Culler, Jonathan D. *Flaubert: The Uses of Uncertainty.* Ithaca, NY: Cornell University Press, 1974.

Cupitt, Don. *Taking Leave of God.* Norwich: Hymns Ancient & Modern Ltd, 2001.

Currie, Gregory. "Narrative and the Psychology of Character." *Journal of Aesthetics and Art Criticism* 67, no. 1 (2009): 61–71.

Daly, Carroll John. *The Snarl of the Beast.* New York: HarperPerennial, 1992.

Daughton, James. "Sketches of the *Poilu*'s World: Trench Cartoons from the Great War." In *World War I and the Cultures of Modernity,* edited by Douglas Peter Mackaman and Michael Mays. Jackson: University Press of Mississippi, 2000.

Davis, J. Madison. "No Man Is a Prophet in His Own Land: Oklahoman Jim Thompson Emerges from the Shadows." *World Literature Today* 81, no. 6 (November–December 2007): 39–40.

de Beauvoir, Simone. *La force de l'âge.* Paris: Gallimard, 1960.

De Fursac, J. R. "Traumatic and Emotional Psychoses: So-called Shell Shock." *American Journal of Insanity* 75 (1918), 19–51.

Dean, Eric. *Shook over Hell: Post-traumatic Stress, Vietnam, and the Civil War.* Cambridge, MA: Harvard University Press, 1997.

Debord, Guy. *Œuvres.* Paris: Gallimard, 2006.

Deming, Barbara. *Running Away from Myself: A Dream Portrait of America Drawn from the Films of the Forties.* New York: Grossman, 1969.

Desnain, Veronique. "Women in French Crime Writing." In *French Crime Fiction,* edited by Claire Gorrara. Cardiff: University of Wales Press, 2009.

Dorpat, Theodore L. *Crimes of Punishment: America's Culture of Violence.* New York: Algora, 2007.

Dreier, Peter, and John Atlas. "A Dystopian Fable about America's Urban Poor." In *The Wire and America's Dark Corners: Critical Essays,* edited by Arin Keeble and Ivan Stacy. Jefferson, NC: McFarland, 2015.

Dussere, Eric. *America Is Elsewhere: The Noir Tradition in the Age of Consumer Culture.* Oxford: Oxford University Press, 2013.

Eagleton, Terry. *Ideology of the Aesthetic.* New York: Wiley, 1990.

Eburne, Jonathan Paul. *Surrealism and the Art of Crime.* Ithaca, NY: Cornell University Press, 2008.

Eisenberg, Nancy. *The Caring Child.* Cambridge, MA: Harvard University Press, 1992.

Eisenzweig, Uri. *Le récit impossible: forme et sens du roman policier.* Paris: C Bourgeois, 1986.

Emanuel, Michelle. *From Surrealism to Less-Exquisite Cadavers: Léo Malet and the Evolution of the French Roman Noir.* Amsterdam: Rodopi, 2006.

Faison, Stephen. *Existentialism, Film Noir, and Hard-Boiled Fiction.* Amherst, NY: Cambria, 2008.

Fay, Warrren. *A Sermon, Delivered January 1, 1822, at the Ordination of the Rev. Joseph Bennet: To the Pastoral Care of the Congregational Church and Society in Woburn, Mass.* Boston: Crocker & Brewster, 1822.

Fénelon, François de Salignac de La Mothe. *Œuvres complètes.* Paris: Briand, 1810.

Field, Stewart. "State, Citizen, and Character in French Criminal Process." *Journal of Law and Society* 33, no. 4 (2006): 522–46.

Finger, John. *Tennessee Frontiers: Three Regions in Transition.* Bloomington: Indiana University Press, 2001.

Finke, Roger, and Rodney Stark. *The Churching of America, 1776–2005: Winners and Losers in Our Religious Economy.* New Brunswick, NJ: Rutgers University Press, 2005.

FitzGerald, Frances. *Way Out There in the Blue: Reagan, Star Wars and the End of the Cold War.* New York: Simon & Schuster, 2001.

Flaubert, Gustave. *Madame Bovary.* Paris: Gallimard, 1972.

——. *Œuvres complètes.* 18 vols. Paris: L. Conard, 1910.

Forter, Greg. *Murdering Masculinities: Fantasies of Gender and Violence in the American Crime Novel.* New York: New York University Press, 2000.

Freedman, Carl, and Christopher Kendrick. "Forms of Labor in Dashiell Hammett's *Red Harvest.*" *Publications of the Modern Language Association of America* 106, no. 2 (March 1991): 209–21.

Freppel, Abbé. *Cours d'eloquence sacrée.* Paris: Bureaux, 1858.

Frommer, Franck. "Jean-Patrick Manchette: le facteur fatal." *Mouvements* 3 (2001): 88–95.

Frommer, Franck, and Marco Oberti. "Dominique Manotti: du militantisme à l'écriture tout en parlant de politique." *Mouvements* 3 (2001): 41–47. http://www.cairn.info/revue-mouvements-2001-3-page-41.htm. Accessed February 16, 2016.

Gaboriau, Émile. *L'affaire Lerouge*. Paris: Ed. Dentu, 1881.

Gaspari, Séverine. "Fred Vargas: une archéozoologue en terrain littéraire." In *Nomadismes des romancières contemporaines de langue française,* edited by Audrey Lasserre and Anne Simon. Paris: Presses de la Sorbonne Nouvelle, 2008.

Geertz, Clifford. *Local Knowledge: Further Essays in Interpretive Anthropology.* New York: Basic Books, 1983.

Gérault, Jean-François. *Jean-Patrick Manchette: parcours d'une œuvre*. Paris: Encrage, 2000.

Giger, Itziar Plazaola, and Jean-Paul Bronckart. "Le temps du polar." *Langue française* 97, no. 1 (1993): 14–42.

Gorrara, Claire. *The Roman Noir in Post-War French Culture: Dark Fictions.* Oxford: Oxford University Press, 2003.

———. "French Crime Fiction: From *genre mineur* to *patrimoine culturel*." *French Studies* 61, no. 2 (2007): 209–14.

Gratton, Johnnie. "Postmodern French Fiction: Practice and Theory." In *The Cambridge Companion to the French Novel: From 1800 to the Present,* edited by Timothy Unwin. Cambridge: Cambridge University Press, 1997.

Grinnell, Jason. "Came to Do Good, Stayed to Do Well." In *The Wire and Philosophy,* edited by David Bzdak, Joanna Crosby, and Seth Vannatta. New York: Open Court, 2013.

Haig, Alexander M. *Caveat: Realism, Reagan, and Foreign Policy.* New York: Macmillan, 1984.

Hamilton, Cynthia S. *Western and Hard-Boiled Detective Fiction in America: From High Noon to Midnight.* New York: Macmillan, 1987.

Hammett, Dashiell. *The Maltese Falcon, The Thin Man, Red Harvest.* New York: Everyman's Library, 2002.

Harman, Gilbert. *Explaining Value and Other Essays in Moral Philosophy.* Oxford: Oxford University Press, 2000.

Hazareesingh, Sudhir. *Political Traditions in Modern France.* Oxford: Oxford University Press, 1994.

Heise, Thomas. "'Going Blood-Simple Like the Natives': Contagious Urban Spaces and Modern Power in Dashiell Hammett's *Red Harvest*." *Modern Fiction Studies* 51 no. 3 (2005): 485–512.

Highsmith, Patricia. *The Talented Mr. Ripley.* New York: Random House, 1955.

———. *Ripley Under Ground.* New York: Doubleday, 1970.

Hitchens, Christopher. "Minority Report." *The Nation* 238, no. 21 (June 2, 1984): 662.

Hobsbawm, Eric. *The Age of Extremes.* New York: Vintage, 1996.

Hocking, William Ernest. *Morale and Its Enemies.* New Haven, CT: Yale University Press, 1918.

Hodgson, Jacqueline. *French Criminal Justice: A Comparative Account of the Investigation and Prosecution of Crime in France.* New York: Hart, 2005.

Hollier, Denis, and R. Howard Bloch, eds. *A New History of French Literature.* Cambridge, MA: Harvard University Press, 1994.

Honneth, Axel. *Pathologies of Reason: On the Legacy of Critical Theory.* New York: Columbia University Press, 2009.

Horsley, Lee. *Twentieth-Century Crime Fiction*. Oxford: Oxford University Press, 2005.

———. *The Noir Thriller*. New York: Palgrave Macmillan, 2009.

Horton, Christine. *Policing Policy in France*. London: Policy Studies Institute, 1995.

Hugo, Victor. *Œuvres posthumes de Victor Hugo*. Paris: J. Hetzel, 1820.

Huntington, Samuel. *The Soldier and the State: The Theory and Politics of Civil-Military Relations*. Cambridge, MA: Harvard University Press, 1957.

Irwin, John T. *Unless the Threat of Death Is Behind Them: Hard-Boiled Fiction and Film Noir*. Baltimore: Johns Hopkins University Press, 2006.

Jackson, Julian. *France: The Dark Years, 1940–1944*. Oxford: Oxford University Press, 2001.

Jacobson, Kristin. "HBO's *The Wire* and Harriet Beecher Stowe's *Uncle Tom's Cabin*." In *The Sentimental Mode: Essays in Literature, Film, and Television*, edited by Jennifer A. Williamson, Jennifer Larson, and Ashley Reed. New York: McFarland, 2014.

Jameson, Fredric. "Realism and Utopia in *The Wire*." *Criticism* 52, no. 3 (2010): 359–72.

Jefferson, Ann. *The Nouveau Roman and the Poetics of Fiction*. Cambridge: Cambridge University Press, 1980.

Jenks, Sylvester. *The Blind Obedience of an Humble Penitent: The Best Cure for Scruples*. London: s.n., 1698.

Johnston, Cristina, and Bill Marshall, eds. *France and the Americas: Culture, Politics, and History*. New York: ABC-CLIO, 2005.

Kalb, Deborah, Gerhard D. Peters, and John Turner Woolley, eds. *State of the Union: Presidential Rhetoric from Woodrow Wilson to George W. Bush*. Washington, DC: CQ Press, 2006.

Keegan, John. *A History of Warfare*. New York: Random House, 2012.

Kennedy, John Pendleton, and Ernest Erwin Leisy. *Horse-Shoe Robinson*. Philadelphia: Carey, Lea & Blanchard, 1835.

Kim, Younghoon. "Rogue Cops' Politics of Equality in *The Wire*." *Journal of American Studies* 47, no. 1 (2013): 189–211.

Kotz, David. *The Rise and Fall of Neoliberal Capitalism*. Cambridge, MA: Harvard University Press, 2015.

Kraepelin, Emil, and Allen Ross Diefendorf. *Clinical Psychiatry: A Text-Book for Students and Physicians*. New York: Macmillan, 1915.

La Berge, Leigh Claire. "Capitalist Realism and Serial Form: The Fifth Season of *The Wire*." *Criticism* 52, no. 3 (2010): 547–67.

Labouret, Guilhem. "Les mutations du discours religieux au XIXe siècle." *Romantisme* 2 (2009): 39–53.

Lacordaire, Henri-Dominique. *Conférences du révérend père Lacordaire*. Brussels: JB de Mortier, 1852.

———. "Mémoire pour le rétablissement en France de l'ordre des frères prêcheurs." In *La liberté de la parole évangélique: écrits, conférences, lettres*, edited by Henri-Dominique Lacordaire, André Duval, and Jean P. Jossua. Paris: Cerf, 1996.

Lacoste, Claudine. "Un substitut théologique: la nature dans *Jocelyn*." In *Romantisme et religion: théologie des théologiens et théologie des écrivains: colloque interdisciplinaires*, edited by Michel Baude and Marc-Mathieu Münch. Paris: Presses universitaires de France, 1980.

Lamartine, Alphonse de. *Œuvres de Lamartine*. Brussels: Société Belge de Librairie, 1840.

——. *Cours familier de littérature: un entretien par mois*. Paris, 1859.

——. *Correspondance de Lamartine*. 8 vols. Paris: Hachette, 1873.

Lamennais, Félicité de. *Œuvres completes de F. de Lamennais*. 12 vols. Paris: Paul Daubrée et Cailleux, 1836–1837.

——. *L'imitation de Jésus-Christ*. Paris: Garnier frères, 1866.

Landry, Jean-Pierre. *Le temps des beaux sermons*. Paris: Librairie Droz, 2006.

Lane, Philip J. "The Existential Condition of Television Crime Drama." *Journal of Popular Culture* 34, no. 4 (2001): 137–51.

Laplanche, Jean, J. B. Pontalis, and Donald Nicholson-Smith. *The Language of Psychoanalysis*. New York: Hogarth, 1973.

Lasch, Christopher. *The Culture of Narcissism: American Life in an Age of Diminishing Expectations*. New York: W. W. Norton, 1991.

Lathrop, Joseph. *Sermons on Various Subjects, Evangelical, Devotional and Practical. Adapted to the Promotion of Christian Piety, Family Religion, and Youthful Virtue* Worcester, MA: Isaiah Thomas, 1809.

Laub, Dori, and Nanette C. Auerhahn. "Knowing and Not Knowing Massive Psychic Trauma: Forms of Traumatic Memory." *International Journal of Psychoanalysis* 74 (1993): 287.

Lee, Susanna. "These Are Our Stories: Trauma, Form, and the Screen Phenomenon of Law and Order." *Discourse* 25, no. 1 (2004): 81–97.

——. *A World Abandoned by God: Narrative and Secularism*. Lewisburg, PA: Bucknell University Press, 2006.

Lemon, Lee T., and Marion J. Reis, eds. *Russian Formalist Criticism: Four Essays*. Lincoln: University of Nebraska Press, 1965.

Lenoir, Eugène. *Étude sur le spiritisme*. Paris: M. Richter, 1888.

Leonard, Frank G. "Cozzens without Sex; Steinbeck without Sin." *Antioch Review* 18, no. 2 (1958): 209–18.

Lévi-Strauss, Claude. *La pensée sauvage*. Paris: Plon, 1962.

——. *The Savage Mind*. Chicago: University of Chicago Press, 1966.

Lukács, Georg. *The Theory of the Novel*. Translated by Anna Bostock. Cambridge, MA: MIT Press, 1971.

MacCannell, Dean, "Democracy's Turn: On Homeless Noir." In *Shades of Noir*, edited by Joan Copjec. London: Verso, 1993.

Macdonald, Ross. *On Crime Writing: The Writer as Detective Hero and Writing the Galton Case*. Santa Barbara, CA: Capra, 1973.

Mackaman, Douglas Peter, and Michael Mays, eds. *World War I and the Cultures of Modernity*. Jackson: University Press of Mississippi, 2000.

Mahan, Jeffrey. "The Hard-Boiled Detective in the Fallen World." *Clues: A Journal of Detection* 1, no. 2 (1980): 90–99.

Malet, Léo. *120, rue de la Gare*. Paris: Fleuve Noir, 1988.

Malmgren, Carl D. "The Crime of the Sign: Dashiell Hammett's Detective Fiction." *Twentieth Century Literature* 45, no. 3 (1999): 371–84.

Manchette, Jean Patrick. *Chroniques.* Edited by Doug Headline and François Guérif. Paris: Rivages, 1996.

———. *Romans noirs.* Paris: Gallimard, 2005.

Manotti, Dominique. "Le roman noir." *Le Mouvement Social* 2, no. 219–220 (April–June 2007): 107–9.

Margolin, Uri. "The Doer and the Deed: Action as a Basis for Characterization in Narrative in Theory of Character." *Poetics Today* 7, no. 2 (1986): 205–25.

Matthews, J. H. "Sade: The Right Person for Surrealism." *Yale French Studies* 35 (1965): 89–95.

McCann, Sean. *Gumshoe America: Hard-Boiled Crime Fiction and the Rise and Fall of New Deal Liberalism.* Durham, NC: Duke University Press, 2000.

McCauley, Michael J. *Jim Thompson: Sleep with the Devil.* New York: Mysterious Press, 1991.

McClymond, Michael J., ed. *Embodying the Spirit: New Perspectives on North American Revivalism.* Baltimore: Johns Hopkins University Press, 2004.

McConnell, Frank. "Detecting Order Among Disorder." *Wilson Quarterly* (Spring 1987): 172–83.

McCoy, Horace. *Kiss Tomorrow Goodbye.* New York: Open Road Media, 2012.

McMillan, Alasdair. "Heroism, Institutions, and the Police Procedural." In *The Wire: Urban Decay and American Television,* edited by Tiffany Potter and C. W. Marshall. New York: Bloomsbury, 2009.

Meeker, Eli. *Sermons, on Philosophical, Evangelical, and Practical Subjects.* Ithaca, NY: Mack & Andrus, 1827.

Michel, Alain, and Arlette Michel. *La littérature française et la connaissance de Dieu.* Paris: Cerf, 2008.

Milgram, Stanley. *Obedience to Authority.* London: Tavistock, 1974.

Miller, Alice. *For Your Own Good: Hidden Cruelty in Child-Rearing and the Roots of Violence.* New York: Macmillan, 2002.

Milton, John R. "The Western Novel: Sources and Forms." *Chicago Review* 16, no. 2 (Summer 1963): 74–100.

Moore, Lewis D. *Cracking the Hard-Boiled Detective: A Critical History from the 1920s to the Present.* New York: McFarland, 2006.

Moyar, Dean. *Hegel's Conscience.* Oxford: Oxford University Press, 2011.

Mullainathan, Sendhil, and Eldar Shafir. *Scarcity: Why Having Too Little Means So Much.* New York: Macmillan, 2013.

Mullen, Anne, and Emer O'Beirne. *Crime Scenes: Detective Narratives in European Culture since 1945.* Amsterdam: Rodopi, 2000.

Müller, Elfriede, and Alexander Ruoff. *Le polar français: crime et histoire.* Paris: La fabrique éditions, 2002.

Murray, Iain. *Revival and Revivalism: The Making and Marring of American Evangelicalism.* New York: Banner of Truth Trust, 1994.

Musset, Alfred. *La confession d'un enfant du siècle.* Paris: Charpentier, 1884.

Myers, Charles. "A Contribution to the Study of Shell Shock: Being an Account of Three Cases of Loss of Memory, Vision, Smell, and Taste, Admitted into the Duchess of Westminster's War Hospital, Le Touquet." *The Lancet* 185, no. 4772 (1915): 316–20.

———. "Contributions to the Study of Shell Shock: Being an Account of Certain Disorders of Cutaneous Sensibility." *The Lancet* 187, no. 4829 (1916): 608–13.

New York Missionary Society. *Interesting Account of Religion in France*. New York: Isaac Collins, 1803.

Nolan, William. *The Black Mask Boys: Masters in the Hard-Boiled School of Detective Fiction*. New York: Mysterious Press, 1985.

O'Brien, Geoffrey. *Hardboiled America: Lurid Paperbacks and the Masters of Noir*. New York: Da Capo, 1997.

Old, Hughes Oliphant. *The Reading and Preaching of the Scriptures in the Worship of the Christian Church*. Volume 6: *The Modern Age*. New York: Eerdmans, 2007.

Panek, LeRoy. *An Introduction to the Detective Story*. New York: Popular Press, 1987.

Payne, Kenneth. "Pottsville, USA: Psychosis and the American 'Emptiness' in Jim Thompson's *Pop. 1280*." *International Fiction Review* 21, nos. 1 and 2 (1994): 127.

Penfold-Mounce, Ruth, David Beer, and Roger Burrows. "*The Wire* as Social Science-Fiction?" *Sociology* 45, no. 1 (2011): 152–67.

Perkins, Anne. "The Nurse and the Mental Patient." *The Nurse: A Monthly Journal of Practical Knowledge* 5 (July–December 1916): 175–79.

Philips, Alastair. *Rififi: French Film Guide*. New York: I. B. Tauris, 2009.

Phillips-Fein, Kim. *Invisible Hands*. New York: W. W. Norton, 2010.

Pippin, Robert B. *The Persistence of Subjectivity: On the Kantian Aftermath*. Cambridge: Cambridge University Press, 2005.

Platten, David. *The Pleasures of Crime: Reading Modern French Crime Fiction*. Amsterdam: Rodopi, 2011.

Poe, Edgar Allan. *Complete Tales and Poems*. New York: Random House, 2012.

Polito, Robert. *Savage Art: A Biography of Jim Thompson*. New York: Knopf, 1995.

Pomeroy, Jonathan. *The Folly of Denying a God; and the Unreasonableness of Infidelity, in General; Held Up to View, in Two Sermons; the Substance of Which Was Preached, Extempore, at Worthington, One Sabbath, Not Long Since*. Northampton, MA: Butler, 1800.

Poole, Sara. "Rompols Not of the Bailey: Fred Vargas and the *polar* as *mini-proto-mythe*." *French Cultural Studies* 12, no. 34 (2001): 95–108.

Prescott, Peter. "The Cirrhosis of the Soul." *Newsweek*, November 17, 1986, 90.

Prince, Gerald. "Narratology, Narrative, and Meaning." *Poetics Today* 12, no. 3 (Autumn 1991): 543–52.

Proust, Marcel. *Un amour de Swann*. Paris: Gallimard, 1954.

———. *Swann's Way*, New York: W. W. Norton, 2013.

Pruche, Benoît. *Existant et acte d'être*. Paris: Desclée, 1977.

Rabinowitz, Paula. *Black and White and Noir: America's Pulp Modernism*. New York: Columbia University Press, 2002.

Raynal, Patrick. "Le roman noir et l'avenir de la fiction." *Les Temps Modernes* 595 (1997): 88–99.

Ricardou, Jean. *Pour une théorie du nouveau roman*. Paris: Seuil, 1971.

Robbe-Grillet, Alain. *Pour un nouveau roman*. Paris: Les Éditions de Minuit, 1963.

——. *For a New Novel: Essays on Fiction.* Translated by Richard Howard. Chicago: Northwestern University Press, 1992.

Rolls, Alistair, ed. *Mostly French: French (in) Detective Fiction.* New York: Peter Lang, 2009.

——. *Paris and the Fetish: Primal Crime Scenes.* Amsterdam: Rodopi, 2014.

Rolls, Alistair, and Deborah A. Walker. *French and American Noir: Dark Crossings.* New York: Palgrave Macmillan, 2009.

Ronell, Avital. "Trauma TV." In *Finitude's Score: Essays for the End of the Millennium.* Lincoln: University of Nebraska Press, 1994.

Rousseau, Jean-Jacques *Œuvres mêlées.* 13 vols. London: Boubers, 1776.

——. *Discours sur l'origine et les fondements de l'inéqalité parmi les hommes.* Paris: Librairie de la Bibliothèque nationale, 1902.

——. *Lettre à Mr. d'Alembert sur les spectacles.* Edited by M. Fuchs. Geneva: Droz, 1948.

Rushton, J. Philippe. "Generosity in Children: Immediate and Long-Term Effects of Modeling, Preaching, and Moral Judgment." *Journal of Personality and Social Psychology* 31, no. 3 (1975): 459–66.

Rzepka, Charles J. *Detective Fiction.* New York: Polity, 2005.

Santner, Eric L. *My Own Private Germany: Daniel Paul Schreber's Secret History of Modernity.* Princeton, NJ: Princeton University Press, 1997.

Sanyal, Debarati. *The Violence of Modernity: Baudelaire, Irony, and the Politics of Form.* Baltimore: Johns Hopkins University Press, 2006.

Sartre, Jean-Paul. *Les mots.* Paris: Gallimard, 1964.

——. *L'être et le néant.* Paris: Gallimard, 1976.

——. *Being and Nothingness.* Translated by Hazel Barnes. New York: Citadel, 2001.

Sass, Louis Arnorsson. "Schreber's Panopticism: Psychosis and the Modern Soul." *Social Research* 54, no. 1 (Spring 1987): 101–47.

——. *Madness and Modernism: Insanity in the Light of Modern Art, Literature, and Thought.* New York: Basic Books, 1992.

——. *The Paradoxes of Delusion: Wittgenstein, Schreber, and the Schizophrenic Mind.* Ithaca, NY: Cornell University Press, 1994.

Saxton, Alexander. *The Rise and Fall of the White Republic: Class Politics and Mass Culture in Nineteenth-Century America.* London: Verso, 2003.

Schatzman, Morton. *Soul Murder: Persecution in the Family.* New York: Random House, 1973.

Schreber, Daniel Paul. *Memoirs of My Nervous Illness.* New York: New York Review of Books, 1955.

Schwartz, Richard B. *Nice and Noir: Contemporary American Crime Fiction.* Columbia: University of Missouri Press, 2002.

Sedgwick, Eve. *Touching Feeling: Affect, Pedagogy, Performativity.* Durham, NC: Duke University Press, 2003.

Seltzer, Mark. "Wound Culture: Trauma in the Pathological Public Sphere." *October* 80 (Spring 1997): 3–26.

Shaffer, Jason. *Performing Patriotism: National Identity in the Colonial and Revolutionary American Theater.* Philadelphia: University of Pennsylvania Press, 2007.

Sheehan, Paul. *Modernism and the Aesthetics of Violence*. Cambridge: Cambridge University Press, 2013.

Sigelman, Lee, and William Jacoby. "The Not-So-Simple Art of Imitation: Pastiche, Literary Style, and Raymond Chandler." *Computers and the Humanities* 30, no. 1 (1996): 11–28.

Simenon, Georges. *Œuvres romanesques*. 25 vols. Paris: Presses de la Cité, 1992.

Singh, Roshan. "*The Wire*: Moral Ambiguity and the Heroic Detective Agency." In *Film and Ethics: What Would You Have Done?*, edited by Jacqui Miller. Newcastle: Cambridge Scholars Publishing, 2013.

Skinner, Robert E. *The New Hard-Boiled Dicks: Heroes for a New Urban Mythology*. New York: Brownstone, 1995.

Smith, Erin. "How the Other Half Read: Advertising, Working-Class Readers, and Pulp Magazines." *Book History* 3 (2000): 204–30.

———. *Hard-Boiled: Working-Class Readers and Pulp Magazines*. Philadelphia: Temple University Press, 2010.

Smith, Johanna M. "Raymond Chandler and the Business of Literature." *Texas Studies in Literature and Language* 31, no. 4 (Winter 1989): 592–610.

Snyder, Claire. *Citizen-Soldiers and Manly Warriors: Military Service and Gender in the Civic Republican Tradition*. New York: Rowman & Littlefield, 1999.

Soulier, Alexandre. *Les Jugements de Dieu contre ceux qui ne croient pas en Jésus-Christ, ou La condamnation de ceux qui n'ont point de Sauveur*. Nîmes: Gaudes, 1824.

Sperry, Len. *Handbook of Diagnosis and Treatment of DSM-IV-TR Personality Disorders*. New York: Psychology Press, 2003.

Spillane, Mickey. *The Mike Hammer Collection*. 3 vols. New York: Penguin, 2001.

Stead, Philip John. "The New Police," In *Police and Society*, edited by David H. Bayley. London: Sage, 1977.

Stendhal. *Le rouge et le noir*. Paris: Gallimard, 2000.

Stewart, Terry. *La mort et l'ange*. Paris: Gallimard, 1948.

Stierle, Karlheinz, and Jean Starobinski. *La capitale des signes: Paris et son discours*. Paris: Les Éditions de la MSH, 2001.

Sue, Eugène. *Les mystères de Paris*. Paris: Presse du New World, 1844.

Tadié, Benoît. *Le polar américain, la modernité et le mal: 1920–1960*. Paris: Presses universitaires de France, 2006.

Thompson, Jim. *The Killer Inside Me*, foreword by Stephen King. New York: Blood and Guts Press, 1989.

———. *Pop. 1280*. New York: Vintage, 1990.

———. *The Killer Inside Me*. New York: Vintage, 1991.

Van Ornum, William. *A Thousand Frightening Fantasies: Understanding and Healing Scrupulosity and Obsessive Compulsive Disorder*. Watsonville, CA: Crossroad, 1997.

Vargas, Fred. *Seeking Whom He May Devour*. Translated by David Bellos. New York: Simon & Schuster, 2004.

———. *Sous les vents de Neptune*. Paris: Viviane Hamy, 2004.

———. *Wash This Blood Clean from My Hand.* Translated by Siân Reynolds. New York: Penguin, 2007.

———. *L'homme aux cercles bleus.* Paris: Viviane Hamy, 2012.

———. *L'homme à l'envers.* Paris: Éditions La Martinière, 2012.

Vercors. *Le silence de la mer et autres récits.* Paris: Albin Michel, 1994.

Verdaguer, Pierre. "The Politics of Food in Post–WWII French Detective Fiction." In *French Food: On the Table, on the Page, and in French Culture,* edited by Lawrence R. Schehr and Allen S. Weiss. New York: Routledge, 2001.

Vest, Jason P. *The Wire, Deadwood, Homicide, and NYPD Blue: Violence Is Power.* New York: ABC-CLIO, 2011.

Vidocq, Eugène. *Mémoires de Vidocq.* Paris: Huillery, 1869.

Vigny, Alfred de. *Stello.* Paris: Charpentier, 1852.

———. *Les destinées: avec une biographie du poète, une présentation générale du recueil, des notices particulières, une analyse méthodique des poèmes, des notes, des documents, des questions, des jugements, des thèmes de réflexion.* Paris: Bordas, 1971.

Vinet, Alexandre. *Chateaubriand.* Paris: L'âge d'homme, 1990.

Walker, John. "City Jungles and Expressionist Reifications from Brecht to Hammett." *Twentieth-Century Literature* 44, no. 1 (Spring 1998): 119–33.

Waller, Gregory A. "Mike Hammer and the Detective Film of the 1980s." *Journal of Popular Film and Television* 13, no. 3 (1985): 108–25.

Walz, Robin. *Pulp Surrealism: Insolent Popular Culture in Early Twentieth-Century Paris.* Berkeley: University of California Press, 2000.

Weber, Jeffrey A., and Johan Eliasson, eds. *Handbook of Military Administration.* New York: CRC Press, 2007.

White, Rob. "Make-Believe, Memory Failure." *Film Quarterly* 62, no. 2 (2008), 4–7.

Whitley, John S. "Stirring Things Up: Dashiell Hammett's Continental Op." *Journal of American Studies* 14, no. 3 (1980): 443–55.

Wister, Owen. *The Virginian: A Horseman of the Plains.* London: Macmillan, 1902.

Wolin, Richard. *The Terms of Cultural Criticism: The Frankfurt School, Existentialism, Poststructuralism.* New York: Columbia University Press, 1992.

Zane, John Maxcy, and Charles J. Reid. *The Story of Law.* New York: Garden City Publishing, 1927.

Zima, Pierre V. *L'ambivalence romanesque: Proust, Kafka, Musil.* Paris: L'Harmattan, 2002.